「反核・写真運動」監修
"Anti-Nuclear Photographers' Movement of Japan"

決定版
広島原爆写真集
The Collection of Hiroshima Atomic bomb Photographs

小松健一・新藤健一 編
Kenichi KOMATSU + Kenichi SHINDO

勉誠出版

はじめに

　戦後70年を迎えた今夏、広島・長崎の原爆写真を後世に残そうと「反核・写真運動」が収集してきた原爆写真集がようやく日の目を見ました。

　収集したオリジナルの原爆写真は30年前に6×9の複製ネガを制作し、10年前に、高解像度のデジタル化を行い、そのネガフィルムとデータは銀行の貸金庫に保管してきました。

　世界の核をめぐる政治状況は複雑です。冷戦時代の米ソは競ってビキニ環礁やカザフスタンで核実験を繰り返してきました。今日、核保有国は米国、ロシア（旧ソ連）、イギリス、フランス、中国の五大国のほか、インド、パキスタン、北朝鮮も保有を表明しています。イスラエルは公式に保有宣言をしていませんが、核保有国とみなされ、イランもそれに順じています。

　国連は1970年3月5日、「核兵器の不拡散に関する条約」（Treaty on the Non-Proliferation of Nuclear Weapons：NPT）を発効させました。締約国は191ヵ国・地域。日本は1976年6月、批准しました。非締約国はインド、パキスタン、イスラエル、南スーダンです。

　しかし、核軍縮は遅々として進みません。2015年4月〜5月、ニューヨークの国連本部で開催されたNPT運用再検討会議では1カ月間に及ぶ長い会議にも関わらず、大国のエゴで合意文書を採択することができなかったのです。これについて潘基文（パン・ギムン）国連事務総長は、世界の核軍縮の要である「実質的成果」を示す最終文書の合意に至らなかったことに遺憾の意を表しました。

　また今年6月1日、長崎大学核兵器廃絶研究センター（RECNA）は、現在の世界の核弾頭の数が約1万5700発であると推計値を発表しました。ロシアの7500発が最も多く、次いで米国が7200発。両国で世界の9割強を占めています。

　NPTでは原子力の平和的利用についても規定しています。条約では締約国の「奪い得ない権利」とともに、原子力の軍事技術への転用を防止するため、非核兵器国が国際原子力機関（IAEA）の保障措置を受諾する義務を規定しています。しかしながら「安全だ」と言われてきた原発にも思わぬ欠陥がありました。米国のスリーマイル島、ソ連のチェルノブイリ事故では生態系や環境にはかりしれない核汚染をもたらし、被ばく者は後遺症に苦しんでいます。

　2011年3月11日の東日本大震災では東京電力福島第一原子力発電所が被災し、福島を中心に放射性物質が飛散、汚染水はいまだに垂れ流し状態になっているのです。

「反核・写真運動」が創設当時に収集した写真は18人の写真家の624点。その後、長崎の原子雲を撮影した松田弘道氏の1点、二瓶禎二氏（文部省学術研究会議 原子爆弾災害調査研究特別委員会に助手として同行）撮影の30点と三菱重工長崎造船所の森末太郎氏が撮影した26点、長崎県の依頼で撮影した、小川虎彦氏の写真17点が追加されました。さらに東京大学の眞島正市教授、菅義夫助教授と筒井俊正助教授、加賀美幾三助手らが撮影した120点が加わり、本書編集中には同盟通信社の中田左都男氏撮影の写真も広島平和記念資料館から27点が見つかりました。そして長崎を撮った山端庸介氏の御子息である山端祥吾氏より新たに約100点の写真の提供がありました。結果的に本書には広島・長崎を合わせておよそ830点が収蔵されています。

　1995年、被爆50年に開催された『「核の恐怖」1945－1995写真展』（東京・コニカプラザ）では本書に掲載した「被爆直後」を撮影した写真に加え「被爆その後」を撮影した大石芳野、児島昭雄、小松健一、佐々木雄一郎、田村茂、丹野章、土田ヒロミ、東松照明、土門拳、長野重一、福島菊次郎、藤川清、細江英公、森下一徹らと、さらにはビキニ、ロシア、ネバダなど世界の核汚染地帯を取材してきた島田興生、新藤健一、豊崎博光、広河隆一、本橋成一、森住卓ら30人の写真も展示され、大きな反響を呼びました。

　『広島原爆写真集』と『長崎原爆写真集』に網羅した写真は私たち「反核・写真運動」のメンバーが見聞してきた筆舌につくし難い原爆の惨状を目撃してきた先達の記録と証言です。
　こうした貴重な遺産を次世代へ確実に引き継ぐとともに、核のない世界平和が一日も早く訪れることを心より願うものです。

2015年 水無月
「反核・写真運動」運営委員会

Introduction

This summer will mark 70 years since the end of the war, and the Atomic Bomb Photo Collection amassed by the "Anti-Nuclear Photographers' Movement of Japan" (whose objective is to hand down photos of the atomic bomb disaster in Hiroshima and Nagasaki to future generations) has finally seen the light of day.

30 years ago, 6x9 duplicate negatives were created from the originally collected atomic bomb photos. 10 years ago, high resolution digital copies of those photos were created, and the negatives and data were stored in a safety deposit box in a bank.

The political situation surrounding nuclear weapons worldwide is complicated. During the cold war era, the United States and Soviet Union repeatedly conducted nuclear weapon testing at Bikini Atoll and Kazakhstan. Today, in addition to the five major nuclear powers (the United States, Russia [former Soviet Union], United Kingdom, France, and China), India, Pakistan, and North Korea have revealed that they possess nuclear weapons. Israel and Iran have made no official announcements but they are recognized as nuclear powers.

On March 5, 1970 the United Nations put the Treaty on the Non-Proliferation of Nuclear Weapons (NPT) into effect. 191 nations and regions signed the treaty. Japan ratified this in June 1976. India, Pakistan, Israel and South Sudan did not sign the treaty.

Nonetheless, nuclear disarmament is making little progress. Although a month-long discussion was held at the NPT Review Conference in April and May 2015 at the UN Headquarters in New York, participants failed to draft a consensus document due to the egos of the major powers. UN Secretary-General Ban Ki-moon expressed disappointment to the failure of reaching an agreement on a final document, supposed to show a "substantive outcome" required for the global nuclear disarmament.

On June 1 of this year, the Research Center for Nuclear Weapons Abolition, Nagasaki University (RECNA) announced that the estimated number of nuclear warhead throughout the world reaches 15,700.. Russia has the most at 7,500, followed by the United States at 7,200. Together, the two nations account for more than 90% of world's nuclear arsenal.

The NPT also stipulates the peaceful use of nuclear energy. In addition to establishing the "inalienable rights" of signatory nations, the treaty says that non-nuclear-weapon states must accept the safeguards of the International Atomic Energy Agency (IAEA) in order to prevent the diversion of nuclear technology to military purpose. Moreover, although atomic power plants has been deemed "safe", unexpected defects were revealed. Accidents on Three Mile Island in the United States and Chernobyl in the Soviet Union have caused immeasurable nuclear contamination to ecological systems and environments, and those who were exposed to radiation continue to suffer the aftereffects.

The TEPCO Fukushima Daiichi Nuclear Power Station was damaged during the Great East

Japan Earthquake on March 11, 2011. Radioactive material was scattered in and out of Fukushima, and contaminated water is still being discharged from the site.

Just after its founding, the "Anti-Nuclear Photographers' Movement of Japan" has collected 624 photos of 19 photographers. Since then, the group has added the first photo of the mushroom cloud in Nagasaki taken by Mr. Hiromichi Matsuda and 30 photos taken by Mr. Teiji Nihei (who accompanied research teams of the Special Committee for Investigation on Atomic Bomb Disaster, National Research Council of Ministry of Education as an assistant), 26 photos by Mr. Suetaro Mori of the Mitsubishi Heavy Industries Nagasaki Shipyard, and 17 photos Mr. Torahiko Ogawa took at the request of Nagasaki prefecture. In addition to those, 120 photos taken by Tokyo University team consisting of Professor Masaichi Majima, Assistant Professors Yoshio Suge and Toshimasa Tsutsui, and Assistant Ikuzo Kagami, were added. And recentry as this volume was being edited, 27 photos taken by Mr. Satsuo Nakata of Domei News Agency were discovered in the Hiroshima Peace Memorial Museum. Approximately 100 new photos were also provided by Mr. Shogo Yamahata, son of Mr. Yosuke Yamahata, who photographed Nagasaki. Overall, this volume contains a total of 830 photos of Hiroshima and Nagasaki.

In 1995, on the 50th year since the atomic bombs disaster, the "Nuclear Fear: 1945-1995" exhibition was held at Konica Plaza in Tokyo. In addition to photos taken "immediately after the explosion" (included in this volume), the Exhibition featured photos by 30 photographers, including those describing the "long lasting aftereffects of the exposure" by Ken Domon, Shigeru Tamura, Kikujiro Fukushima, Akira Tanno, Shigeichi Nagano, Shomei Tomatsu, Eiko Hosoe, Ittetsu Morishita, Yoshino Oishi, Kenichi Komatsu and others. It also exhibited photos taken by those who covered radiation contaminated zones around the world (such as the Bikini Atoll, Russia and Nevada) including Kosei Shimada, Hiromatsu Toyosaki, Ryuichi Hirokawa, Seiichi Motohashi, Takashi Morizumi and Kenichi Shindo. The exhibition generated enthusiastic responses.

The photos contained in this Hiroshima and Nagasaki atomic bomb photo collections are records and testimonies of those who witnessed firsthand the indescribable devastation caused by the atomic bombs. The members of the "Anti-Nuclear Photographers' Movement of Japan" learn a lot from these photos.

We hope that future generations will inherit this distressing but precious legacy, and that the day all of humankind will enjoy world peace without nuclear weapons will come soon.

June 2015
"Anti-Nuclear Photographers' Movement of Japan" Steering Committee

目次

Contents

はじめに
「反核・写真運動」運営委員会

Introduction
"Anti-Nuclear Photographers' Movement of Japan" Steering Committee 002

凡例 008

決定版
広島原爆写真集
The Collection of Hiroshima Atomic bomb Photographs 009

対談
「原爆を撮った男たち」の証言
松本栄一　林 重男　（聞き手・小松健一） 224

解説
「広島の原爆を撮った男」
新藤健一 234

あとがき
小松健一・新藤健一 243

撮影者一覧 245

凡例

●本書では、「反核・写真運動」が収集・保管していた原爆写真について、
　原則として撮影された年月日順に配列した。
　ただし、レイアウトの都合上、若干前後を入れ替えている場合もある。

●キャプションは、撮影者本人の残したメモ、関連する既刊書籍、
　「広島平和記念資料館　平和データベース」「長崎原爆資料館　収蔵品検索」等の
　ウェブサイトなどを参照しつつ、新たに判明した事実も加え、小松健一が執筆した。

●キャプション末には、判明している範囲で、撮影年月日と撮影場所、撮影者を記した。

●詳細な場所が特定できなかった写真は、市名のみを表記した。

●収集・保管した写真は網羅的に収録することを目指したが、
　ほぼ同じカットが複数枚ある写真や、撮影時の条件等が悪く鮮明に写っていない写真、
　経年による劣化が激しい写真については適宜割愛した。

●撮影場所等の新事実、錯誤等、写真に関する情報がありましたら、編集部にお寄せください。

決定版
広島原爆写真集

The Collection of Hiroshima Atomic bomb Photographs

爆心地から 6500m。広島市の東北東約 7km の水分峡（みくまり峡）へ遊びにいっていて広島市上空に B29 が 1 機、落下傘が浮いているのを見た。間発閃光、飛行機は猛スピードで逃げる。異様な色を放って雲の柱がたちのぼった。轟音と爆風がきた。2 枚撮影の 1 枚目である。2 枚目は雲が画面いっぱいに広がり、形がわからなかった＝ 1945 年 8 月 6 日、広島県安芸郡府中町水分峡から（撮影：山田精三）

6500m from the ground zero. When I went on vacation to Mikumarikyou, 7km east-northeast of Hiroshima City, I saw a B29 bomber and a parachute in the sky above the city. Immediately, a flash was emitted and the aircraft escaped at high speed. A pillar of oddly-colored smoke rose into the sky. The roar and the blast wave occurred. This photo is the first of a pair. In the second photo, something was photographed on the full screen, but its shape is unclear = Photographed on August 6th 1945 at Mikumarikyou, Fuchu-cho, Aki-gun, Hiroshima Prefecture by Seizo Yamada

爆心地から約7000m。炸裂2分後＝1945年8月6日、広島県安佐郡古市町神田橋（撮影：松重三男）
Around 7000m from the ground zero. Two minutes after the explosion = Photographed on August 6th 1945 at Kandabashi, Furuichi-cho, Asa-gun, Hiroshima Prefecture by Mitsuo Matsushige

爆心地から約2600mの広島陸軍兵器補給廠へ中学4年で卒業して引続き動員でいた。
比治山の上空にオレンジ色の煙があがった。
「なにかあった」と思い少しして2階にかけのぼり、窓からのぞいて、北西方向4枚続けて撮影する。
(レンガの建物当時二号館)①= 1945年8月6日、広島市霞町から爆心地上空 (撮影:深田敏夫)

After graduating from junior high school at 4th year grade, I was working still at Hiroshima army weapon supply depot, approximately 2600 meters from the ground zero. I saw an orange smoke above Mt.Hiji from this depo. Realizing something has happened, I ran up to the second floor of the brick building (then Building No.2) in a few minutes and looked out of the window towards northwest direction. There I took 4 photographs. Photograph No.1, = taken at the building at Kasumi-cho, Hiroshima-City by me, Toshio Fukada, shows the sky above the ground zero on August 6th 1945

爆心地から約2600mの広島陸軍兵器補給廠へ中学4年で卒業して引続き動員でいた。比治山の上空にオレンジ色の煙があがった。
「なにかあった」と思い少しして2階にかけのぼり、窓からのぞいて、北西方向4枚続けて撮影する。
(レンガの建物当時二号館)②＝1945年8月6日、広島市霞町から爆心地上空（撮影：深田敏夫）

After graduating from junior high school at 4th year grade, I was working still at Hiroshima army weapon supply depot, approximately 2600 meters from the ground zero. I saw an orange smoke above Mt.Hiji from this depo. Realizing something has happened, I ran up to the second floor of the brick building (then Building No.2) in a few minutes and looked out of the window towards northwest direction. There I took 4 photographs. Photograph No.2, = taken at the building at Kasumi-cho, Hiroshima-City by me, Toshio Fukada, shows the sky above the ground zero on August 6th 1945

爆心地から約2600mの広島陸軍兵器補給廠へ中学4年で卒業して引続き動員でいた。
比治山の上空にオレンジ色の煙があがった。「なにかあった」と思い少しして2階にかけのぼり、窓からのぞいて、北西方向4枚続けて撮影する。
(レンガの建物当時二号館)③＝ 1945年8月6日、広島市霞町から爆心地上空(撮影：深田敏夫)

After graduating from junior high school at 4th year grade, I was working still at Hiroshima army weapon supply depot, approximately 2600 meters from the ground zero. I saw an orange smoke above Mt.Hiji from this depo. Realizing something has happened, I ran up to the second floor of the brick building (then Building No.2) in a few minutes and looked out of the window towards northwest direction. There I took 4 photographs. Photograph No.3, = taken at the building at Kasumi-cho, Hiroshima-City by me, Toshio Fukada, shows the sky above the ground zero on August 6th 1945

爆心地から約 2600m の広島陸軍兵器補給廠へ中学 4 年で卒業して引続き勤けでいた。
比治山の上空にオレンジ色の煙があがった。「なにかあった」と思い少しして 2 階にかけのぼり、窓からのぞいて、北西方向 4 枚続けて撮影する。
(レンガの建物当時二号館) ④= 1945 年 8 月 6 日、広島市霞町から爆心地上空 (撮影：深田敏夫)

After graduating from junior high school at 4th year grade, I was working still at Hiroshima army weapon supply depot, approximately 2600 meters from the ground zero. I saw an orange smoke above Mt.Hiji from this depo. Realizing something has happened, I ran up to the second floor of the brick building (then Building No.2) in a few minutes and looked out of the window towards northwest direction. There I took 4 photographs. Photograph No.4, = taken at the building at Kasumi-cho, Hiroshima-City by me, Toshio Fukada, shows the sky above the ground zero on August 6th 1945.

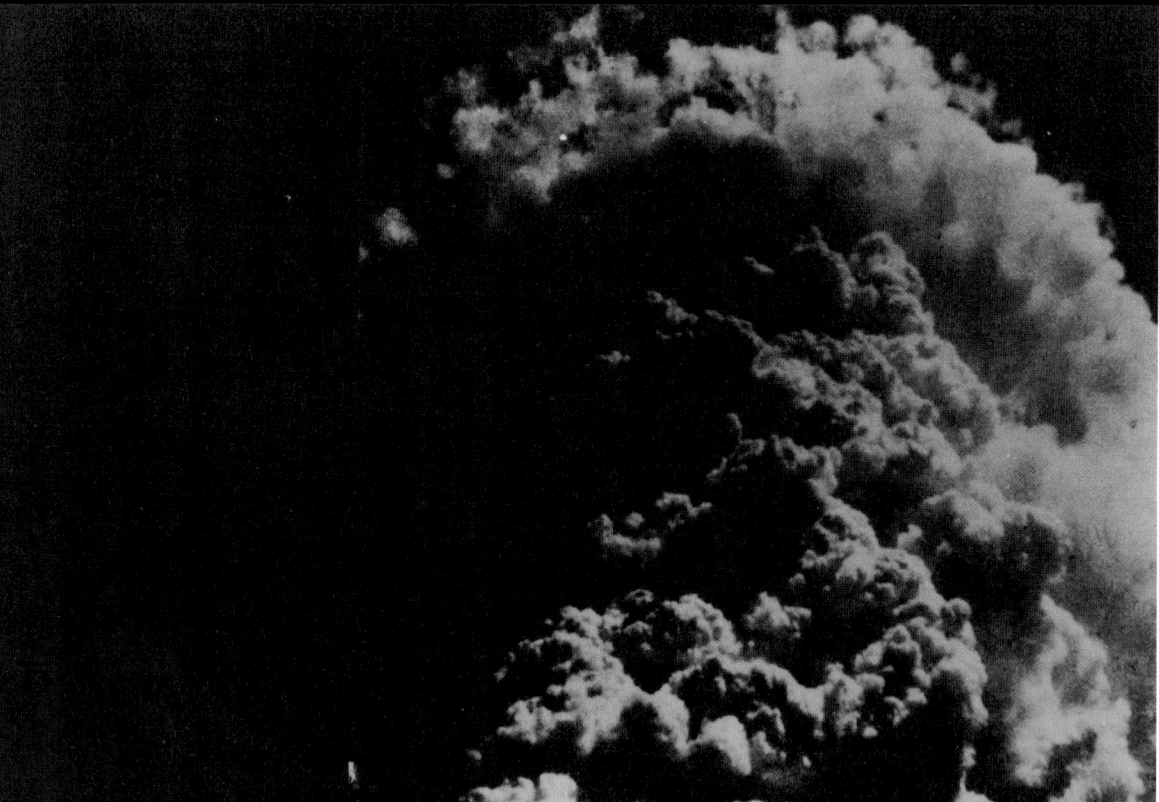

広島市の爆心地から約4kmの宇品町の陸軍船舶練習部構内から炸裂後15分に撮影したキノコ雲
= 1945年8月6日(撮影:木村権一)

The mushroom cloud, 4km from the ground zero. About 15 minutes after the explosion
= Photographed on August 6th 1945 at Ujina-machi, Hiroshima City by Gon'ichi Kimura

爆心地から約7000m。約30分後= 1945年8月6日、広島県安佐郡古市町神田橋(撮影:松重三男)

Around 7000m from the ground zero. About 30 minutes after the explosion = Photographed on August 6th 1945
at Kandabashi, Furuichi-cho, Asa-gun, Hiroshima Prefecture by Mitsuo Matsushige

炸裂後約1時間たった頃には、広島市の大半が炎上した。船舶練習部本部三階屋上西端から撮影。
西に向って広島市デルタ地域のほぼ全景が写っている。中央部が爆心地方向＝1945年8月6日、広島市（撮影：木村権一）
Most areas of Hiroshima City were burned within 1 hour after the explosion.
Photographed from the west end of the roof of three-story building of Marine Training HQ in Hiroshima City.
Almost all the delta areas of the city can be seen westward. The ground zero is at the center of this photograph.
＝ Photographed on August 6th 1945 by Gon'ichi Kimura

爆心地から南々東約 2270m の
御幸橋西詰。
当時宇品警察署管内千田町
巡査派出所前で急設された臨時治療所。
建物疎開作業中被爆した
広島女子商業学校・
県立第一中学校生徒が多くいた。
治療に当っているのは警察官 2 人。
当時この派出所には永田巡査部長がいた。
負傷者に糧抹廠からもってきた油を
塗布して応急治療に当る
＝ 1945 年 8 月 6 日、午前 11 時前、
広島市千田町三丁目御幸橋西詰
（撮影：松重美人）

West end of the Miyuki Bridge, which is approximately 2270 meters south-southeast of the ground zero. A temporary aid station was quickly set up outside the Senda-machi police box, which was then under the jurisdiction of Ujina Police Station. Many students from Hiroshima Girls' Commercial School and First Hiroshima Prefectural Junior High School were treated here by 2 police officers. Those students were victim of the bomb while dismantling buildings nearby in order to prevent a big fire by possible air-raid. The police box was then resided by a Sergeant named Nagata. Cooking oil from military supply depot was used for the treatment of burn injury. = Photographed at the west end of Miyuki Bridge at 3 cho-me, Senda-machi, Hiroshima City by Yoshito Matsushige

あまりにも残酷で、
初めの1枚目のシャッターを
切るまでに30分は躊躇し、
この辺りをうろうろした。
この2枚目を撮影の時は
いくぶん心も落ち着いていた。
この派出所前から
御幸橋上両側には死者、
負傷者で埋まっていた。
夕方から軍のトラックで宇品、
似ノ島へ運ぶ
＝1945年8月6日
午前11時過ぎ頃、
広島市千田町3丁目御幸橋西詰
（撮影：松重美人）

I wandered around this place for 30 minutes, hesitating to take the first photograph. I was shocked by such brutality. By the time I took this second photograph, I was a little bit calmer. Corpses and injured victims lined on both sides of the Miyuki bridge up to in front of this police box. In that evening, Military truck came and carried them away to Ujina and Ninoshima island.
= Photographed at around 11AM on August 6th 1945 at the west end of the Miyuki Bridge, 3-chome, Senda-machi, Hiroshima City by Yoshito Matsushige

当日撮影の3番目。爆心地から約2600m。この地域は火災からはのがれたが、爆風の損傷は惨たんである。
妻が貴重品の整理をしているのを撮影する＝1945年8月6日、広島市翠町、撮影者の住居（撮影：松重美人）

Third photograph of that day. Approximately 2600 meters from ground zero.
This area was untouched by the fire but severely damaged by the blast wave. Photographer's wife is sorting out valuables.
= Photograph taken on August 6th, 1945 at photographer's house in Midori-machi, Hiroshima City by Yoshito Matsushige

撮影者の居住する家の前の電車道をへだてる向側に西消防署皆実出張所があった。木造の3階建ては爆風で倒壊。
望楼で執務の消防士は倒壊と共に落ち、2階にいた4、5人は下敷。重傷1人、軽傷数人小隊長林喜代一。
6日夜から重・軽傷者数人が家で1週間ぐらい治療＝1945年8月6日、広島市翠町（撮影：松重美人）

There used to be the Nishi Fire Department Minami branch across the tram road in front of photographer's house. The wooden 3 story building was destroyed by the blast wave. The watchtower collapsed with the fire fighters on duty and 4 to 5 people on the second floor were buried under the debris. 1 person was severely injured and several slightly wounded. Platoon leader was Kiyokazu Hayashi. From the night of the 6th August, several wounded people stayed at this photographer's house for treatment. = Photographed on August 6th 1945 at Midori-machi, Hiroshima City by Yoshito Matsushige

爆心地から南々東2500mの宇品線電車周り角で、当日の夕方には宇品警察から被爆者に罹災証明が出され、罹災者はその証明で戦時非常用の救援食糧（カンパン）をもらった。罹災証明を書いているのは宇品署藤田徳夫巡査。当日この場には当時の須沢署長他5、6人の署員がいた＝1945年8月6日、広島市皆実町六丁目字品線電車回り角（撮影：松重美人）

In the evening of August 6th, at the turning point of Ujina tram line, 6-chome, Minami-machi, Hiroshima City, 2500 meters south-southeast from the ground zero, Certificates for bomb victims were issued and distributed by Ujina Police Station. With that certificate, victims were given emergency food such as hardtack which was originally for military emergency use. Person writing those certificates is police constable named Tokuo Fujita. At this site, there were about 5 to 6 police officers including Ujina Police Station Chief named Suzawa.
= Photographed on August 6th 1945 by Yoshito Matsushige

トラックで被爆した人達を安全な市郊外へ急送した＝1945年8月6日、広島県安佐郡安古市町（撮影：松重三男）

The bomb victims were rushed by truck to the city suburbs which were considered to be safer
= Photographed on August 6th 1945 at Yasufuruichi-cho, Asa-gun, Hiroshima Prefecture by Mitsuo Matsushige

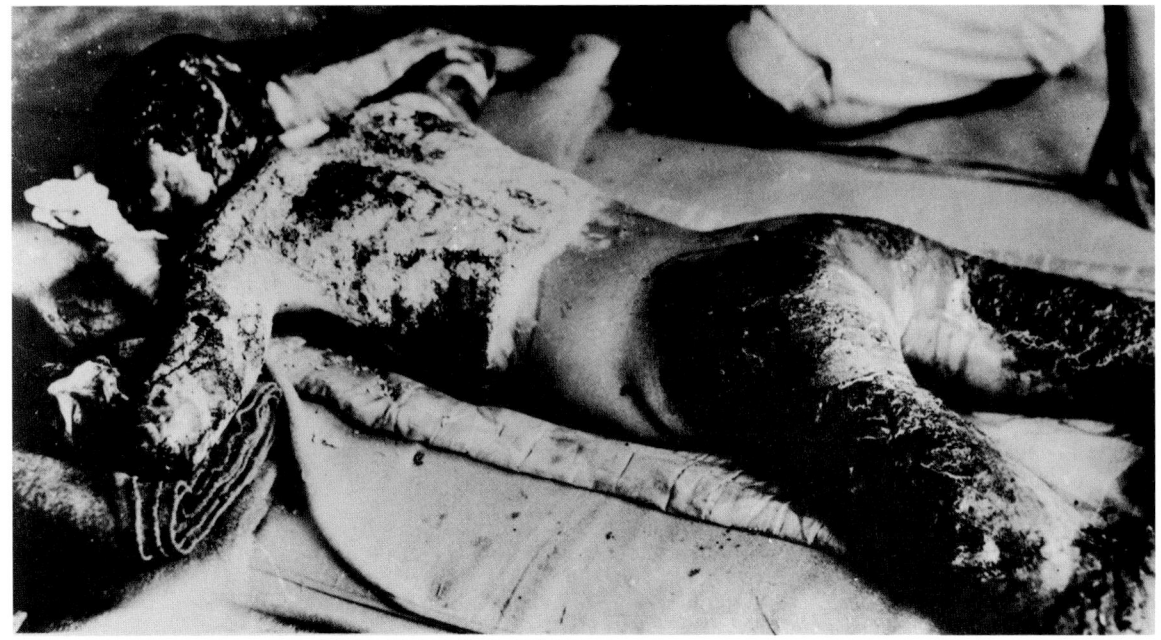

全身熱傷の被爆者＝1945年8月7日、広島湾似島検疫所（撮影：尾糠政美）
A bomb victim with whole body burned = Photographed on August 7th 1945 at Ninoshima Quarantine Office, Aki-gun, Hiroshima Prefecture by Masami Onuka

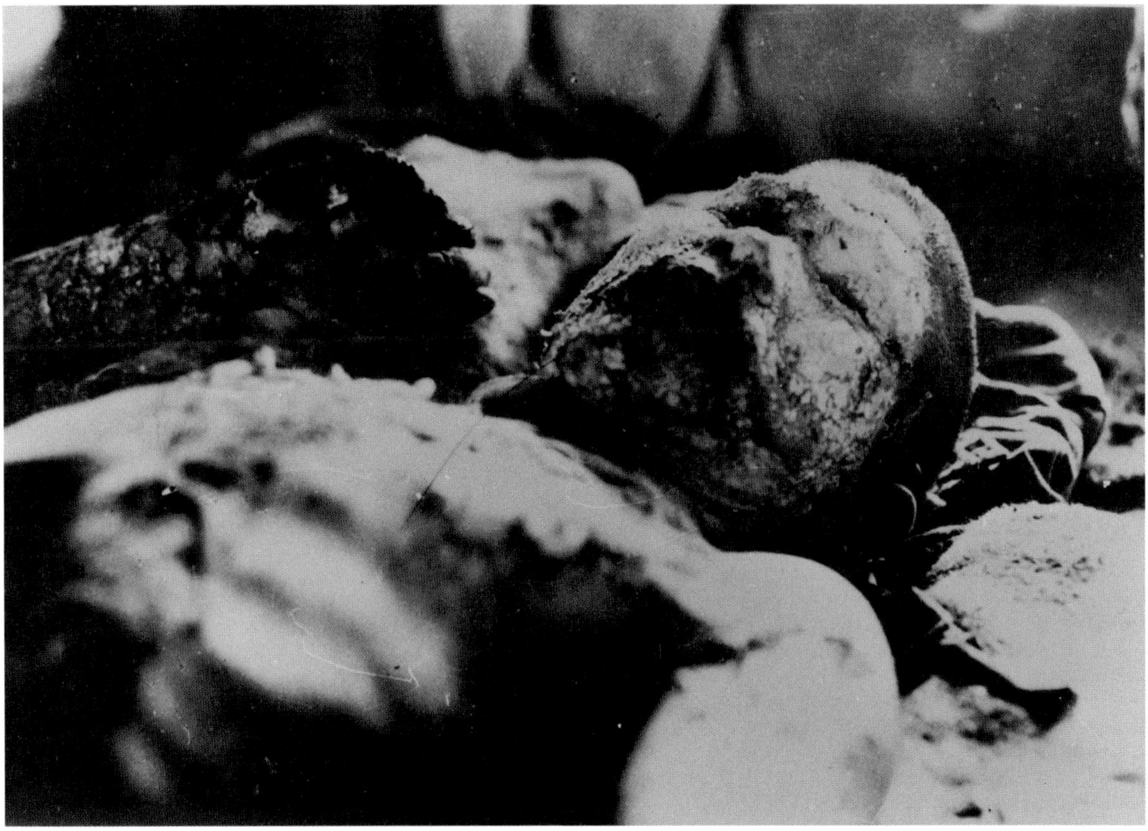

熱傷の被爆者＝1945年8月7日、広島湾似島検疫所（撮影：尾糠政美）
An bomb victim with burns = Photographed on August 7th 1945 at Ninoshima Quarantine Office, Aki-gun, Hiroshima Prefecture by Masami Onuka

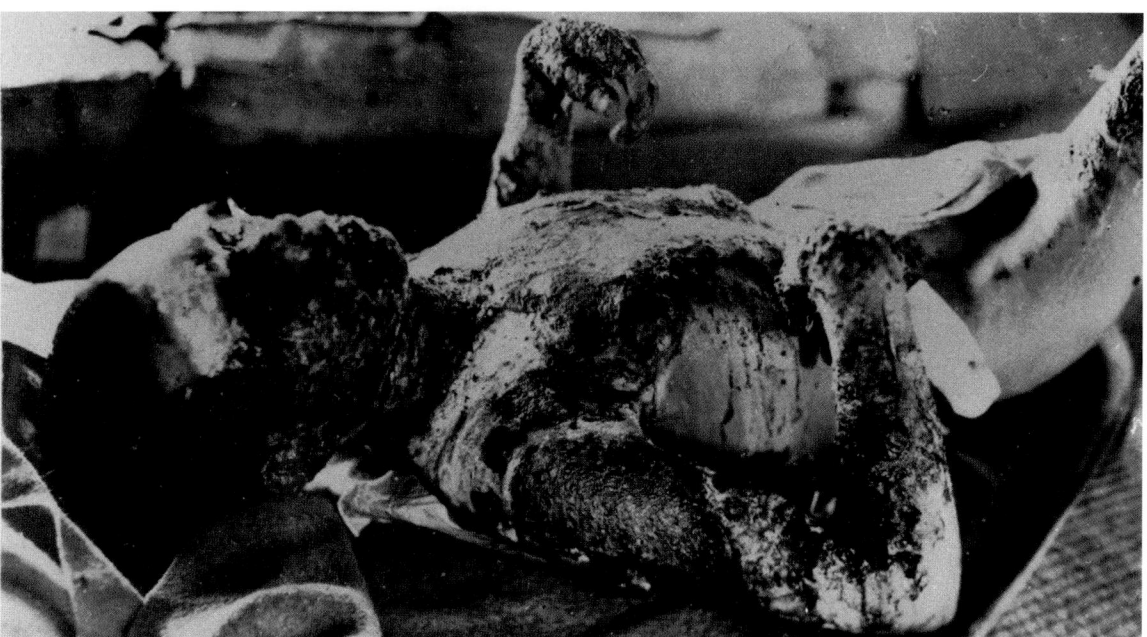

似島検疫所のあった似島は市街地から海上4000m。臨時救護所になり、熱線で全身焼けただれた人々の多くが広島港からここに運ばれた
＝1945年8月7日、広島湾似島検疫所（撮影：尾糠政美）

Ninoshima Island, where the Ninoshima Quarantine Office was located, is 4,000m from the center of Hiroshima City.
It was used as an emergency evacuation center for a large number of victims whose whole bodies were burnt by thermal radiation. They were transported here through the Port of Hiroshima = Photographed on August 7th 1945 at Ninoshima Quarantine Office, Aki-gun, Hiroshima Prefecture by Masami Onuka

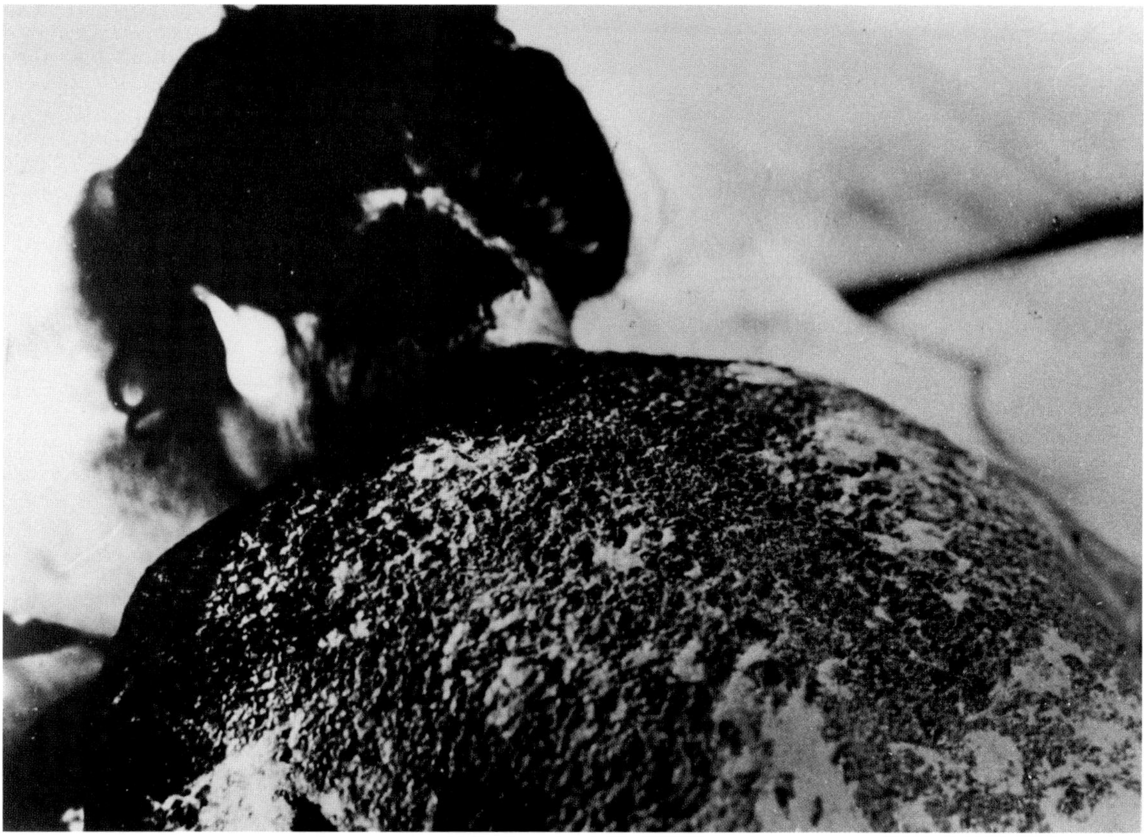

熱傷の婦人＝1945年8月7日、広島湾似島検疫所（撮影：尾糠政美）

A woman with burns = Photographed on August 7th 1945 at Ninoshima Quarantine Office, Aki-gun, Hiroshima Prefecture by Masami Onuka

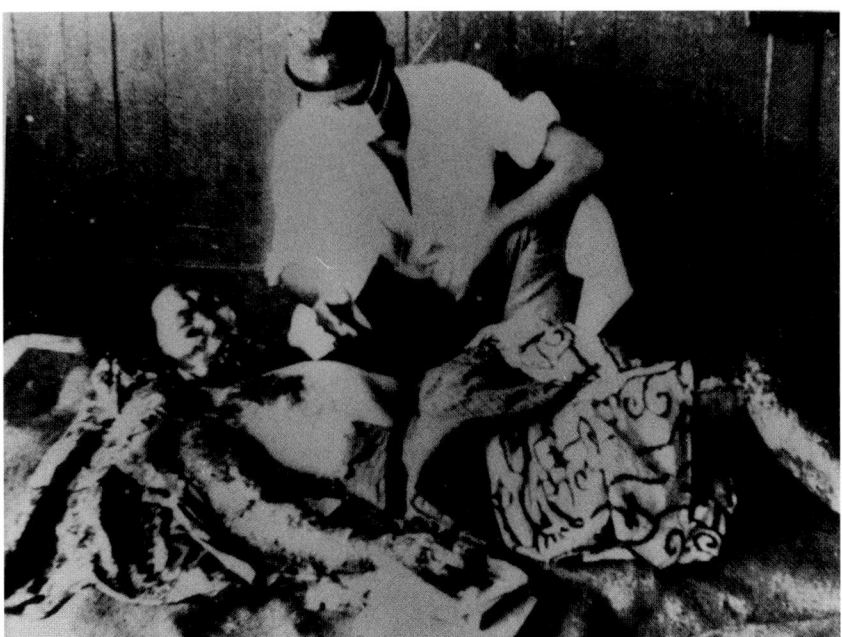

市立第一国民学校段原一帯は火災からはのがれたが、爆風で校舎は半壊。
窓や壁にむしろをおおい負傷者を収容した＝ 1945 年 8 月、爆心地から約 2600m の広島市段原山崎町（撮影：尾糠政美）
Although the Danbara district of Hiroshima City did not catch fire, the No.1 Municipal Primary School there was half collapsed
by the blast wave. The broken windows and walls were covered with straw mats and the injured victims were accommodated
in this school = Photographed at Danbara -Yamazakicho, Hiroshima City, appropriately 2600m from the ground zero in August 1945
by Masami Onuka

爆心地から 1000m（広島市基町白島より）の広島連隊区司令部（地区司令部、当時の司令官は藤井少将）の焼け跡につくられた仮司令部事務所
＝ 1945 年 8 月 7 日、広島連隊区司令部（撮影：岸田貢宜）
Japan army's temporary command office built on the site of the burnt-out Hiroshima Regiment HQ (commander at the time was major general Fujii).
Located 1000 meters from the ground zero = Photographed on August 7th 1945 by Mitsugi Kishida

被爆の翌日、倒れている鉄塔やコンクリートの下には死体があり、爆心地から近い、広島市の商店街でもあったこの辺りは死臭ただよう、もっともひどい惨状であった＝1945年8月7日、本通り中央角から北方の広島市紙屋町、立町方面を望む（撮影：岸田貢宜）

The day after the bomb. Dead bodies seen under the collapsed steel towers and concretes. This area, Hiroshima's shopping street near the ground zero, showed the most dreadful devastation with stench of death in the air = Photographed on August 7th 1945 at the corner of the central part of Hondori street, Hiroshima City, looking north toward Kamiya-cho and Tate-machi area by Mitsugi Kishida

爆心地から約1700m、広島市信用組合本部前。被爆建物で数カ所残っているなかの一つである。賀茂海軍衛生学校の職員、生徒が救護活動にあたった＝1945年8月7日、広島市横川町三丁目（撮影：岸田貢宜）

In front of Hiroshima Credit Union HQ, about 1700m from the ground zero. The HQ was one of the few buildings to have survived the blast. Kamo Naval Medical School staff members and students were taking part in relief works
= Photographed on August 7th 1945 at 3 Cho-me, Yokogawa-cho, Hiroshima City by Mitsugi Kishida

爆心地から約400m。建物右は安田銀行、左は大林組(現山口銀行)、中央は下村時計店、その後方に比治山の北端部が見える。手前に足を折り曲げた少年らしい死体がある＝1945年8月7日、広島市本通りを通して東方を望む(撮影：岸田貢宜)

Around 400m from the ground zero. The building on the right is Yasuda Bank. On the left is the Obayashi-Gumi (current Yamaguchi Bank). In the center is Shimomura clock shop and behind the shop, the northern edge of Hiji Mountain can be seen. A corpse is seen in front. The corpse with legs bent seems to be one of a young boy = Photographed on August 7th 1945, looking eastward through the Hondori Street, Hiroshima City by Mitsugi Kishida

余燼がまだ熱かった。軍隊、消防団、警防団が出て道路のとりかたづけをしていた。
同じ場所を10月に写した佐々木雄一郎氏の写真と比較してみると直後の壊滅状況がよくわかる＝1945年8月7日、
爆心地から500mの広島市本通りから、爆心地方向を見る（撮影：岸田貢宜）

The embers were still hot. The army, fire brigade and civil defence unit were clearing the debris on the roads.
Comparing with the photos of the same location taken later in October by Yuichiro Sasaki, this photo shows the severity of the devastation at this place, 500m from the ground zero, immediately after the blast = Photographed on August 7th 1945, looking the direction of the ground zero through the Hondori street, Hiroshima City, by Mitsugi Kishida

爆後初めて撮影されたとされる原爆ドーム。
下流の元安橋から撮影された
＝1945年8月、広島県産業奨励館
（撮影：松重美人）

Known to be the first photograph of the Hiroshima Prefectural Industrial Promotion Hall (the Atomic Bomb Dome) right after the bomb explosion.
= Photographed from the downstream side of Motoyasu Bridge by Yoshito Matsushige

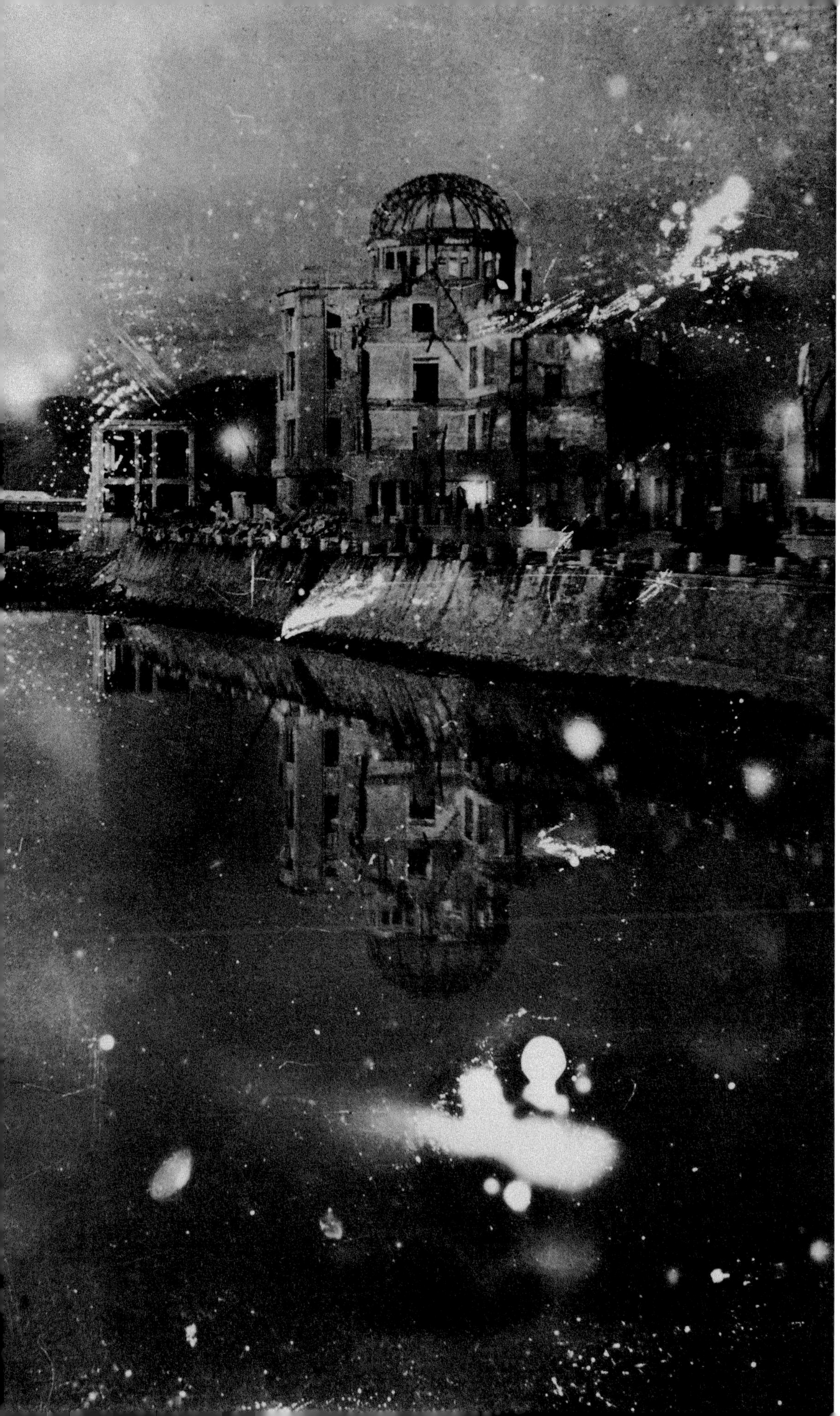

右後方は横川橋。現在の広島市基町1番地辺り。爆心地から約1070m。広島第二陸軍病院の廃虚跡、
本川河畔にテント張りの小屋を建て、火傷者や負傷者を収容した＝1945年8月9日、広島第二陸軍病院太田川畔テント救護所（撮影：川原四儀）
Yokokawa Bridge is on the right top. This area is currently 1-banchi, Motomachi, Hiroshima City. Approximately 1070 meters from the ground zero.
Tented huts for injured and burnt victims were built on the ruins of Hiroshima second Army Hospital along the riverbanks of so-called Honkawa (Ota river).
= Photographed on August 9th 1945 by Yotsugi Kawahara

爆心地から2500mの地域で、建物の全壊は80％という＝1945年8月9日、広島第二陸軍病院三滝分院（撮影：川原四儀）
80% of the buildings were completely destroyed within 2,500 meters radius of the ground zero.
= Photographed on August 9th 1945 at Mitaki Branch of the Hiroshima Second Army Hospital by Yotsugi Kawahara

爆風を北東から受け、棟瓦のところで渦を巻き、屋根瓦をはぎとる＝1945年8月9日（撮影：川原四儀）
Blast wave, coming in from northeast, created whirlpool around the roof and stripped tiles off.
= Photographed on August 9th 1945 by Yotsugi Kawahara

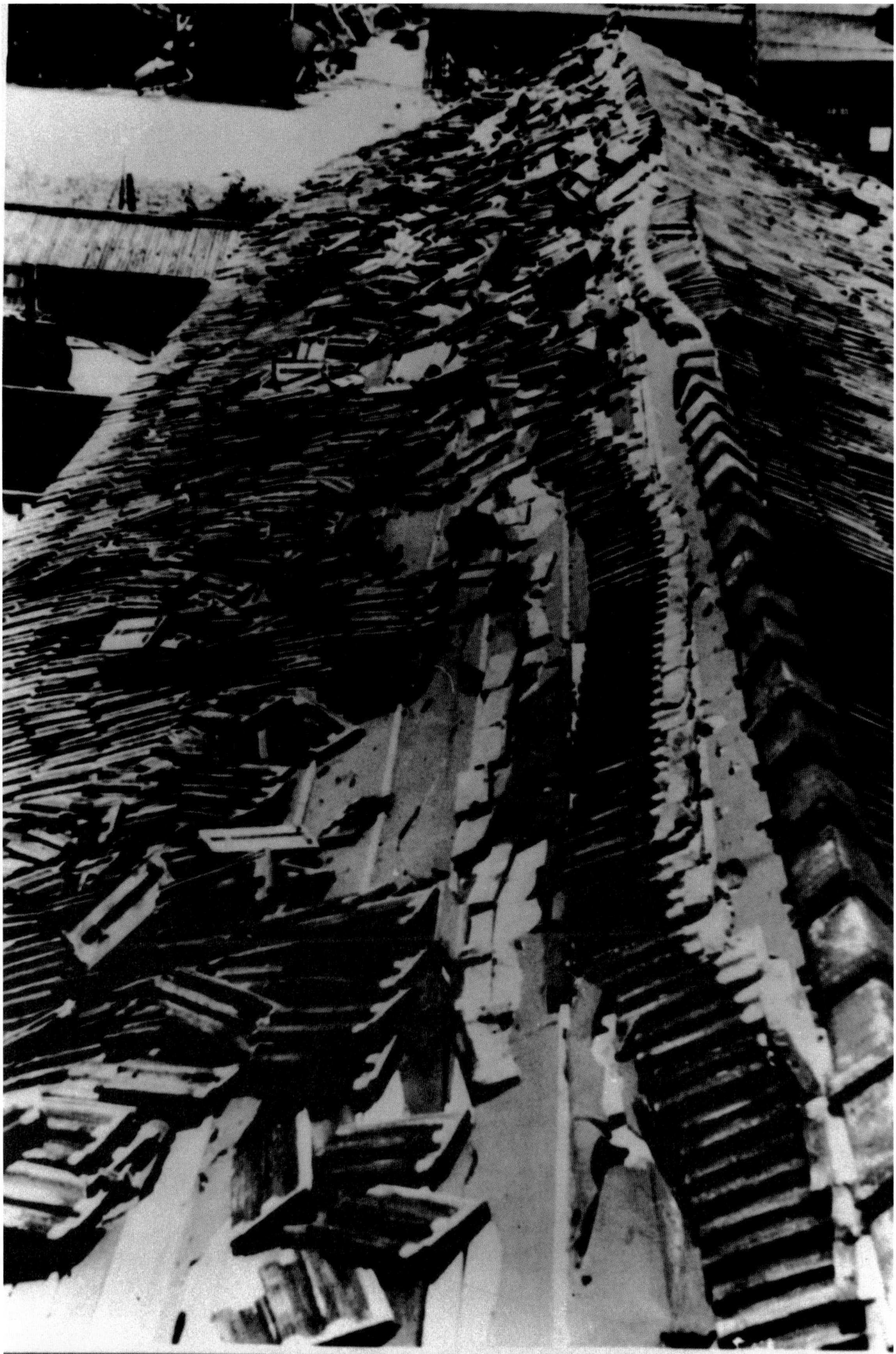

ここの収容者は10日位して大野陸軍病院に移される＝1945年8月9日、広島第二陸軍病院太田川畔テント救護所（撮影：川原四儀）
The inpatients here will be moved, after 10 days, to Ohno Army hospital.
= Photographed on August 9th 1945 at Hiroshima Second Army Hospital first-aid tent station along the riverbanks of Ota river by Yotsugi Kawahara

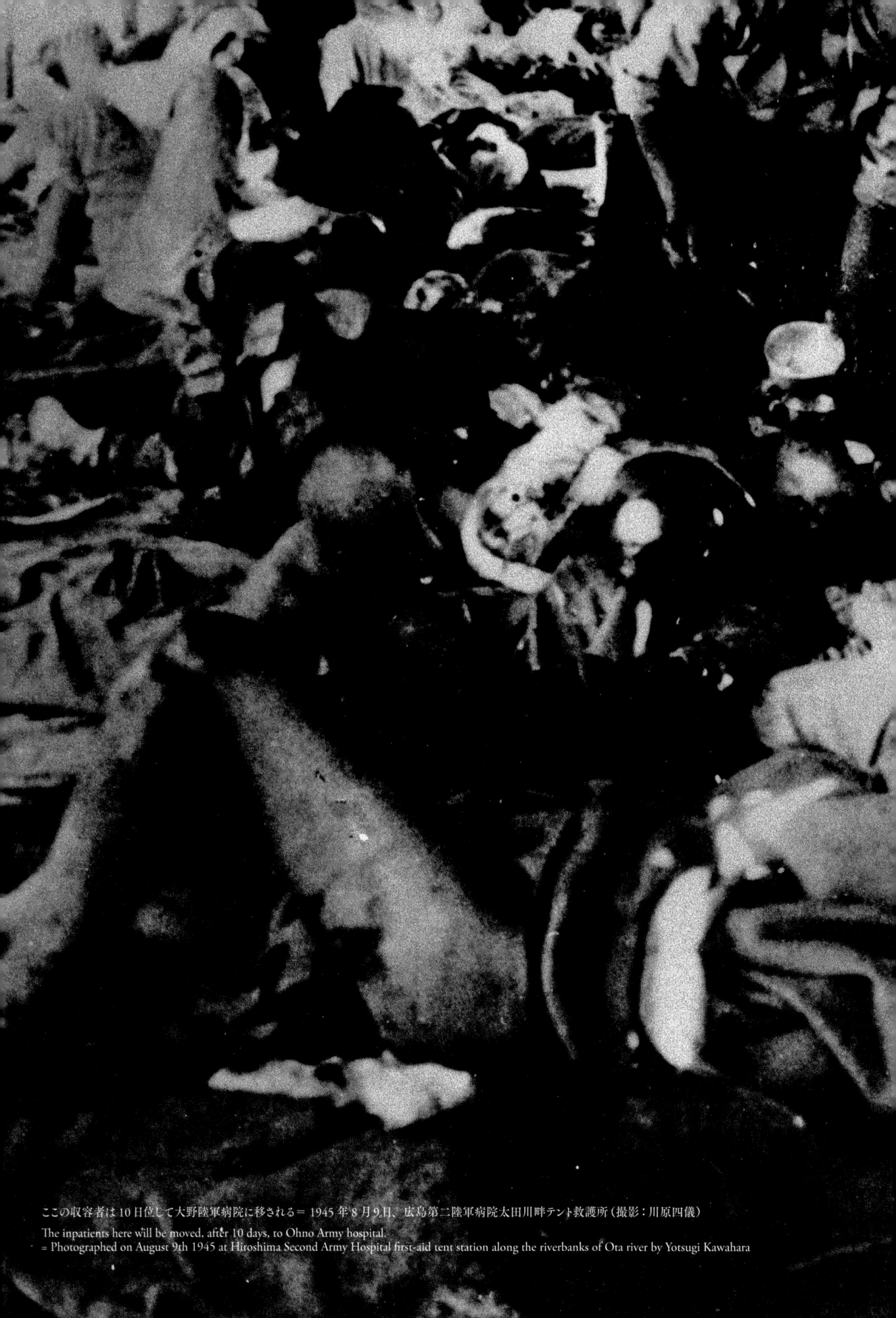

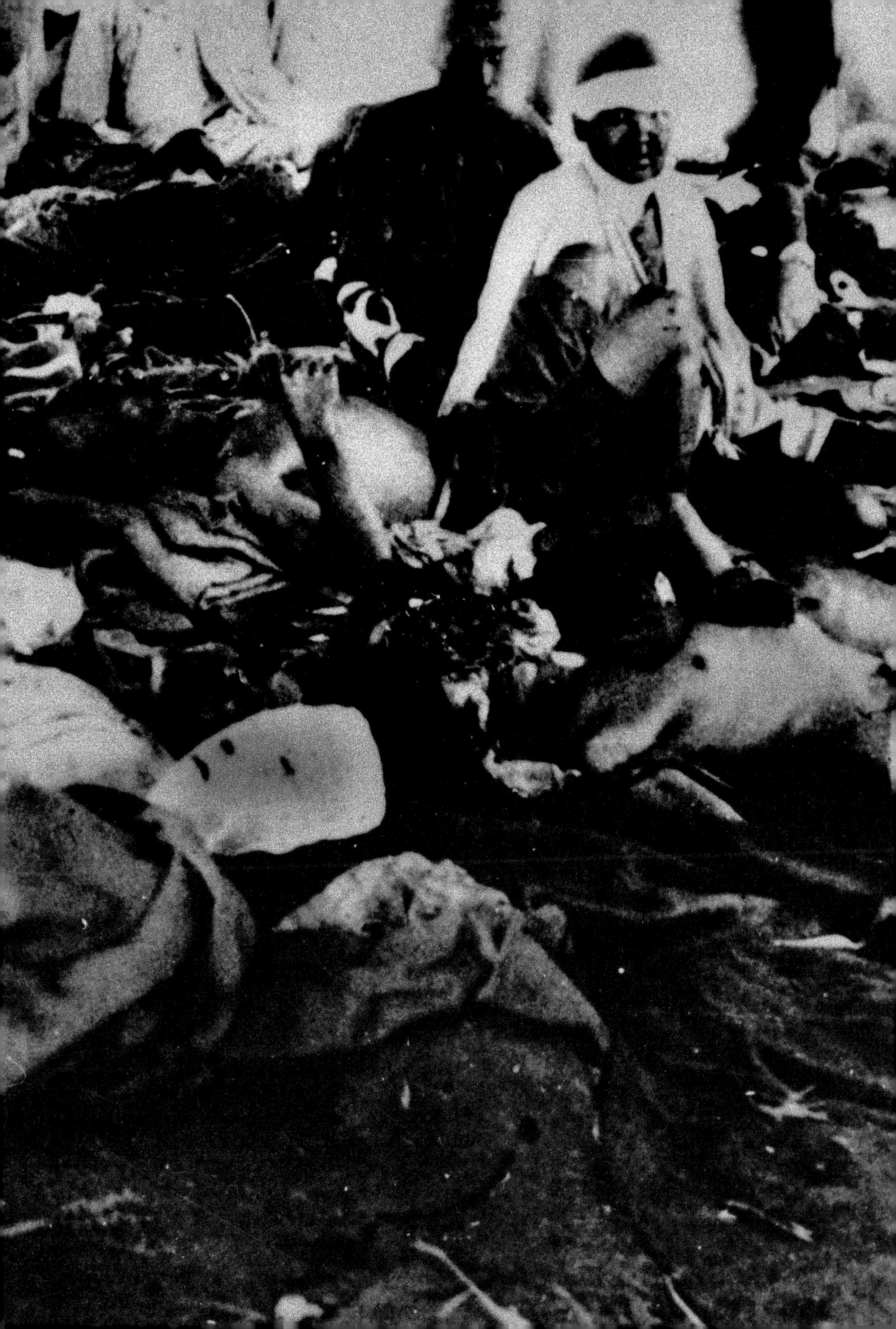

8月9日、午後3時頃軍隊や周辺町村から救護隊が広島市内に入った。
遠方からは岡山、山口、島根、鳥取、兵庫、大阪、県内の警察官90人、警防団員2,700人、大竹海兵団からも救護隊が派遣された。
後方の建物は芸備銀行本店と住友銀行広島支店＝1945年8月9日、広島市紙屋町付近（撮影：岸田貢宜）

Around 3pm on 9th August, rescue teams from the Japan army and neighboring towns and villages entered Hiroshima City. Teams also came from far away Prefectures such as Okayama, Yamaguchi, Shimane, Tottori, Hyogo and Osaka. 90 police officers and 2,700 members of the civil defense unit within Hiroshima Prefecture , and relief teams from Otake Kaiheidan (Marine Guard) also entered the city. The buildings behind are Geibi Bank HQ and Sumitomo Bank Hiroshima Branch
= Photographed on August 9th 1945 at Kamiya-cho, Hiroshima City by Mitsugi Kishida

広島の陸軍船舶司令部は臨時救護本部になり、収容者の氏名が玄関脇の壁に張り出された＝1945年8月10日頃（撮影：川原四儀）

Names of inpatients posted on the sidewall of the entrance of Japan Army Shipping HQ which was used as a temporary relief HQ.
= Photographed on August 10th 1945 by Yotsugi Kawahara

爆心地から 700 〜 800m。西練兵場付近の死体＝ 1945 年 8 月 10 日、広島城付近（撮影：中田左都男 同盟通信）

700 to 800 meters from the ground zero. A corpse near the Nishi Military Exercise Grounds = August 10, 1945, near the Hiroshima Castle, Hiroshima City (Photo: Satsuo Nakata, Domei News Agency)

爆心地から 500m。西練兵場付近の死体＝ 1945 年 8 月 10 日、広島城付近（撮影：中田左都男 同盟通信）

500 meters from the ground zero. A corpse near the Nishi Military Exercise Grounds = August 10, 1945, near Hiroshima Castle (Photo: Satsuo Nakata, Domei News Agency)

爆心地から 1000m。日本放送協会広島中央放送局＝ 1945 年 8 月 10 日か 11 日、広島市上流川町（撮影：中田左都男 同盟通信）
1,000 meters from the ground zero. Japan Broadcasting Corporation (NHK) Hiroshima Central Broadcasting Station
= August 10 or 11, 1945, Kaminagarekawa-cho, Hiroshima City (Photo: Satsuo Nakata, Domei News Agency)

爆心地から 2500m。大洲町付近の木造家屋＝ 1945 年 8 月 10 日か 11 日、広島市大洲町（撮影：中田左都男 同盟通信）
2,500 meters from the ground zero. A wooden house near Ozu-machi, Hiroshima City = August 10 or 11, 1945
(Photo: Satsuo Nakata, Domei News Agency)

爆心地から980m。広島城の堀のハス＝1945年8月10日か11日、広島市基町（撮影：中田左都男 同盟通信）
980 meters from the ground zero. Lotuses in the moat of the Hiroshima Castle = August 10 or 11, 1945, Moto-machi, Hiroshima City
 (Photo: Satsuo Nakata, Domei News Agency)

熱線を浴び、爆風により倒れた樹木＝1945年8月10日か11日、広島市（撮影：中田左都男 同盟通信）
A tree covered in heat rays, felled by the blast wave = August 10 or 11, 1945, Hiroshima City
(Photo: Satsuo Nakata, Domei News Agency)

爆心地から1700m。石油配給統制倉庫＝1945年8月10日か11日、広島市横川町（撮影：中田左都男 同盟通信）

1,700 meters from the ground zero. Warehouse for the control of Oil distribution = August 10 or 11, 1945, Yokogawa-cho, Hiroshima City (Photo: Satsuo Nakata, Domei News Agency)

吹きとばされた窓＝1945年8月10日か11日、広島市（撮影：中田左都男 同盟通信）

A blown out window = August 10 or 11, 1945, Hiroshima City (Photo: Satsuo Nakata, Domei News Agency)

爆心地から1370m。広島逓信病院の鉄のドア＝1945年8月10日か11日、広島市基町（撮影：中田左都男 同盟通信）
1,370 meters from the ground zero. The iron door of the Hiroshima Teishin Hospital = August 10 or 11, 1945, Moto-machi, Hiroshima City (Photo: Satsuo Nakata, Domei News Agency)

爆風で裂けた木＝1945年8月10日か11日、広島市（撮影：中田左都男 同盟通信）
A tree split apart by the blast wave = August 10 or 11, 1945, Hiroshima City (Photo: Satsuo Nakata, Domei News Agency)

爆心地から1620m。脱線した山陽本線の貨車＝1945年8月10日か11日、山陽本線神田川鉄橋（撮影：中田左都男 同盟通信）
1,620 meters from the ground zero. A freight car derailed on the Sanyo Main line = August 10 or 11, 1945, Kandagawa railway bridge of the Sanyo Main line, Hiroshima City (Photo: Satsuo Nakata, Domei News Agency)

爆心地から 870m。中国新聞社屋上から東南方向を望む。
斜屋町久保田本店の煙突が残る＝1945 年 8 月 10 日か 11 日、広島市上流川町（撮影：中田左都男 同盟通信）
870 meters from the ground zero. Southeast view from the roof of Chugoku Shinbun-sha.
The smokestacks of the brewery named Kubota Honten still standing in Chigiya-cho, Hiroshima City = August 10 or 11, 1945,
Kaminagarekawa-cho, Hiroshima (Photo: Satsuo Nakata, Domei News Agency)

爆心地から 1200m。水田のイネ＝1945 年 8 月 10 日か 11 日、広島市（撮影：中田左都男 同盟通信）
1,200 meters from the ground zero. Rice plants in a paddy field = August 10 or 11, 1945, Hiroshima City
(Photo: Satsuo Nakata, Domei News Agency)

爆心地から840m。全焼した路面電車（400形）＝1945年8月10日か11日、広島市八丁堀付近（撮影：中田左都男 同盟通信）
840 meters from the ground zero. A tram car (Type 400) completely destroyed by fire = August 10 or 11, 1945, near Hacchobori, Hiroshima City (Photo: Satsuo Nakata, Domei News Agency)

爆心地から3000m。東練兵場付近の木造家屋＝1945年8月10日か11日、広島市東練兵場付近（撮影：中田左都男 同盟通信）
3,000 m from the ground zero. A wooden house near the Higashi Military Exercise Grounds = August 10 or 11, 1945, Hiroshima City (Photo: Satsuo Nakata, Domei News Agency)

爆風で裂けた木＝1945年8月10日か11日、広島市（撮影：中田左都男 同盟通信）
A tree split apart by the blast wave = August 10 or 11, 1945, Hiroshima City (Photo: Satsuo Nakata, Domei News Agency)

爆心地から3000m。木造家屋＝1945年8月10日か11日、広島市（撮影：中田左都男 同盟通信）
3,000 m from the ground zero. A wooden house = August 10 or 11, 1945, Hiroshima City (Photo: Satsuo Nakata, Domei News Agency)

爆心地から 1380m。常葉橋、饒津神社方面。広島逓信局から＝ 1945 年 8 月 10 日か 11 日、広島市基町（撮影：中田左都男 同盟通信）

1,380 meters from the ground zero. View toward Tokiwa bridge and Nigitsu Shrine, from Hiroshima Teishin-kyoku (Tele-communication Office) = August 10 or 11, 1945, Moto-machi, Hiroshima City (Photo: Satsuo Nakata, Domei News Agency)

爆心地から 1900m。広島駅構内内部 = 1945 年 8 月 10 日か 11 日、広島市松原町（撮影：中田左都男 同盟通信）
1,900 meters from the ground zero. Inside Hiroshima Station = August 10 or 11, 1945, Matsubara-cho, Hiroshima City
(Photo: Satsuo Nakata, Domei News Agency)

爆心地から1000m。壊れた階段＝1945年8月10日か11日、広島市（撮影：中田左都男 同盟通信）

1,000 meters from the ground zero. Some destroyed stairs = August 10 or 11, 1945, Hiroshima City (Photo: Satsuo Nakata, Domei News Agency)

爆心地から 1620m。山陽本線神田川鉄橋での復旧作業 = 1945 年 8 月 10 日か 11 日、山陽本線神田川鉄橋（撮影：中田左都男 同盟通信）
1,620 meters from the ground zero. Restoration work on Kandagawa railway bridge of the Sanyo Main line
= August 10 or 11, 1945, Hiroshima City (Photo: Satsuo Nakata, Domei News Agency)

爆心地から 800m。正面左が中国新聞社新館の西面、その手前の鉄骨が小田政商店倉庫
= 1945 年 8 月 10 日か 11 日、広島市胡町（撮影：中田左都男 同盟通信）
800 meters from the ground zero. The west side of the new building of the Chugoku Shinbun-sha is in the front left.
The iron frame in front is the warehouse of a draper, Odamasa Shoten = August 10 or 11, 1945, Ebisu-cho, Hiroshima City
(Photo: Satsuo Nakata, Domei News Agency)

爆心地から870m。中国新聞社屋上から東方向、稲荷町方面を望む。正面右の建物は広島東警察署。
正面向こうに稲荷町電車専用橋。右下の建物は日本勧業銀行広島支店
＝ 1945年8月10日か11日、広島市上流川町（撮影：中田左都男 同盟通信）
870 meters from the ground zero. Eastward view from the rooftop of the Chugoku Shinbun-sha toward Inari-machi, Hiroshima City.
The building on the front right is the Hiroshima Higashi Police Station. The front back is the railroad bridge at Inari-machi.
The building on the bottom right is the Hiroshima branch of Nihon Kangyo Bank = August 10 or 11, 1945, Kaminagarekawa-cho,
Hiroshima City (Photo: Satsuo Nakata, Domei News Agency)

広島市街＝ 1945年8月10日か11日（撮影：中田左都男 同盟通信）
Downtown area of Hiroshima City = August 10 or 11, 1945 (Photo: Satsuo Nakata, Domei News Agency)

爆心地から 2030m。大正橋北側付近から広島駅方面＝ 1945 年 8 月 10 日か 11 日、大正橋北側から
（撮影：中田左都男 同盟通信）

2,030 meters from the ground zero. View toward the Hiroshima Station from the north side of the Taisho bridge
= August 10 or 11, 1945, Hiroshima City (Photo: Satsuo Nakata, Domei News Agency)

爆心地から 870m。中国新聞社屋上から東南東方向を望む。
手前は日本勧業銀行広島支店＝ 1945 年 8 月 10 日か 11 日、広島市上流川町（撮影：中田左都男 同盟通信）

870 meters from the ground zero. East-southeast view from the rooftop of the Chugoku Shinbun-sha. The building to the front is the Hiroshima branch of Nihon Kangyo Bank = August 10 or 11, 1945, Kaminagarekawa-cho, Hiroshima City (Photo: Satsuo Nakata, Domei News Agency)

爆心地から870m。中国新聞社から北方の上流川通りを望む
＝1945年8月10日か11日、広島市上流川町（撮影：中田左都男 同盟通信）
870 meters from the ground zero. Northward view of the Nagarekawa Street from the Chugoku Shinbun-sha
= August 10 or 11, 1945, Kaminagarekawa-cho, Hiroshima City
(Photo: Satsuo Nakata, Domei News Agency)

手前縦に2本見えるのは中国新聞社本館3階の破壊された窓枠。
南の全焼全壊地区を見る。写真上部中央に遮る物もなく、多くの被爆者が収容された広島市金輪島がくっきり見える。
写真中央斜めの道が流川通り、左から比治山南端その下に久保田本店の煙突（この煙突の頂上部は切り取って
広島平和記念資料館で保存展示している）＝1945年8月11日、中国新聞社から南に向って（撮影：川原四儀）
The vertical pillars are debris of 3rd floor window frames of Chugoku Shimbun Honkann (main building).
To the south, whole area was completely ruined. Nothing blocked the view. Kanawa Island, where atomic bomb victims were placed, can be seen clearly.
The road, crossing the center of this photo, is Nagarekawa street. Mt. Hiji is seen on the upper-left and the chimney of Kubota HQ is at the bottom of this
mountain. The chimney has been cut half and it's upper part is now displayed at Hiroshima Peace Memorial Museum.
= Photographed southward from Chugoku Shimbun-sha on August 11th 1945 by Yotsugi Kawahara

火傷、熱線によって、着物の模様の黒い部分が光を吸収して肌に焼きつく＝1945年8月15日頃、広島市（撮影：陸軍船舶司令部写真部）
The dark colored parts of the kimono clothes absorbed more energy of thermal radiation, causing the patterns to be burned on the victim's skin.
= Photographed around August 15th 1945 by Photographer Team of the Japan Army Shipping HQ

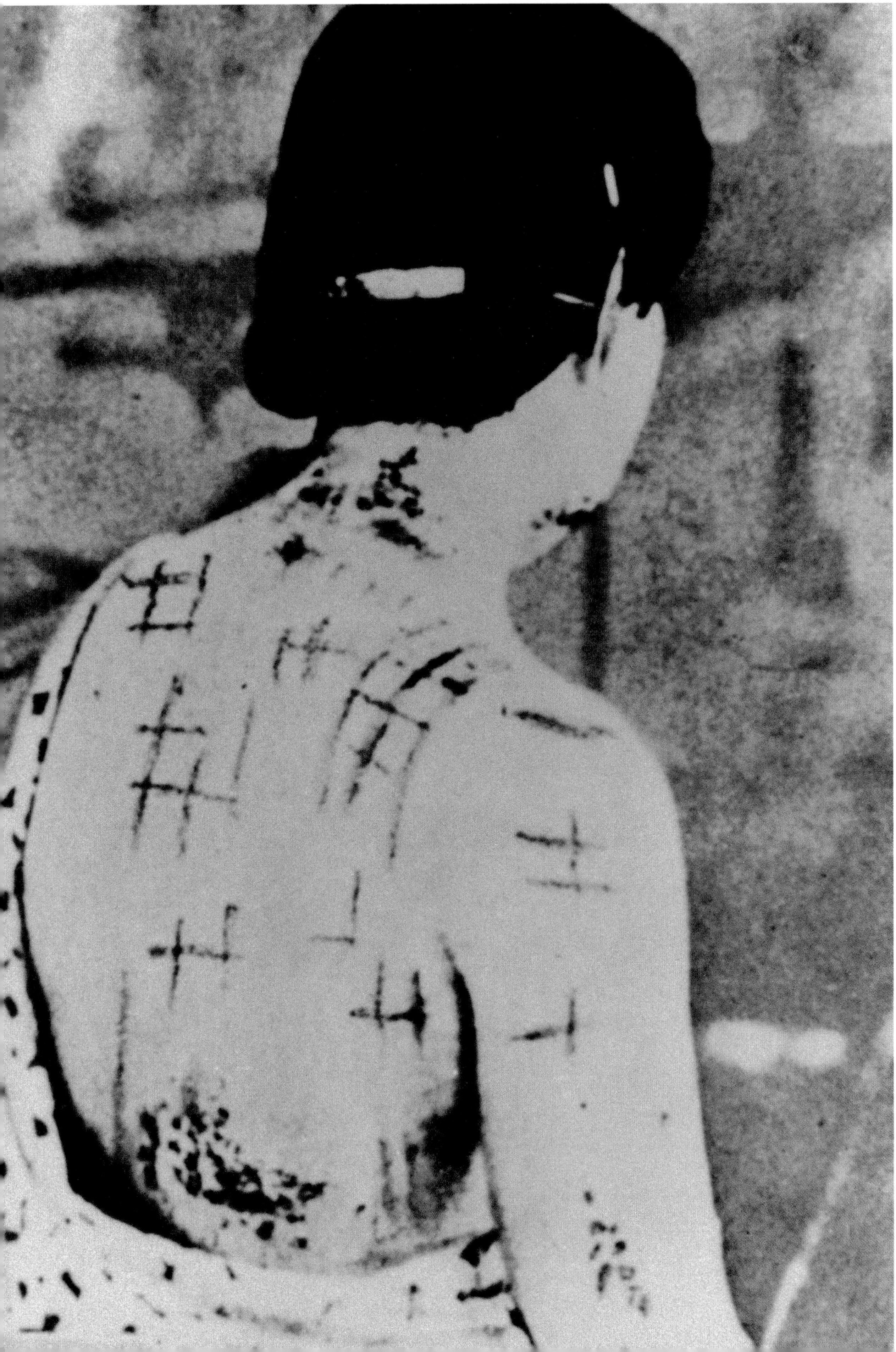

広島市紙屋町交差点で被曝した路面電車。後方の建物左がキリンビヤホール、右が大林組、安田銀行
＝1945年8月中旬（撮影：川原四儀）

Debris of a tram car exposed to radioactivity at the crossing of Kamiya-cho, Hiroshima City. The building on the left is Kirin Beer Hall, on the right Obayashi-Gumi and Yasuda Bank. = Photographed in mid-August 1945 by Yotsugi Kawahara.

一面瓦礫と化した木造住宅や店舗などの跡。手前細い露地道は、一応瓦礫が片づけられ、救護に入市した人だろうか、歩きやすそうに見える。
左上部に広島流川教会、右上部に広島東警察署が見える＝1945年8月中旬、広島市山口町から西に向って（撮影：川原四儀）

Ruins of wooden houses and stores all covered by debris. In front, persons who probably entered Hiroshima City for rescue work,
walk somewhat comfortably on the narrow road where debris are cleared. On upper left you can see Hiroshima Nagarekawa church and on upper right,
Hiroshima Higashi Police Station. = Photographed westward from Yamaguchi-cho, Hiroshima City in mid-August 1945 by Yotsugi Kawahara

中国軍管区司令長官官舎や
広島第一陸軍病院第一分院など、
西練兵場西側にあった木造の
建物は爆風で倒壊し、
高熱火災で全焼、
焼けた庭木や街路樹が
立ちつくしていた。
中央部左から
広島県産業奨励館、
広島県商工経済会など
＝ 1945 年 8 月 20 日
（撮影：尾木正己）

All the wooden buildings on the west side of the Army's Nishi Training Ground, including the official residence of the Chugoku Area Army Commander-in-Chief and No.1 Branch of No. 1 Hiroshima Army Hospital, were collapsed by the blast wave and burned down by high-temperature fires. Burnt trees in gardens and streets still stood. Hiroshima Prefectural Industrial Promotion Hall (the Atomic Bomb Dome), Hiroshima Prefecture Chamber of Commerce and Economy building and others are seen on the left
= Photographed on August 20th 1945 by Masami Oki

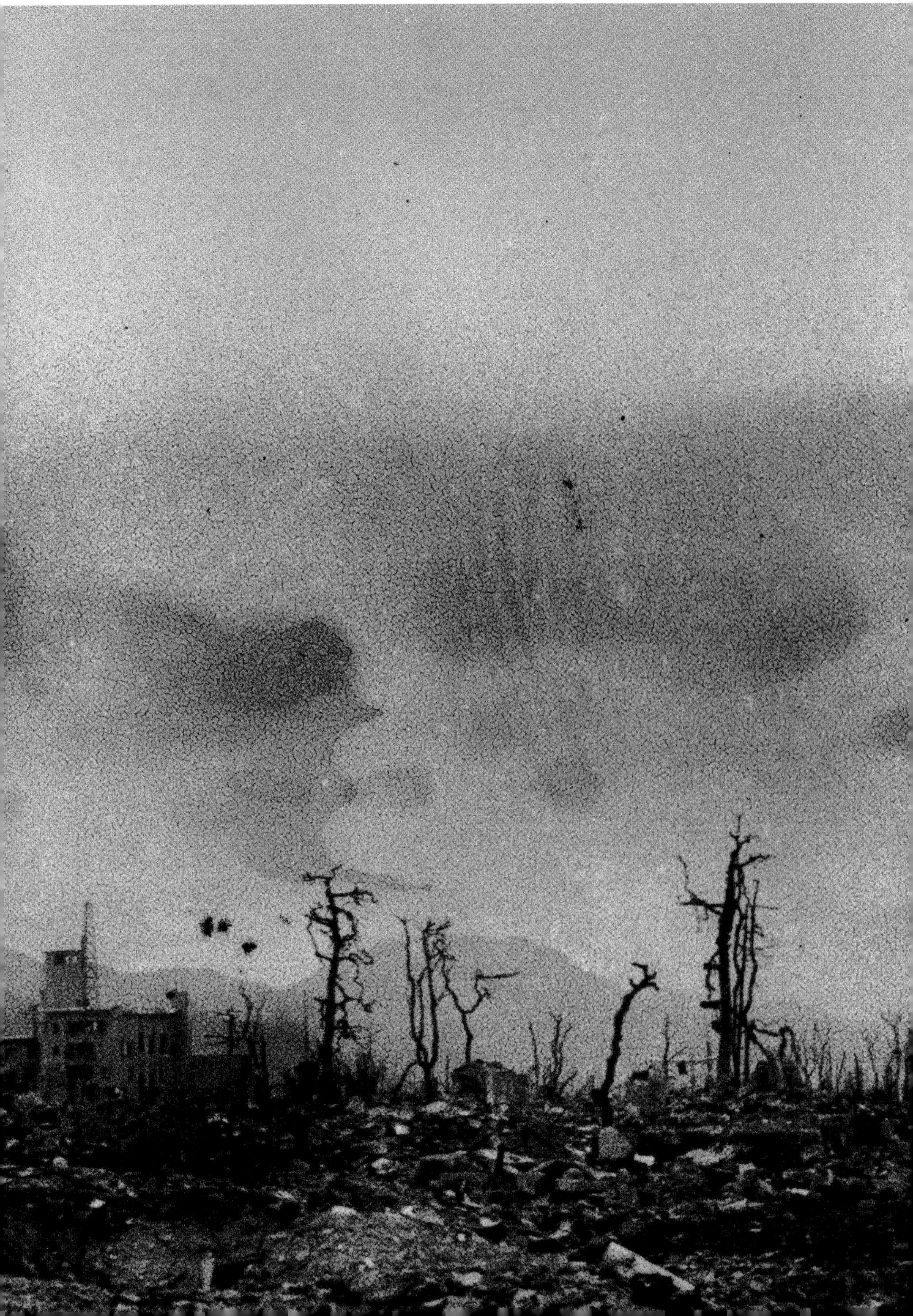

町工場や木造住宅の密集した爆心に近いこの地域は、熱線と爆風、
その後の火災で全焼全壊した。左手前焼けた松の木らしい残骸付近が
空鞘神社前。その奥左から千代田生命広島支店など、
その右広島商工経済会、農林中央金庫広島支所など。その右、
広島県産業奨励館、本川国民学校＝1945年8月20日、
空鞘神社付近から南東に向かって（撮影：尾木正己）

This district near the ground zero, densely-packed with small factories and wooden houses, was completely burned down and destroyed by the thermal radiation, blast wave and the following fire. A burnt tree, possibly pine, still stood in front of destroyed Sorasaya Shrine. From left to right in the back are Hiroshima Branch of Chiyoda Seimei, Hiroshima Prefecture Chamber of Commerce and Economy, Norin Chuo Kinko Hiroshima Office and others. To the right of that, Hiroshima Prefectural Industrial Promotion Hall (the Atomic Bomb Dome), Honkawa Primary School = Photographed on August 20th 1945, facing southeast from the area near Sorasaya Shrine by Masami Oki

全焼全壊した家屋の跡に消息を知らせる伝言の板が立ててある。
写真手前右側多くの自転車の残骸が残され自転車店の跡と思われる。
写真左から広島商工経済会、その奥福屋百貨店、芸備銀行本店、
千代田生命広島支社など、中央に広島県産業奨励館、
右端窓が打ち破られた建物は本川国民学校＝1945年8月20日、
広島市鷹匠町香川自転車店付近から東南東（爆心）に向かって
（撮影：尾木正己）

A board informing the whereabouts of the family is stood at the place of their completely burnt and destroyed houses. The wreckage of many bicycles on the right front tells that a bicycle shop was here. At left, Hiroshima Chamber of Commerce and Economy, and in the back of it, Fukuya Department Store, Geibi Bank HQ, Hiroshima Branch of Chiyoda Seimei etc. At the center, Hiroshima Prefectural Industrial Promotion Hall (the Atomic Bomb Dome) can be seen. The building with the right side of window broken is Honkawa Primary School = Photographed on August 20th 1945 from the area near Kagawa bicycle shop in Takajo-machi, Hiroshima City, toward the east-southeast direction (toward the ground zero) by Masami Oki

画面右側、相生橋西側と中島地区へ繋がる中央の橋の欄干は、
爆風で吹き飛ばされ、市内電車の電柱も倒れ込んでいる。
右手前から倒れ込みながらも残った相生橋左岸側の欄干、その後に
日本赤十字社広島支部。その南側にあった同支部木造建物は
全焼全壊した＝1945年8月20日、相生橋中央部から西に1/3の
地点で、北側歩道付近から南東に向かって（撮影：尾木正己）

On the right of this photograph, the railing of the center bridge that links the west side of Aioi Bridge with the Nakajima district, Hiroshima City, was blown off by the blast, and the power poles for trams fell down. On the front left, the railings of the left bank side of Aioi Bridge fell down but still remain. Hiroshima Branch of Japanese Red Cross Society can be seen behind the railings. The wooden building of this Branch, located on the south side of the main building, was completely burned down and destroyed = Photographed on August 20th 1945 at the north-side footpath of Aioi Bridge toward the southeast direction by Masami Oki

北（日本赤十字社広島支部東側）から南に向かって。。
被爆時爆心直下のこの建物はほとんど真上からの爆風で
倒壊は免れたものの、一瞬にして大破、
熱線は木質の天井で発火し全焼した＝1945年8月20日、
広島県産業奨励館（原爆ドーム）（撮影：尾木正己）

Southward view of Hiroshima Prefectural Industrial Promotion Hall (the Atomic Bomb Dome) from the east side of Hiroshima Branch of Japanese Red Cross Society. Though the atomic bomb exploded just above this Hall, it has not been fully collapsed because blast wave came directly from above. However, it was completely ruined in a moment and its wooden ceiling was ignited by thermal radiation. The building was burnt down = Photographed on August 20th 1945 by Masami Oki

左手前に日本赤十字社広島支部の残骸が見え、その右建物の
基礎だけになった所は全焼全壊した同支部の木造建物跡。
中央部には広島県産業奨励館、その右奥の建物群は
袋町電車道りの明治生命広島支店、広島富国館など。
右端元安川の奥は広島市役所など、その前の橋は元安橋。
元安川の花崗岩の石垣は火災で黒く焼けた跡が残り、
潮の干いた河原には瓦礫の散乱した様子が見られる＝1945年8月20日、
相生橋東詰（左岸側）から南南東に向って（撮影：尾木正己）

The ruin of Hiroshima Branch of Japanese Red Cross Society can be seen on the left. On the right, only foundation of the wooden building of this Red Cross remains. At the center, Hiroshima Prefectural Industrial Promotion Hall (the Atomic Bomb Dome), and on the right behind the hall, the buildings of Meiji Seimei Hiroshima Branch, Hiroshima Fukokukan and others along the Fukuro-machi tram street, Hiroshima City. Motoyasu River can be seen on the right and Hiroshima City Municipal Office and others are behind the river. In front of them, Motoyasu Bridge can be seen. The stone wall of the river bank, made of granite, shows black burnt marks by the fire. At low tide, scattered debris can be seen on the riverbed = Photographed on August 20th 1945 facing south-southeast direction from the east end of the Aioi Bridge (left bank side) by Masami Oki

1928(昭和3)年に建った大きな時計台を組み込んだ鉄筋2階建ての
建物は本通りのランドマークだった。コンクリートの両壁が構造材の役をなし、
重い時計台を直接支えていたこの建物は、被爆時爆風でもろくも崩れ、
アーチ窓の2階部分と時計台を残して座屈し、南東側へ倒れ込んだ
＝1945年8月20日、広島市本通り西から東（キリンビヤホール）に向って
（撮影：尾木正己）

Shimomura Clock Shop. This reinforced concrete two-story building with a large clock tower, which was incorporated in 1928, was the landmark of Hondori street, Hiroshima City. The building with two concrete walls, which is acting as constructional material directly supporting the heavy clock tower, easily collapsed by the blast wave and fell down in south-easterly direction. Only the second floor with the arched window and the clock tower remained = Photographed eastward from Hondori street, Hiroshima City on August 20th 1945 by Masami Oki

日本貯蓄銀行広島支店。被爆により広島県農業会は、大手町通りに
面した円柱が特徴的な玄関部分と、事務所部分が崩落して分解した。
この写真はその玄関部分から南に向って撮影したものである。
中央に見えるかつて2階建てだった日本貯蓄銀行広島支店は、
爆風で1階部分だけ残して崩壊し、金庫室だけが形をとどめ、
8月16日からの日本銀行内仮店舗での営業に役立った
＝1945年8月20日、広島県農業会広島支所東側玄関付近から南
（日本貯蓄銀行広島支店）に向って（撮影：尾木正己）

Hiroshima Branch of Japan Savings Bank (center) seen southward from the entrance part of Hiroshima Prefecture Agriculture Association building, whose office building and entrance with characteristic columns facing Otemachi street, collapsed and wholly disintegrated. Japan Savings Bank Hiroshima Branch used to be a two-story building. It collapsed by the blast wave. Only the ground floor and the bank vault remained. The vault was used for the operation of the Bank of Japan Temporaly Branch from August 16th = Photographed southward (toward Japan Savings Bank Hiroshima Branch) from the east entrance of Hiroshima Branch of Hiroshima Prefectural Agriculture Association on August 20th 1945 by Masami Oki

全焼した貨車。写真上部屋根のように見える部分は国鉄山陽本線の
鉄路。写真には写っていないが左側に山陽本線神田川鉄橋があり、
被爆時鉄橋上に49両編成の貨物列車がさしかかり転覆炎上したが、
直ちに復旧させるため、京橋（神田）川や車のガード南側道路に
転落させ鉄路を確保、直ちに開通させた＝1945年8月20日、
広島市二葉ノ里山陽本線饒津ガード北側（饒津神社側）から
南南西に向って（撮影：尾木正己）

Completely burned-down freight cars. The roof-like structure at the top of the photograph is the railway track of Japan National Railway's Sanyo mainline. Though it is not shown in this photograph, there was the Kanda River Railway Bridge for the Sanyo mainline on the left side. At the time of the explosion, a freight train of 49 cars had just started to pass the bridge, which was overturned and burst into frames. For the quick re-opening of the line, the wreckage of the train was pushed into the river or the road on the south side of the guard rail. The line was re-opened a short time later = Photographed toward south-southwest from the north side of Nigitsu fence of the Sanyo mainline railway at Futabanosato (Nigitsu Shrine side), Hiroshima City on August 20th 1945 by Masami Oki

鉄骨3階建てで増築された店舗兼倉庫の呉服問屋の建物は、爆風でねじれ、その後の高熱火災で、全焼全壊した。
この建物の残骸は時間とともに鉄の重みで次第に沈みその姿を変え原爆の高熱火災の威力の象徴のように多くの人達によって記録された。
当時貴重だったこの残骸は、鉄材として何者かに持ち去られた。右の建物は内部を全焼した中国新聞社新館、その奥に広島流川教会
＝1945年8月20日、南から北北東（広島流川教会）に向って（撮影：尾木正巳）

The three-story extended building with reinforced concrete, used as a shop and warehouse for a kimono wholesaler, was twisted by the blast wave
and burned down and collapsed completely by high-temperature fires. The debris of the building, gradually collapsed under the weight of the steel, was rembered
by many as a symbol of the terrifying power of high-temperature fires. However, these steel materials, which was valuable at that time, were stolen by someone
as metal scrap. The building on the right is the new wing of Chugoku Shinbun-sha, the interior of which was completely burned down.
Behind the building, Hiroshima Nagaregawa Church can be seen = Photographed toward north-northeast side (toward Hiroshima Nagaregawa Church)
from the south on August 20th 1945 by Masami Oki

広島瓦斯本社。爆心方向の壁、天井は爆風で崩壊し、全焼した＝1945年8月20日、北東側の広島市大手町筋から（撮影：尾木正巳）
The HQ of Hiroshima Gas. The wall and the ceiling facing the ground zero collapsed and burned down by the blast wave
= Photographed on August 20th 1945. at the northeast side of Otemachisuji, Hiroshima City by Masami Oki

石造物だけ残った民家の庭。瓦礫、家財道具の散乱が甚だしく、
石灯ろう・植木等の残骸から大邸宅が予想される＝1945年8月20日、
広島市十日市町付近、北方を望む（撮影：尾木正己）

Only stoneworks remained at this garden of a house. It seems that there once stood a large wealthy house since a large amount of debris and household items lay scattered around. You can also see the remains of stone garden lanterns and garden trees = Photographed northward from Tokaichi-machi, Hiroshima City on August 20th 1945 by Masami Oki

小町北端にあった国泰寺の宇品線電車道（西）側道路に面してあった
大クスノキ、宇品線電車軌道敷設の際にも、軌道を少し迂回させ
歩道を嵩上げし、市民に親しまれた大クスノキを守ったが、
原爆のエネルギーには勝てず爆風で倒れ、その後の火災で発火し、
消失枯死した。その後この老クスノキは根から堀りかえされ銘木として、
市内の家具店に保管されていたが、篆刻作家の安達春江によって、
刻字作品としてよみがえった＝1945年8月20日、
広島市尾道町北隅から東に向って（撮影：尾木正巳）

A huge camphor tree, facing the west side of Ujina tramway near Kokutai Temple in the north edge of Komachi, Hiroshima City, felled by the blast wave and burned by the following fire. The ancient tree, which was popular to the local people and once saved by having the route of the tramway diverted and a footpath raised when Ujina Tram Line had opened, could not withstand the energy of atomic bomb. The tree were pulled out by the root and kept as a precious wood in a furniture shop in the city and was subsequently used for artworks by Harue Adachi, a renowned seal carver = Photographed on August 20th 1945 eastward from the north end of Onomichi-cho, Hiroshima City by Masami Oki

饒津神社中門手前の参道西側から北に向って。二葉山の西麓に、
1835（天保6）年藩主浅野斉粛により壮健された南北に長い境内地に
老松群と100余基の石灯籠に囲まれた宏壮な木造の社殿群は、
熱線と爆風により、本殿・唐門など一瞬にして倒壊炎上。
石造物を残して全て灰燼に帰した。写真手前のように境内いたるところに
瓦礫が散乱し、後方の境内林も枯木が林立し、火災のすさまじさを
物語っている＝1945年8月20日、広島市（撮影：尾木正己）

Northward view from the west side of the approach in front of the Chumon gate of Nigitsu Shrine. A group of large wooden shrine buildings constructed by the order of the Local Lord Gensai Asano in 1835 and surrounding ancient pine trees, as well as more than 100 stone lanterns in the garden at the west side foot of Futabayama mountain, were completely destroyed by the blast wave and thermal radiation. The Inner Shrine and Karamon gate were also destroyed. Everything except the stoneworks turned into ashes. The debris scattered everywhere in the premises, and the charred trees standing tell the ferocity of the fire = Photographed toward Inner Shrine from Chumon gate at Nigitsu Shrine on August 20th 1945 by Masami Oki

山手町、山陽本線鉄道路線の柵。山陽本線。
鉄道路線敷枕木使用の鉄道沿線の柵が熱閃光により自然着火し燃えた
＝1945年8月末、爆心地から約2100m西方の広島市山手町（撮影：北勲）

Fences for Japan National Raiway Sanyo mainline at Yamate-cho, Hiroshima City. The fencing along the railway line, using wood crossties, was spontaneously ignited by the high temperature flash rays.
= Photographed in the end of August 1945 at Yamate-cho, approximately 2100m west of the ground zero by Isao Kita

広島市立第一国民学校救護所。比治山によって爆風がさえぎられ、また火災もまぬがれた段原地区には避難者が殺到。その収容に学校が、格好の場になった。治療には陸軍暁部隊から軍医、郊外から応援の医師があたった
＝1945年8月末頃、爆心地から東南東約2600mの段原山崎町市立第一国民学校（撮影：陸軍船舶司令部写真班）

Emergency evacuation center at No.1 Municipal Primary School in Danbara-Yamazakicho, Hiroshima City, located 2600m east-southeast of the ground zero. A large number of people fleeing the city center rushed to the Danbara area, where the blast was blocked thanks to Hijiyama hills and no fire occurred. The school immediately became an emergency center. Military doctors from Japan Army Akatsuki regiment as well as doctors from the suburbs treated the patients = Photographed in the end of August 1945 at No.1 Municipal Primary School by Photographer Team of the Japan Army Shipping HQ

1945年8月末頃、広島市（撮影：陸軍船舶司令部写真班）
In the end of August 1945. Hiroshima City. Photographed by Photographer Team of the Japan Army Shipping HQ

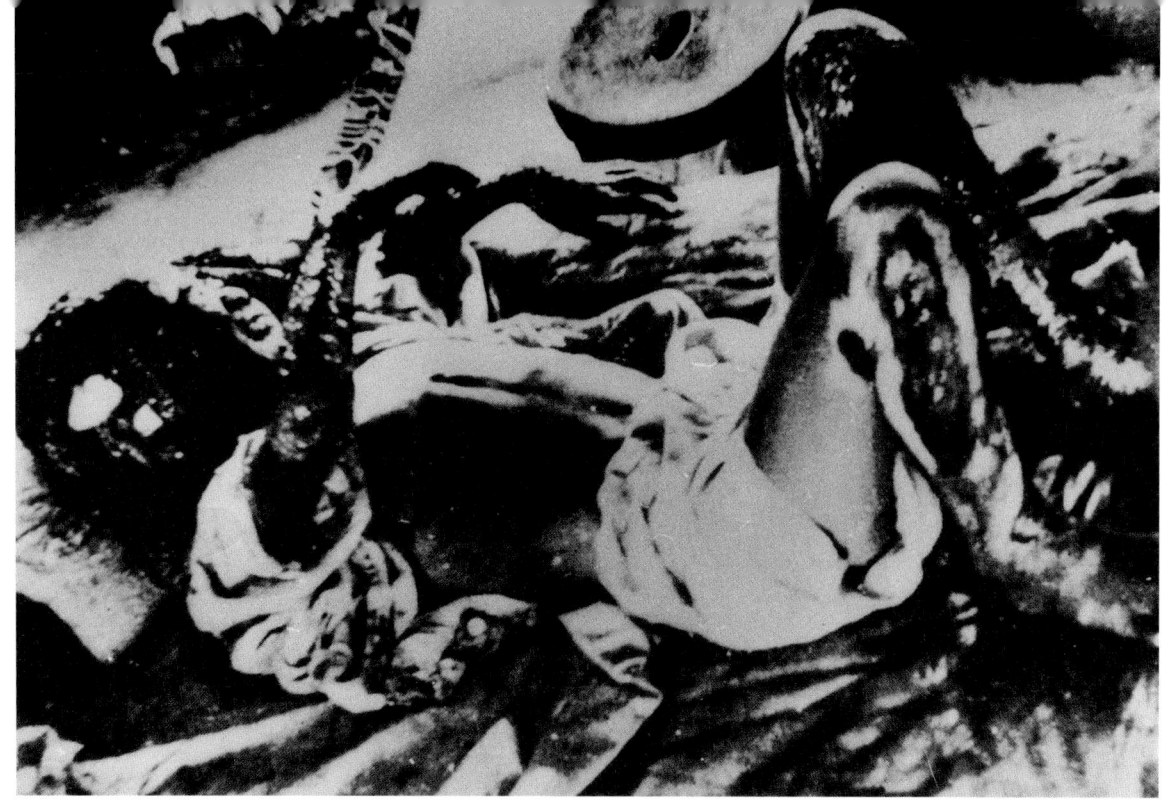

挺身隊として出動作業中に被爆した女子中学生。体全面火傷で苦悶。
被爆直後の撮影だが収容所不明＝1945年8月末頃、広島市（撮影：陸軍船舶司令部写真班）
A junior high school girl injured while working as a member of volunteer corps. Suffering from whole body burn.
The photograph was taken at an unidentified evacuation center in Hiroshima City immediately after the explosion
= Photographed in the end of August 1945 by Photographer Team of the Japan Army Shipping HQ

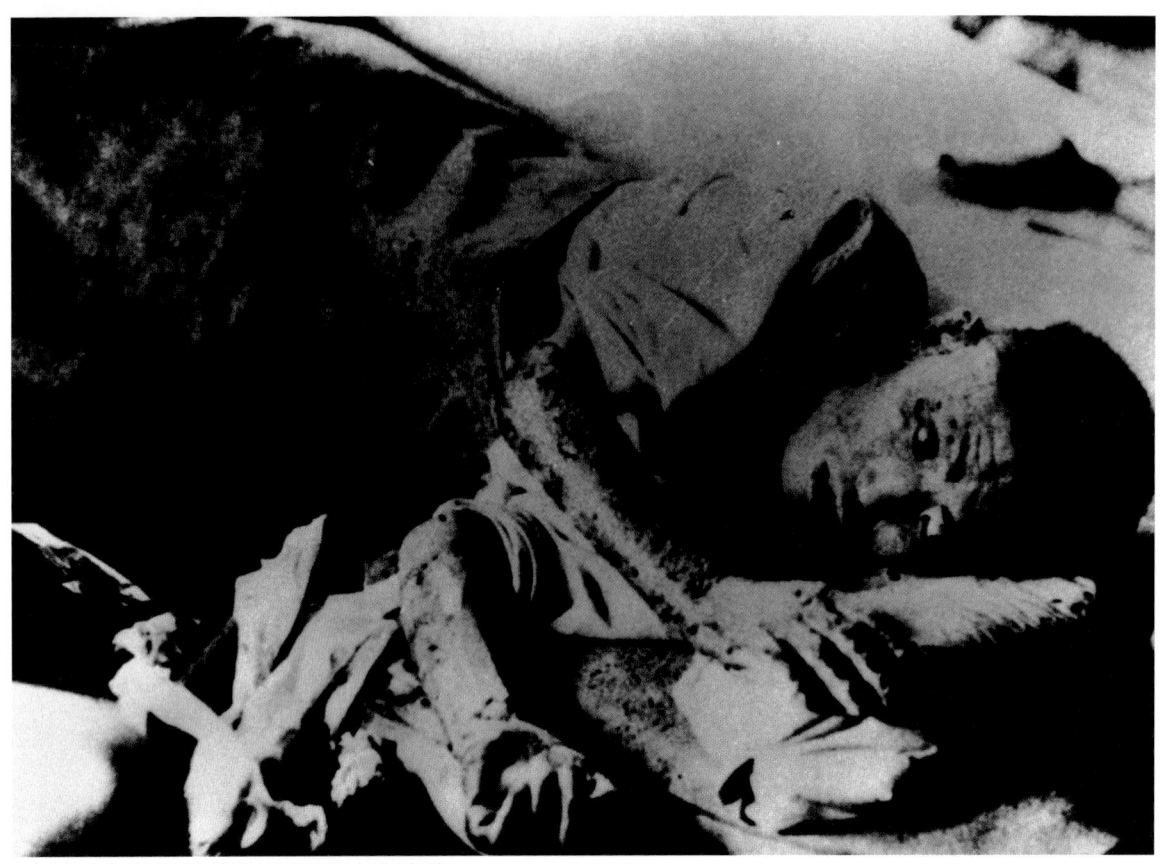

1945 年 8 月末頃、広島市（撮影：陸軍船舶司令部写真班）
In the end of August 1945. Hiroshima City. Photographed by Photographer Team of the Japan Army Shipping HQ

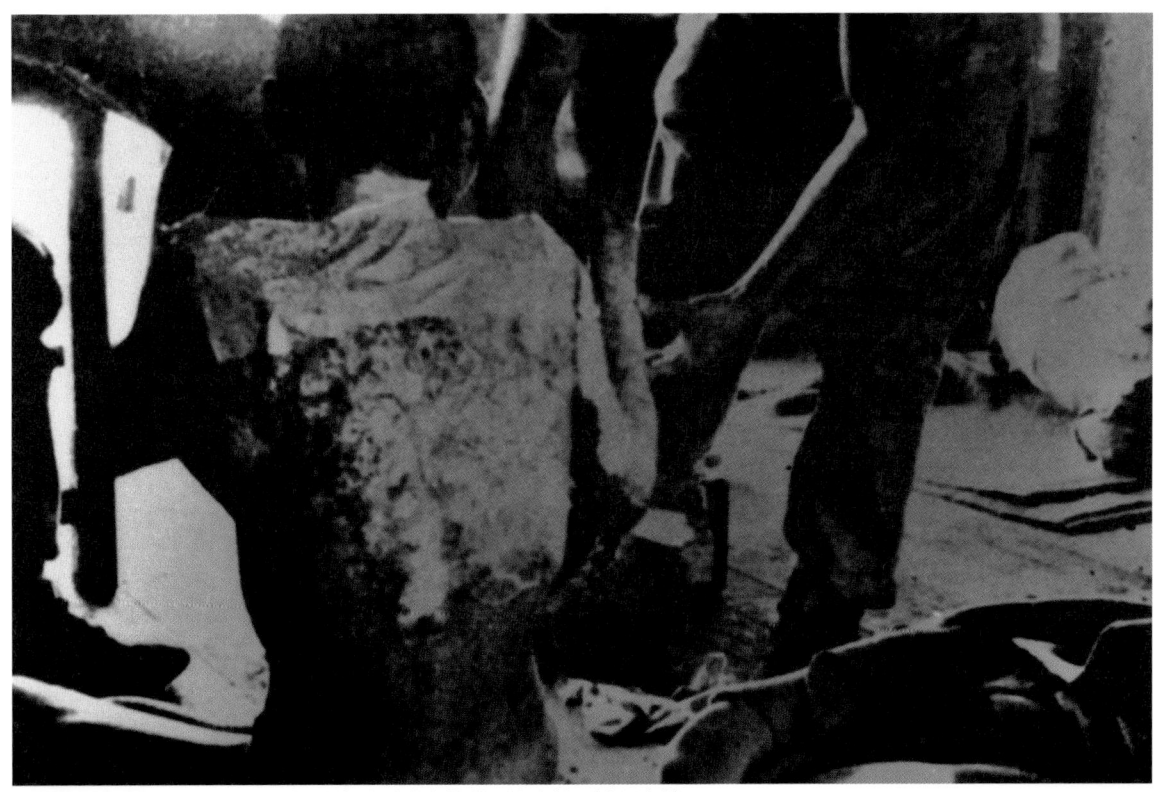

背全面に火傷を負う若い兵士＝ 1945 年 8 月末頃、広島市（撮影：陸軍船舶司令部写真班）
A young soldier with burn covering his whole backside. = In the end of August 1945. Hiroshima City.
= Photographed by Photographer Team of the Japan Army Shipping HQ

現在の広島護国神社前広場南側の石垣の内部に残る。
本土決戦に備え石垣の内部に掘り抜かれた半地下防空作戦室。
この地下壕に動員勤務していた2人の比治山高等女学校の3年生の
女子挺身隊員によって広島壊滅の一報が打電された＝1945年8月末、
中国軍管区司令部防空作戦室（撮影：川原四儀）

Inside view of the stone walls of south side square in front of the Hiroshima Gokoku shrine in Hiroshima City. Stone wall was dug out to build Semi-basement air defense operation room for the expected final battle on mainland. 2 of third year students from Hijiyama Girl's High school, who work in this underground vault as member of volunteer corps, cabled the first telegraph informing the destruction of Hiroshima. = Photographed in the end of August 1945 at Chugoku Military District HQ air defense operation room by Yotsugi Kawahara

爆心地から東南東360mの本通り。帝国銀行広島支店。
爆風で天井も床も吹き抜かれたが火災の中で大金庫は残った
＝1945年8月末頃、帝国銀行広島支店内部（撮影：川本俊雄）

Hondori Street at 360 meters east south-east of the ground zero. The walls and ceilings of Teikoku Bank Hiroshima Branch were blown away by the blast wave but the vault survived the fire. = Photographed in the end of August 1945 by Toshio Kawamoto

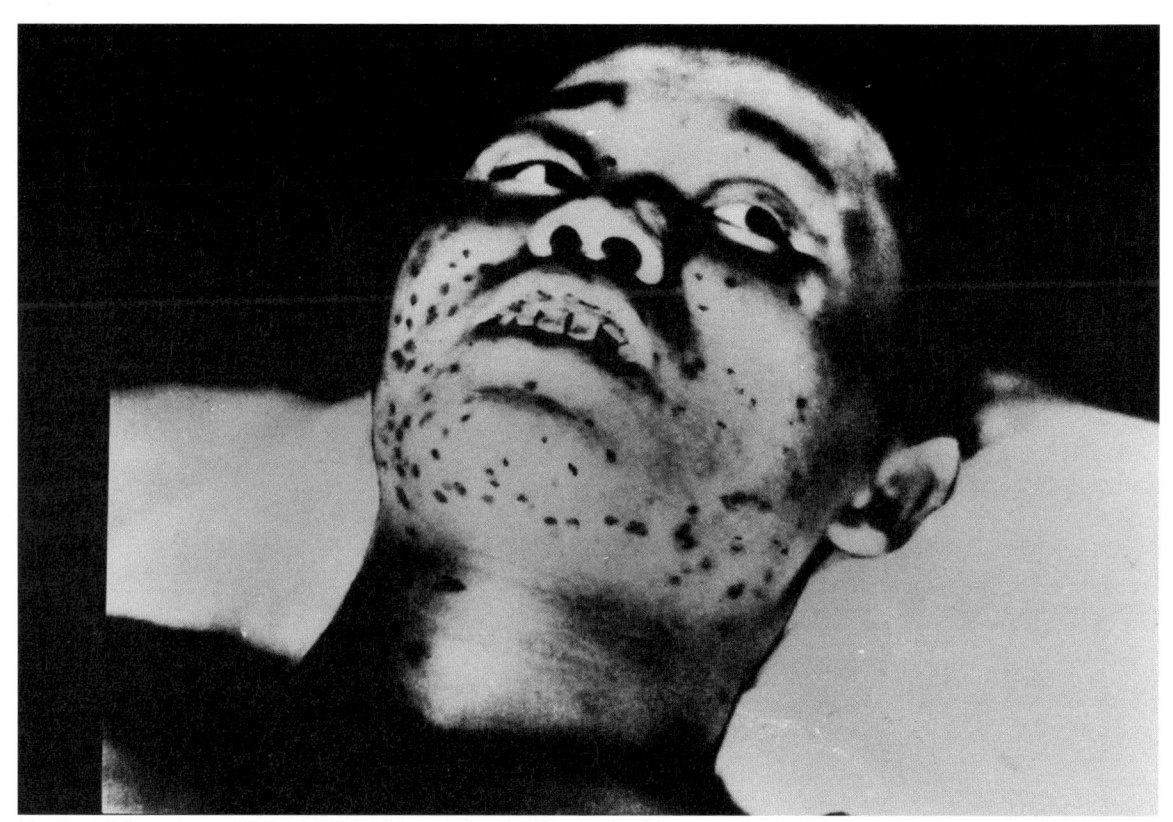

爆心地から南東に1500mの広島赤十字病院中央部＝1946年2月（撮影：木村権一）
The central part of the Hiroshima Red Cross Hospital, located 1,500 meters southeast of the ground zero = Photographed in February 1946 by Gonichi Kimura

米軍による DDT の散布？を自宅 2 階から、崇徳中学校講堂方向に撮影。
煙突は飯田染工場。後方煙突は加土染工場。
楠木町四丁目太田川沿い大芝公園土手に向って
(南東方向) = 1945 年 9 月頃、広島市大芝町
大芝公園付近から (撮影：深田敏夫)

US soldier spraying somethig, probably DDT (insectiside). Photograph taken from the second floor of the photographer's house, toward Sotoku middle school auditorium.
The chimneys are those of Iida dyeing factory and Kado dyeing factory (behind).
= Photographed toward Oshiba park riverbank at 4 cho-me, Kusunoki-machi, Hiroshima City, along the Ota river in September 1945 by Toshio Fukada

写真手前焼け跡は東洋座、その上電車通りの影は福屋百貨店のもの。中央部には全焼全壊した広島電鉄市内電車 (430 型) の
残骸、その上は木造で跡形もなくなった歌舞伎座の焼け跡と、その前 (電車通り側) は建物疎開の跡。
被爆前このあたりに仁丹の巨大な広告塔があった。道路上には救護隊や罹災者の消息を尋ねる人達が見える
= 1945 年 9 月頃、広島市上流川町中国新聞社新館屋上から北西 (八丁堀福屋旧館) 方向 (撮影：川原四儀)

On front is the burnt Toyo-za Cinema, and above left, burnt Fukuya department store casts shadows on tram road. In the center is the debris of totally destroyed tram car (type 430) of Hiroshima Electric Railway Co.,Ltd. . Above right is Kabuki-za Theater which burnt to the ground because of its wooden structure. Open space in front of this theater, along Densha (tram) street, are places where buildings evacuated before the Atomic bomb. There was a huge advertising tower of Jintan (Japanese medical product) in this area before the destruction.
On the road you can see members of rescue teams and people checking for the whereabout of their friends and relatives. = Photographed in September 1945 from the rooftops of Chugoku Shinbun-sha Shinnkan (new annex), Kaminagarekawa-cho, Hiroshima City, facing northwest towards the old building of Haccho-bori Fukuya department store by Yotsugi Kawahara

外国人の目から見ると、市の中心に墓があるのが異様に映る。
その依頼で撮影したもの＝ 1946 年 9 月頃、旧中国新聞社 3 階から宇品方向を望む（撮影：松重美人）

This photo was taken by the request of a foreigner who thought cemeteries in the middle of the city starnge.
= Photographed in September 1946 from the third floor of former HQ of Chugoku Shimbun-sha toward Ujina direction by Yoshito Matsushige

爆心地から北東 1380m の京橋の欄干上から撮影する。
3 枚続き。当時の中国新聞社・福屋新館・福屋旧館・日本勧業銀行広島支店が、
ガレキの中に残る＝ 1946 年 9 月頃、広島市京橋から（撮影：松重美人）

This photo was taken, 3 in a row, from the top of Kyobashi bridge rail, 1380 meters northeast of the ground zero, toward the Hirosima city center.
There used to be buildings of Chugoku Shimbun-sha, Fukuya depatment store New and Old Wing, and Nihon Kangyo Bank Hiroshima branch.
= All of them were destroyed. Photographed by Yoshito Matsushige

橋げたが風圧で移動、橋台が橋脚からはずれて通行危険となった。
9月と10月の風水害で完全に落橋した。
対岸は広島市中島本町(いまの平和記念公園) = 1945 年 9 月上旬、
本川橋(撮影:松本栄一)

It became too dangerous to cross the bridge as the girder was moved by the pressure of the blast wave and the abutment was detached from the pier. The bridge completely collapsed bnecause of the damages by storm and flood in September and October. Nakajima-honmachi, Hiroshima City (currently the Hiroshima Peace Memorial Park) can be seen on the opposite side = Photographed at the beginning of September 1945 at Motokawa Bridge by Eiichi Matsumoto

1945 年 9 月上旬、広島の爆心地付近の元安川西詰から東に向って
(撮影:松本栄一)

Eastward view from the west end of Motoyasu Bridge near the ground zero at the beginning of September 1945 by Eiichi Matsumoto

爆心地から東へ 850m。火災の熱により崩れ曲がった繁華街にあった
映画館・太陽館 = 1945 年 9 月上旬、広島市下鉄砲町(撮影:松本栄一)

850m east of the ground zero. Taiyokan Cinema in downtown Hiroshima City, which was destroyed and twisted by the heat from fire = Photographed at the beginning of September 1945 at Moto-machi, Hiroshima City by Eiichi Matsumoto

広島は商都であると同時に軍都でもあった。
各種軍関係施設が集まっていた基町の歩兵第一補充隊兵器庫近くで
散乱する機関銃や鉄カブト。爆心地から約 800m
= 1945 年 9 月上旬、広島市基町(撮影:松本栄一)

Hiroshima was a commercial as well as a military center. Machine guns and iron helmets scattered around the arsenal of the Infantry's First Replacement Depot in the Motomachi district, Hiroshima City, where military facilities were concentrated. Approximately 800m from the ground zero = Photographed at the beginning of September 1945 at Motomachi by Eiichi Matsumoto

相生橋の欄干は爆風によって斜めになっていた。左建物は本川国民学校＝1945年9月上旬、広島市（撮影：二瓶禎二）

The railing of Aioi Bridge was slanted by the blast wave. The building on the left is Honkawa Primary School
= Photographed at the beginning of September 1945 by Teiji Nihei

爆心地から南230m。広島瓦斯本社＝1945年9月上旬、広島市大手町（撮影：文部省学術研究会議 原子爆弾災害調査研究特別委員会）

230 meter south of the hypocenter. Hiroshima Gas Head Office = Early September 1945, Ote-machi (Photo: Special Committee for the Investigation of A-bomb Damages of the Scientific Research Council, Ministry of Education)

1945年9月7日〜12日頃までの間に撮影、広島市（撮影：文部省学術研究会議 原子爆弾災害調査研究特別委員会）

Photographed around September 7th - 12th 1945 in Hiroshima City by Special Committee for the Investigation of A-bomb Damages

1945年9月7日～12日頃までの間に撮影、
広島市（撮影：文部省学術研究会議 原子爆弾災害調査研究特別委員会）
Photographed around September 7th - 12th 1945 in Hiroshima City
by Special Committee for the Investigation of A-bomb Damages

1945年9月7日～12日頃までの間に撮影、
広島市（撮影：文部省学術研究会議 原子爆弾災害調査研究特別委員会）
Photograph taken on around September 7th - 12th 1945 in Hiroshima City by
Special Committee for the Investigation of A-bomb Damages

1945年9月7日～12日頃までの間に撮影、
広島市（撮影：文部省学術研究会議 原子爆弾災害調査研究特別委員会）
Photograph taken on around September 7th - 12th 1945 in Hiroshima City
by Special Committee for the Investigation of A-bomb Damages

1945年9月7日～12日頃までの間に撮影、
広島市（撮影：文部省学術研究会議 原子爆弾災害調査研究特別委員会）
Photograph taken on around September 7th - 12th 1945 in Hiroshima City
by Special Committee for the Investigation of A-bomb Damages

1945年9月7日～12日頃までの間に撮影、
広島市（撮影：文部省学術研究会議 原子爆弾災害調査研究特別委員会）
Photograph taken on around September 7th - 12th 1945 in Hiroshima City
by Special Committee for the Investigation of A-bomb Damages

1945年9月7日〜12日頃までの間に撮影、
広島市（撮影：文部省学術研究会議
原子爆弾災害調査研究特別委員会）

Photograph taken on around September
7th - 12th 1945 in Hiroshima City by Special
Committee for the Investigation of A-bomb
Damages

1945年9月7日〜12日頃までの間に撮影、広島市
（撮影：文部省学術研究会議　原子爆弾災害調査研究特別委員会）

Photograph taken on around September 7th - 12th 1945 in Hiroshima City
by Special Committee for the Investigation of A-bomb Damages

1945年9月7日〜12日頃までの間に撮影、広島市
（撮影：文部省学術研究会議　原子爆弾災害調査研究特別委員会）

Photograph taken on around September 7th - 12th 1945 in Hiroshima City
by Special Committee for the Investigation of A-bomb Damages

広島駅正前＝1945年9月8日〜23日頃（撮影；松本栄一）
In front of the Hiroshima Station. = Photographed around September 8th to 23rd 1945 by Eiichi Matsumoto

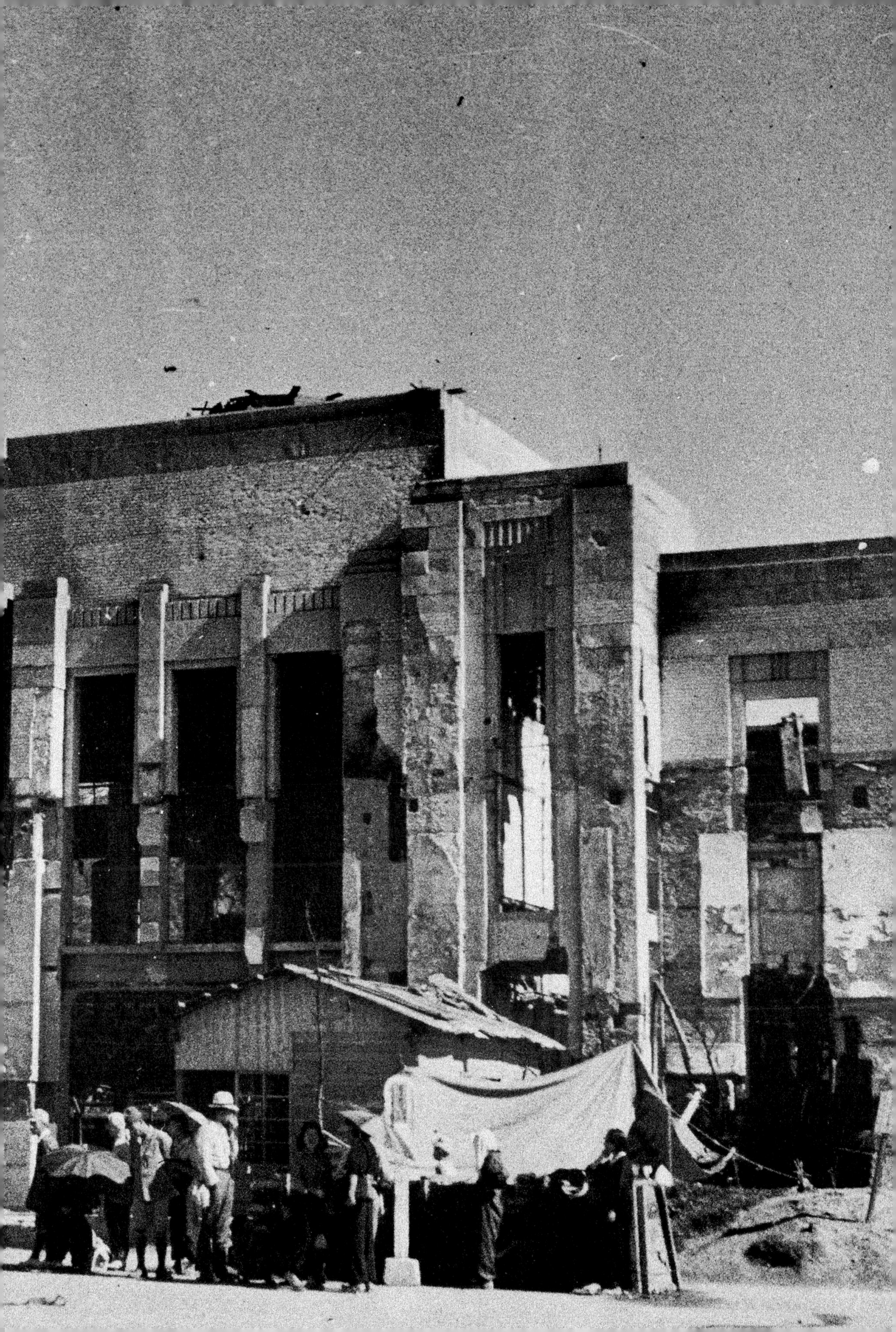

爆心地から100m。元安川にかかる元安橋
＝1945年9月8日～23日頃（撮影：松本栄一）

100m from the ground zero. Motoyasu Bridge over the Motoyasu River, Hiroshima City. = Phpgraphed around September 8th to 23rd 1945 by Eiichi Matsumoto

左からの爆風で薙ぎ倒された欄干＝1945年9月8日～23日頃、
御幸橋（撮影：松本栄一）

The railing fallen down to the ground by the blast wave from the left. = Photographed around September 8th to 23rd 1945 on Miyuki Bridge, Hiroshima City by Eiichi Matsumoto

爆圧で折れた鉄筋コンクリートのはり。爆心から200メートルほどの日赤広島県支部の倉庫2階天井は、
爆圧で屋上がすり鉢状に凹んだ＝1945年9月8日～23日頃、広島市猿楽町（撮影：松本栄一）

The beams of reinforced concrete crooked by the blast wave. At the Hiroshima Prefecture Red Cross warehouse about 200 meters from the ground zero, the ceiling of the second floor has been indented by the blast wave. = Photographed around September 8th to 23rd 1945 at the east end of Aioi Bridge, Hiroshima City by Eiichi Matsumoto

爆心地から約1.5kmの広島赤十字病院＝1945年9月8日〜23日頃
（撮影：松本栄一）

Hiroshima Red Cross Hospital, about 1.5km from the ground zero.
= Photographed around September 8th to 23rd 1945 by Eiichi Matsumoto

爆心地から約1.5kmの広島赤十字病院＝1945年9月8日〜23日頃
（撮影：松本栄一）

Hiroshima Red Cross Hospital, about 1.5km from the ground zero.
= Photographed around September 8th to 23rd 1945 by Eiichi Matsumoto

広島赤十字病院。爆風によって窓枠が飴のように曲がっていた
＝1945年9月上旬、広島市千田町
（撮影：文部省学術研究会議 原子爆弾災害調査研究特別委員会）

Hiroshima Red Cross Hospital.
The window frame was bent like melted candy by the blast wave
= Photographed at the beginning of September 1945 at Senda-machi,
Hiroshima City by Special Committee for the Investigation of A-bomb Damages

中国新聞社屋上から広島駅方面を望む＝1945年9月8日〜23日頃、
広島市上流川町（撮影：松本栄一）

View toward the Hiroshima Station area from the rooftop of the Chugoku
Shimbun-sha building. = Photographed around September 8th to 23rd 1945
at Kaminagarekawa-cho, Hiroshima City by Eiichi Matsumoto

広島文理大学遠望＝ 1945 年 9 月 8 日〜 23 日頃（撮影：松本栄一）

View of the Hiroshima Imperial University Teachers College at a distance
= Photographed around September 8th to 23rd 1945 by Eiichi Matsumoto

広島文理大学遠望＝ 1945 年 9 月 8 日〜 23 日頃（撮影：松本栄一）

View of the Hiroshima Imperial University Teachers College at a distance
= Photographed around September 8th to 23rd 1945 by Eiichi Matsumoto

吹き抜けた爆風のため窓枠が外側に飛ばされている
＝ 1945 年 9 月 8 日〜 23 日頃、広島本川国民学校西校舎の西側
（撮影：松本栄一）

The window frames were blown out by the blast wave
= Photographed around September 8th to 23rd 1945 on the west side
of the west building of Honkawa Primary School by Eiichi Matsumoto

爆風でできた壁の亀裂＝ 1945 年 9 月上旬、広島市
（撮影：文部省学術研究会議
原子爆弾災害調査研究特別委員会）

A wall crack caused by the blast wave = Photographed at the
beginning of September 1945 in Hiroshima City by Special
Committee for the Investigation of A-bomb Damages

中国配電本社ビルの爆風によって飛んだ雨とい＝1945年9月上旬、広島市小町
（撮影：文部省学術研究会議 原子爆弾災害調査研究特別委員会）

The gutters of Chugoku Haiden HQ Building blown off by the blast wave = Photographed at the beginning of September 1945 at Komachi, Hiroshima City by Special Committee for the Investigation of A-bomb Damages

爆心地から南へ 800m。中国配電本社ビル。北側の雨どいが、爆風によってちぎれ飛んでいた＝ 1945 年 9 月上旬、広島市小町
（撮影：文部省学術研究会議　原子爆弾災害調査研究特別委員会）

800m south of the ground zero. Chugoku Haiden HQ Building. The Gutters on the north side were torn off
= Photographed at the beginning of September 1945 at Komachi Hiroshima City by Special Committee for the Investigation of A-bomb Damages

広島赤十字病院＝ 1945 年 9 月中旬、広島市千田町
（撮影：文部省学術研究会議 原子爆弾災害調査研究特別委員会）

Hiroshima Red Cross Hospital = Mid-September 1945,
Senda-machi, Hiroshima City (Photo: Special Committee for Investigation on
Atomic Bomb Disaster, National Research Council of Ministry of Education)

破壊した玄関のドア＝ 1945 年 9 月中旬、
広島市（撮影：文部省学術研究会議 原子爆弾災害調査研究特別委員会）

Destroyed entrance door = Photographed in mid-September 1945 in
Hiroshima City by Special Committee for the Investigation of
A-bomb Damages

広島赤十字病院＝ 1945 年 9 月中旬、広島市千田町
（撮影：文部省学術研究会議 原子爆弾災害調査研究特別委員会）

Hiroshima Red Cross Hospital = Photographed in mid-September 1945
at Senda-machi, Hiroshima City by Special Committee for the Investigation of
A-bomb Damages

1945年9月中旬、広島市
(撮影:文部省学術研究会議 原子爆弾災害調査研究特別委員会)
Photographed in mid-September 1945 in Hiroshima City by Special Committee for the Investigation of A-bomb Damages

爆心地から680m。中国配電本店の玄関。雨といも完全に潰れている
= 1945年9月上旬、広島市小町
(撮影:文部省学術研究会議 原子爆弾災害調査研究特別委員会)
680m from the ground zero. The entrance of Chugoku Haiden HQ Building. Gutters are completely crushed = Photographed at the beginning of September 1945 at Komachi, Hiroshima City by Special Committee for the Investigation of A-bomb Damages

1945年9月中旬、広島市
(撮影:文部省学術研究会議 原子爆弾災害調査研究特別委員会)
Photographed in mid-September 1945 in Hiroshima City. Photographed by Special Committee for the Investigation of A-bomb Damages

広島赤十字病院 = 1945年9月中旬、広島市千田町
(撮影:文部省学術研究会議 原子爆弾災害調査研究特別委員会)
Hiroshima Red Cross Hospital. = Photographed in mid-September 1945 at Senda-machi, Hiroshima City by Special Committee for the Investigation of A-bomb Damages

墓石の爆風圧の被災状況など調査する班員たち。計5人のチームだった
= 1945年9月上旬、広島市
(撮影:文部省学術研究会議 原子爆弾災害調査研究特別委員会)
5 man team investigating the damage of gravestones by the blast wave = Photographed at the beginning of September 1945 in Hiroshima City by Special Committee for the Investigation of A-bomb Damages

爆心地から130m。爆風でくずれた元安橋の東詰め近くの石柱の上部。
後方に広島県産業奨励館が見える＝1945年9月上旬（撮影：文部省学術研究会議 原子爆弾災害調査研究特別委員会）

130m from the ground zero. Top part of the middle column near the east end of Motoyasu Bridge, Hiroshima City collapsed due to the blast wave.
Hiroshima Prefectural Industrial Promotion Hall (the Atomic Bomb Dome) is seen behind the bridge.
= Photographed at the beginning of September 1945 by Special Committee for the Investigation of A-bomb Damages

爆心地付近に架かる相生橋。左奥は広島県商工経済会
＝ 1945 年 9 月上旬、相生橋北参道西より
（撮影：文部省学術研究会議　原子爆弾災害調査研究特別委員会）

Aioi Bridge near the ground zero. Hiroshima Prefecture Chamber of Commerce and Economy are seen on upper left = Photographed at the beginning of September 1945 from the west side of Aioi Bridge North Approach by Special Committee for the Investigation of A-bomb Damages

中国配電本社ビルの爆風によってちぎれた雨とい＝ 1945 年 9 月上旬、広島市小町（撮影：文部省学術研究会議　原子爆弾災害調査研究特別委員会）

The gutters at Chugoku Haiden HQ Building torn by the blast wave = Photographed at the beginning of September 1945 at Komachi, Hiroshima City by Special Committee for the Investigation of A-bomb Damages

広島商工会議所の屋上から相生橋を見おろす。手前右の残骸は櫓下変電所＝1945年9月上旬
（撮影：文部省学術研究会議 原子爆弾災害調査研究特別委員会）

Looking down Aioi Bridge from the rooftop of Hiroshima Chamber of Commerce building. The ruin on the right is Yagurashita electrical substation
= Photographed at the beginning of September 1945 by Special Committee for the Investigation of A-bomb Damages

爆風に耐えて残った広島護国神社の狛犬を調査する菅義夫班員＝1945年9月中旬（撮影：文部省学術研究会議 原子爆弾災害調査研究特別委員会）

Yoshio Suge, a member of the Special Committee for the Investigation of A-bomb Damages, studying the Komainu (stone-carved guardian dog) at Hiroshima Gokoku Shrine, Hiroshima City. The Komainu survived the blast wave = Photographed in mid-September 1945 by Special Committee for the Investigation of A-bomb Damages

相生橋の標柱の被害状況を調べる班員たち＝1945年9月上旬
（撮影：文部省学術研究会議　原子爆弾災害調査研究特別委員会）

Team members studying the damage of the station pole at Aioi Bridge, Hiroshima City = Photographed at the beginning of September 1945 by Special Committee for the Investigation of A-bomb Damages

爆風で上部が破壊された相生橋の標柱＝1945年9月上旬
（撮影：文部省学術研究会議　原子爆弾災害調査研究特別委員会）

The station pole of Aioi Bridge, Hiroshima City. The top part of the pole was destroyed by the blast wave = Photographed at the beginning of September 1945 by Special Committee for the Investigation of A-bomb Damages

護国神社の石灯篭に刻まれた熱線の痕を調査する班員たち
＝1945年9月中旬、広島市基町
（撮影：文部省学術研究会議　原子爆弾災害調査研究特別委員会）

Team members studying the damage on the stone lantern by thermal radiation = Photographed at Motomachi, Hiroshima City in mid-September 1945 by Special Committee for the Investigation of A-bomb Damages

原爆の爆風にも耐え残った広島護国神社の狛犬を調査する
＝1945年9月中旬
（撮影：文部省学術研究会議　原子爆弾災害調査研究特別委員会）

View of Inner Shrine of the Hiroshima Gokoku Shrine, Hitoshima City, from the rooftop of Hiroshima Chamber of Commerce building = Photographed in mid-September 1945 by Special Committee for the Investigation of A-bomb Damages

広島護国神社参道を望む＝1945年9月中旬
（撮影：文部省学術研究会議 原子爆弾災害調査研究特別委員会）

View of the Approach road to the Hiroshima Gokoku Shrine,
Hiroshima City = Photographed in mid-September 1945
by Special Committee for the Investigation of A-bomb Damages

広島護国神社参道を望む＝1945年9月中旬
（撮影：文部省学術研究会議 原子爆弾災害調査研究特別委員会）

View of the Approach road to the Hiroshima Gokoku Shrine,
Hiroshima City = Photographed in mid-September 1945
by Special Committee for the Investigation of A-bomb Damages

広島商工会議所屋上から護国神社本殿方面を望む
＝1945年9月上旬（撮影：文部省学術研究会議
原子爆弾災害調査研究特別委員会）

View of Inner Shrine of the Hiroshima Gokoku Shrine,
Hitoshima City, from the rooftop of Hiroshima Chamber
of Commerce building = Photographed at the beginning of
September 1945 by Special Committee for the Investigation
of A-bomb Damages

広島商工会議所屋上より市街地の東方面を望む
= 1945 年 9 月上旬（撮影：文部省学術研究会議
原子爆弾災害調査研究特別委員会）

View of the east side of the Hiroshima City from the
rooftop of Hiroshima Chamber of Commerce building
= Photographed at the beginning of September 1945
by Special Committee for the Investigation of A-bomb
Damages

広島商工会議所屋上より爆心地から市の東南方面を望む
= 1945 年 9 月上旬（撮影：文部省学術研究会議
原子爆弾災害調査研究特別委員会）

View of the southeast side of the Hiroshima City including
the ground zero, from the rooftop of Hiroshima Chamber
of Commerce building = Photographed at the beginning
of September 1945 by Special Committee for the
Investigation of A-bomb Damages

爆心地から北西へ 180m。手前は日本赤十字社
広島支部倉庫と元安川、本川を望む = 1945 年 9 月上旬
（撮影：文部省学術研究会議
原子爆弾災害調査研究特別委員会）

180m northwest of the ground zero. The warehouse of
Japanese Red Cross Hiroshima Office, Motoyasu River
and Hon River are seen in the front = Photographed at the
beginning of September 1945 by Special Committee for
the Investigation of A-bomb Damages

広島商工会議所屋上から T 字型が特徴の相生橋を見る。
後方の建物は本川国民学校 = 1945 年 9 月上旬
（撮影：文部省学術研究会議
原子爆弾災害調査研究特別委員会）

View of T-shape Aioi Bridge from the rooftop of
Hiroshima Chamber of Commerce building. The building
in the back is Honkawa Primary School = Photographed
at the beginning of September 1945 by Special Committee
for the Investigation of A-bomb Damages

一面焼け野原となった広島市内。正面の白っぽい建物は、帝国銀行広島支店
＝ 1945 年 9 月上旬（撮影：文部省学術研究会議 原子爆弾災害調査研究特別委員会）

Part of the Hiroshima City, completely burnt to the ground. The Whitish color building in the front is Hiroshima Branch of Teikoku Bank
= Photographed at the beginning of September 1945 by Special Committee for the Investigation of A-bomb Damages

太田川下流、西北方面を望む＝1945年9月上旬
（撮影：文部省学術研究会議
原子爆弾災害調査研究特別委員会）

View of the northwest side of the Hiroshima City, at the downstream of Ota River = Photographed at the beginning of September 1945 by Special Committee for the Investigation of A-bomb Damages

広島商工会議所屋上より、手前元安川と本川を望む
＝1945年9月上旬（撮影：文部省学術研究会議
原子爆弾災害調査研究特別委員会）

View of Motoyasu River (front) and Hon River from the rooftop of Hiroshima Chamber of Commerce building = Photographed at the beginning of September 1945 by Special Committee for the Investigation of A-bomb Damages

広島商工会議所屋上より市街地を望む＝1945年9月上旬
（撮影：文部省学術研究会議　原子爆弾災害調査研究特別委員会）

View of Hiroshima City from the rooftop of Hiroshima Chamber of Commerce building = Photographed at the beginning of September 1945 by Special Committee for the Investigation of A-bomb Damages

広島商工会議所屋上より市街地の西方面を望む。
左は相生橋＝1945年9月上旬
（撮影：文部省学術研究会議　原子爆弾災害調査研究特別委員会）

View of the west side of the Hiroshima City center from the rooftop of Hiroshima Chamber of Commerce building. Aioi Bridge is on the left = Photographed at the beginning of September 1945 by Special Committee for the Investigation of A-bomb Damages

広島市内の東方面を望む。
正面の高い建物は福屋百貨店＝1945年9月上旬
（撮影：文部省学術研究会議　原子爆弾災害調査研究特別委員会）

View of the east side of the Hiroshima City center. The tall building in front is Fukuya Department Store = Photographed at the beginning of September 1945 by Special Committee for the Investigation of A-bomb Damages

広島商工会議所屋上より市街地北方面を望む。
手前は護国神社本殿跡＝1945年9月上旬
（撮影：文部省学術研究会議　原子爆弾災害調査研究特別委員会）

View of the north side of the Hiroshima City center from the rooftop of Hiroshima Chamber of Commerce building. The part in front is the ruin of Inner Shrine of the Hiroshima Gokoku Shrine = Photographed at the beginning of September 1945 by Special Committee for the Investigation of A-bomb Damages

広島商工会議所屋上より太田川をはさんで市の北方面を望む
＝ 1945 年 9 月上旬
（撮影：文部省学術研究会議 原子爆弾災害調査研究特別委員会）

View of the north side of the Hiroshima City and Ota River
from the rooftop of the Hiroshima Chamber of Commerce building
= Photographed at the beginning of September 1945 by Special Committee
for the Investigation of A-bomb Damages

広島市の東方面を望む。手前右は広島県産業奨励館と
元安川＝ 1945 年 9 月上旬
（撮影：文部省学術研究会議 原子爆弾災害調査研究特別委員会）

View of the east side of the Hiroshima City.
Hiroshima Prefectural Industrial Promotion Hall (the Atomic Bomb Dome)
and Motoyasu River are seen on the right
= Photographed at the beginning of September 1945 by Special Committee
for the Investigation of A-bomb Damages

爆心地から 180m。日本生命広島支店の正面
＝ 1945 年 9 月中旬、広島市大手町
（撮影：文部省学術研究会議 原子爆弾災害調査研究特別委員会）

180m from the ground zero. The frontal view of the Hiroshima Branch
of Nihon Seimei = Photographed at Otemachi, Hiroshima City
in mid-September 1945 by Special Committee for the Investigation
of A-bomb Damages

爆心地から70mの西向寺の墓地から広島県産業奨励館を望む
＝ 1945年9月上旬（撮影：文部省学術研究会議 原子爆弾災害調査研究特別委員会）
View of Hiroshima Prefectural Industrial Promotion Hall (the Atomic Bomb Dome)
from Saikou-ji Cemetery, 70m from the ground zero.
＝ Photographed at the beginning of September 1945
by Special Committee for the Investigation of A-bomb Damage

広島県産業奨励館（原爆ドーム）。
下の黒い部分はフィルムが感光したのだろうか
＝ 1945 年 9 月上旬（撮影：文部省学術研究会議
原子爆弾災害調査研究特別委員会）

Hiroshima Prefectural Industrial Promotion Hall
(the Atomic Bomb Dome). The black part of this
photo may have resulted from the film being exposed.
= Photographed at the beginning of September 1945
by Special Committee for the Investigation of A-bomb
Damage

爆心地から 1.5km。広島赤十字病院正面
＝ 1945 年 9 月上旬、広島市千田町
（撮影：文部省学術研究会議 原子爆弾災害調査研究特別委員会）

1.5 km from the ground zero. Front of Hiroshima Red Cross Hospital = Early
September 1945, Senda-machi, Hiroshima City (Photo: Special Committee
for Investigation on Atomic Bomb Disaster, National Research Council of
Ministry of Education)

爆風で壊れたビルの窓
＝ 1945 年 9 月上旬、広島市
（撮影：文部省学術研究会議 原子爆弾災害調査研究特別委員会）

Windows of a building destroyed by the blast wave = Early September 1945,
Hiroshima City (Photo: Special Committee for Investigation on Atomic
Bomb Disaster, National Research Council of Ministry of Education)

爆風による墓石のずれなどを調査する菅義夫班員＝1945年9月上旬、
広島市（撮影：文部省学術研究会議 原子爆弾災害調査研究特別委員会）

A member of the Special Committee for Investigation on Atomic Bomb
Disaster, Yoshio Suga investigating gravestones displaced by the blast wave
= Early September 1945, Hiroshima City (Photo: Special Committee for
Investigation on Atomic Bomb Disaster, National Research Council of
Ministry of Education)

爆風でずれた墓石＝1945年9月上旬、広島市
（撮影：文部省学術研究会議 原子爆弾災害調査研究特別委員会）

A gravestone displaced by the blast wave = Early September 1945, Hiroshima
City (Photo: Special Committee for Investigation on Atomic Bomb Disaster,
National Research Council of Ministry of Education)

被災した市内を調査する班員＝1945年9月上旬、広島市（撮影：文部省学術研究会議 原子爆弾災害調査研究特別委員会）

Team members investigating the devastated city = Early September 1945, Hiroshima City
(Photo: Special Committee for Investigation on Atomic Bomb Disaster, National Research Council of Ministry of Education)

文部省学術研究会議原子爆弾災害調査研究特別委員会の「広島長崎における輻射温度および爆風圧」の調査班の助手として参加した
加賀美幾三氏が撮影した広島県産業奨励館＝1945年9月上旬（撮影：加賀美幾三）

The Hiroshima Prefectural Industrial Promotion Hall (the Atomic Bomb Dome) photographed by Ikuzo Kagami,
who assisted the "radiation temperature and bomb blast pressure" investigation team formed by the Special Committee for Investigation
on Atomic Bomb Disaster, National Research Council of Ministry of Education = Early September 1945 (Photo: Ikuzo Kagami)

広島県産業奨励館と元安川＝1945年9月上旬（撮影：文部省学術研究会議　原子爆弾災害調査研究特別委員会）
Hiroshima Prefectural Industrial Promotion Hall (the Atomic Bomb Dome) and Motoyasu River.
= Photographed at the beginning of September 1945 by Special Committee for the Investigation of A-bomb Damage

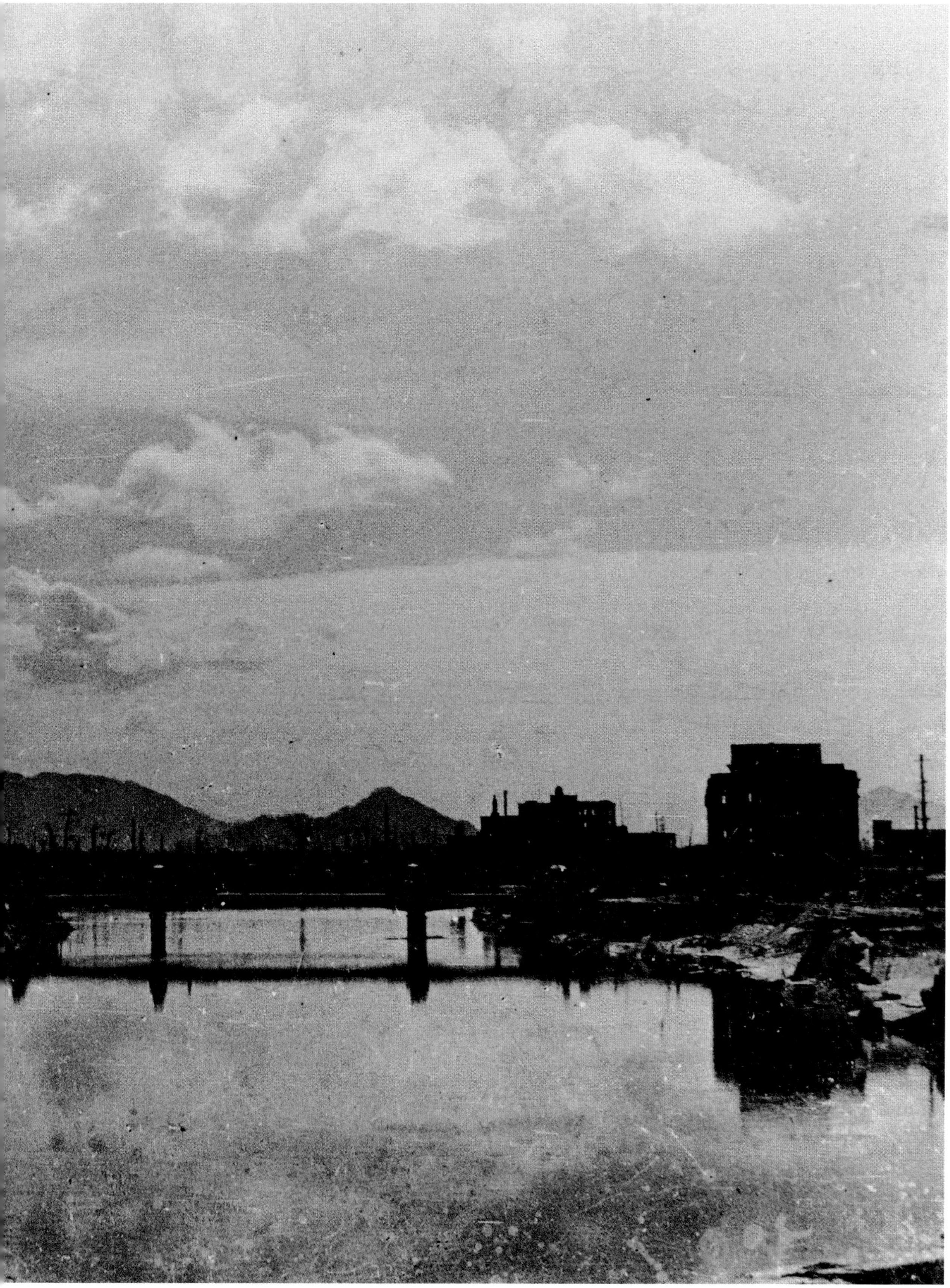

広島商工会議所屋上から手前は相生橋。市の西方面を望む
= 1945年9月中旬、広島市基町（撮影：松本栄一）

View of the west side of the Hiroshima City from the rooftop of the Hiroshima Chamber of Commerce and Industry in Motomachi. Aioi Bridge is in front. = Photographed in mid-September 1945 by Eiichi Matsumoto

広島県産業奨励館と元安川を望む。遠くに広島湾が見える= 1945年9月上旬
（撮影：文部省学術研究会議 原子爆弾災害調査研究特別委員会）

Hiroshima Prefectural Industrial Promotion Hall and Motoyasu River.
= Phptpgraphed at the beginning of September 1945 by Special Committee for the Investigation of A-bomb Damage

広島商工会議所屋上から太田川の対岸の市内西方面を望む=
1945年9月中旬、広島市基町（撮影：松本栄一）

View of the west side of the Hiroshima City, beyond the Ota River, from the roof of Hiroshima Chamber of Commerce and Industry in Motomachi.
= Photographed in mid-September 1945 by Eiichi Matsumoto

広島商工会議所屋上から、護国神社をはじめ広島市基町一帯を見る。
正面に爆風でなぎ倒された大鳥居が見える= 1945年9月中旬
（撮影：松本栄一）

View of the Hiroshima Gokoku Shrine and the Motomachi, Hiroshima City from the rooftop of Hiroshima Chamber of Commerce and Industry.
The big Torii (entrance gate to the shrine) fallen down by the blast can be seen in the front. = Photographed in mid-September 1945 by Eiichi Matsumoto

広島商工会議所屋上から。左側の相生橋、そして西方を望む
＝ 1945 年 9 月中旬、広島市基町（撮影：松本栄一）

View of Aioi Bridge and the west side of the Hiroshima City from the rooftop of the Hiroshima Chamber of Commerce and Industry in Motomachi.
= Photographed in mid-September 1945 by Eiichi Matsumoto

広島商工会議所屋上から市の東方面を望む。右手の広い敷地は
西練兵所があった場所＝ 1945 年 9 月中旬、広島市基町（撮影：松本栄一）

View of the east side of the Hiroshima City from the rooftop of Hiroshima Chamber of Commerce and Industry in Motomachi.
The large area on the left used to be the Nishi Military Exercise Grounds.
= Photographed in mid-September 1945 by Eiichi Matsumoto

爆心地北西 200m の所にあった
広島商工会議所屋上から北方面を望む。
流れるのは太田川
＝ 1945 年 9 月中旬、広島市基町
（撮影：松本栄一）

Northward view of the Hiroshima City from the rooftop of Hiroshima Chamber of Commerce and Industry in Motomachi, Hiroshima City, 200m northwest of the ground zero. The Ota River runs.
= Photographed in mid-September 1945 by Eiichi Matsumoto

広島商工会議所屋上から市の東北方面を望む。正面には護国神社本殿があった＝ 1945 年 9 月中旬、広島市基町（撮影：松本栄一）

View of the northeast side of the Hiroshima City from the rooftop of the Hiroshima Chamber of Commerce and Industry in Motomachi, Hiroshima City. There was the Main shrine of the Hiroshima Gokoku Shrine in front. = Photographed in mid-September 1945 by Eiichi Matsumoto

広島商工会議所屋上から市の北方面を望む。左側奥に広島城が見える ＝ 1945 年 9 月中旬、広島市基町（撮影：松本栄一）

View of the north side of the Hiroshima City from the rooftop of Hiroshima Chamber of Commerce and Industry in Motomachi. On the left back, Hiroshima Castle can be seen. = Photographed in mid-September 1945 by Eiichi Matsumoto

中国新聞社屋上から市内の北方面を望む＝ 1945 年 9 月中旬、広島市上流川町（撮影：松本栄一）

View of the north side of the Hiroshima City from the rooftop of the Chugoku Shimbun-sha building in Motomachi.
= Photographed in mid-September 1945 by Eiichi Matsumoto

爆心地から東南東 900m にあった中国新聞社屋上から市内の北方面を望む
＝ 1945 年 9 月中旬、広島市上流川町（撮影：松本栄一）

View of the north side of the Hiroshima City from the rooftop of the
Chugoku Shimbun-sha building in Kaminagarekawa-cho.
900m east-southeast of the ground zero.
= Photographed in mid-September 1945 by Eiichi Matsumoto

中国新聞屋上から市街地を望む＝ 1945 年 9 月中旬、
広島市上流川町（撮影：松本栄一）

View of the Hiroshima City from the rooftop of the Chugoku Shimbun-sha
building in Kaminagarekawa-cho.
= Photographed in mid-September 1945 by Eiichi Matsumoto

中国新聞屋上から市街地を望む＝ 1945 年 9 月中旬、広島市上流川町
（撮影：松本栄一）

View of the Hiroshima City from the rooftop of the Chugoku Shimbun-sha
building in Kaminagarekawa-cho.
= Photographed in mid-September 1945 by Eiichi Matsumoto

中国新聞屋上から牛田山方面を望む。左中央にある建物は
広島中央放送局＝ 1945 年 9 月中旬、広島市上流川町（撮影：松本栄一）

View of the Ushita mountain area of the Hiroshima City from the rooftop of
the Chugoku Shimbun-sha building in Kaminagarekawa-cho.
The building at center left was the Hiroshima Central Broadcasting Station.
= Photographed in mid-September 1945 by Eiichi Matsumoto

爆心地から東南東へ900m、中国新聞社屋上から市内を見る。手前は、日本基督教団広島流川教館＝1945年9月中旬、広島市上流川町（撮影：松本栄一）
View of the Hiroshima City from the rooftop of the Chugoku Shimbun-sha building in Kaminagarekawa-cho, 900m east-southeast of the ground zero. In front is Hiroshima Nagarekawa Hall of the United Church of Christ in Japan. = Photographed in mid-September 1945 by Eiichi Matsumoto

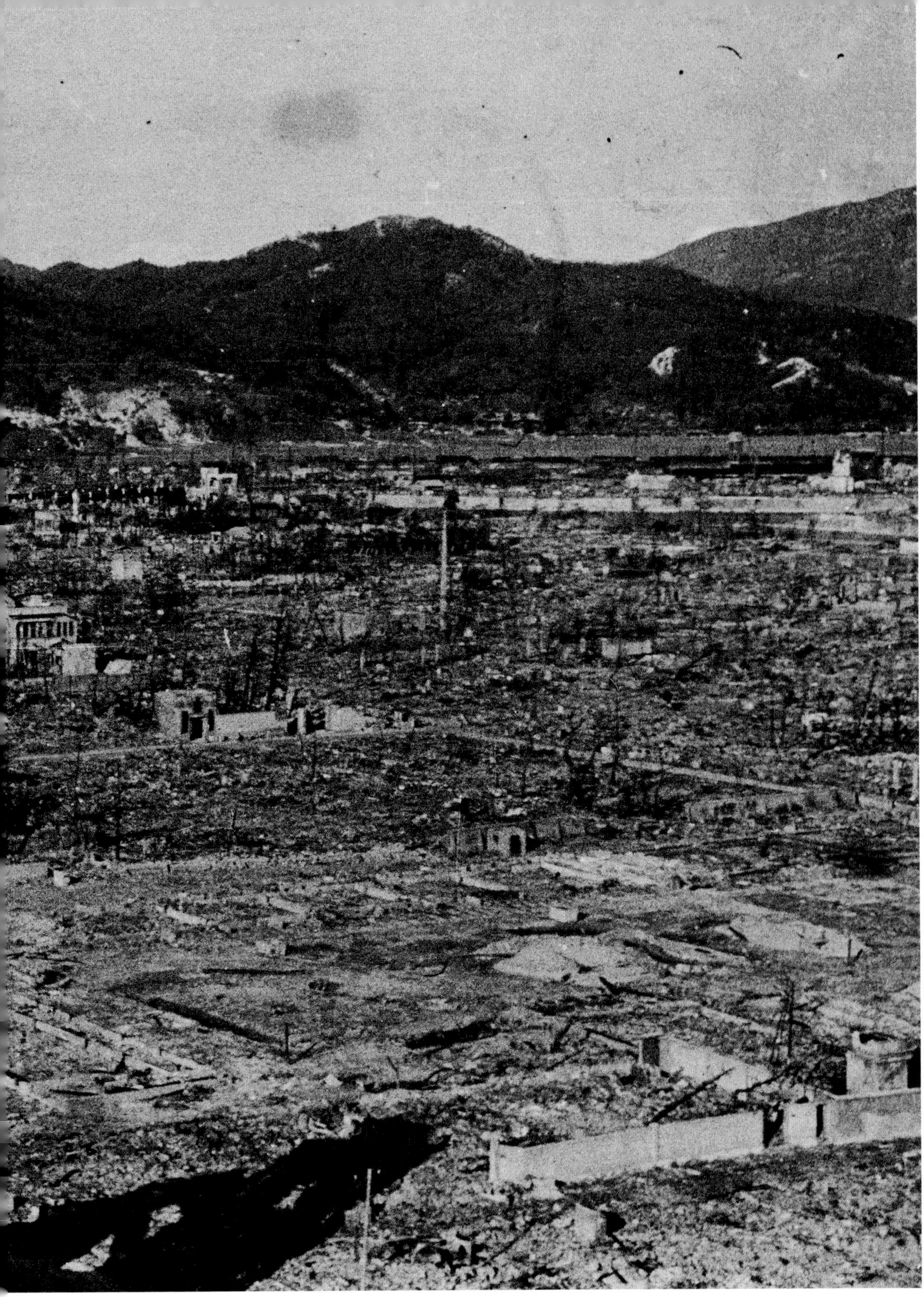

肉親を探しているのか、呆然と佇つ男性＝1945年9月中旬、
広島市（撮影：松本栄一）

A dazed man, probably looking for his relatives.
= Photographed in Hiroshima City in mid-September 1945 by Eiichi Matsumoto

爆風によって破壊されたビル＝1945年9月中旬、
広島市（撮影：松本栄一）

The building destroyed by the blast wave.
= Photographed in Hiroshima City in mid-September 1945 by Eiichi Matsumoto

広島瓦斯本社＝1945年9月中旬、
広島市大手町三丁目（撮影：松本栄一）

The HQ of Hiroshima Gas, 3 chome, Otemachi, Hiroshima City.
= Photographed in mid-September 1945 by Eiichi Matsumoto

爆心地から南へ210m。広島瓦斯本社＝1945年9月中旬、
広島市大手町三丁目（撮影：松本栄一）

210m south of the ground zero. The HQ of Hiroshima Gas, 3 chome, Otemachi, Hiroshima City. = Photographed in mid-September 1945 by Eiichi Matsumoto

爆心地から東南東 350m。広島市本通りにあった帝国銀行広島支店
＝1945 年 9 月中旬（撮影：松本栄一）

350m east-southeast of the ground zero. Hiroshima Branch of the Bank of Japan at Hondori street, Hiroshima City.
= Photographed in mid-September 1945 by Eiichi Matsumoto

爆心地より東 700m のコンクリート 2 階建てのこの建物は、
中心部に柱のないマッチ箱のような構造だったため、
側面から受けた爆圧で、膝を折るように 1 階がつぶれた。
後方の建物はキリンビヤホール＝ 1945 年 9 月中旬、
広島市平田屋町本通りの下村時計店（撮影：松本栄一）

700m east of the ground zero. This two-story concrete building of the Shimomura Clock Shop, Hirataya-machi Hondori, Hiroshima City, had no central pillar, just like a matchbox. The first floor warped and crumbled by the blast wave from the lateral side. The building in the back was Kirin Beer Hall. = Photographed in mid-September 1945 by Eiichi Matsumoto

帝国銀行広島支店の正面入口＝ 1945 年 9 月中旬（撮影：松本栄一）

The front entrance of Hiroshima Branch of the Bank of Japan in Hiroshima City. = Photographed in mid-September 1945 by Eiichi Matsumoto

帝国銀行広島支店の内部＝ 1945 年 9 月中旬（撮影：松本栄一）

Inside Hiroshima Branch of the Bank of Japan.
= Photographed in mid-September 1945 by Eiichi Matsumoto

日本貯蓄銀行広島支店。建物の一部が残っただけで粉々になった。
通りを歩く人々が見える＝1945年9月中旬、
広島市大手町（撮影：松本栄一）

Hiroshima Branch of the Nippon Chotiku Bank in Otemachi,
Hiroshima City. Almost entire building was blown to pieces.
People walking on the streets can be seen
= Photographed in mid-September 1945 by Eiichi Matsumoto

爆心地から170m。燃料会館＝1945年9月中旬、広島市中島本町
（撮影：松本栄一）

170m from the ground zero. Nenryo Kaikan (Fuel Hall)
in Nakajima Honmachi, Hiroshima City
= Photographed in mid-September 1945 by Eiichi Matsumoto

本来の外観はまったくわからないほど崩壊している＝1945年9月中旬、
広島市（撮影：松本栄一）

The completely collapsed building with the original exterior not recognized
= Photographed in Hiroshima City in mid-September 1945
by Eiichi Matsumoto

橋の欄干も吹き飛んでいた＝1945年9月中旬、
広島市（撮影：松本栄一）

The bridge rails were blown away = Photographed in Hiroshima City
in mid-September 1945 by Eiichi Matsumoto

完全に壊れて、わずかに土台部分のみが残った＝ 1945 年 9 月中旬、広島市（撮影：松本栄一）
Building completely collapsed and only the foundation remains = Photographed in Hiroshima City in mid-September 1945 by Eiichi Matsumoto

原形がわからないほど破壊された建物＝ 1945 年 9 月中旬、広島市（撮影：松本栄一）

The completely destroyed building with the original shape not recognized = Photographed in Hiroshima City in mid-September 1945 by Eiichi Matsumoto

窓枠の破損はほとんど見られなかったが、壁面に影ができていたビル ＝ 1945 年 9 月中旬、広島市（撮影：松本栄一）

A shadow was burned into the wall of the building. Almost no damage on the window frames = Photographed in Hiroshima City in mid-September 1945 by Eiichi Matsumoto

国泰寺の大楠と隣りにあった日本銀行広島支店＝1945年9月中旬、広島市小町（撮影：松本栄一）
Hiroshima Branch of the Bank of Japan and a large camphor tree at Kokutai Temple in Komachi, Hiroshima City
= Photographed in mid-September 1945 by Eiichi Matsumoto

爆心地から東へ700km。
広島福屋百貨店（左）からキリンビアホールを見る
＝1945年9月中旬、広島市八丁堀付近
（撮影：松本栄一）

700m east of the ground zero.
View of Kirin Beer Hall from Hiroshima Fukuya Department Store (left) near Hacchobori, Hiroshima City = Photographed in mid-September 1945 by Eiichi Matsumoto

爆心地から南南東の 400m。国泰寺墓地＝ 9 月中旬、広島市小町（撮影：松本栄一）

400m south-southeast of the ground zero. The Graveyard at the Kokutai Temple in Komachi, Hiroshima City
= Photographed in mid-September 1945 by Eiichi Matsumoto

爆心地から 710m。福屋百貨店本館＝ 1945 年 9 月中旬、広島市胡町（撮影：松本栄一）

710m from ground zero. The main building of Fukuya Department Store
= Photographed in mid-September 1945 at Ebisucho, Hiroshima City by Eiichi Matsumoto

爆心地から東へ約830m。福屋百貨店旧館横の残がい。建物内は完全に類焼していた＝1945年9月中旬、広島市胡町（撮影：松本栄一）
Approximately 830m east of the ground zero. The remains of a building in Ebisu-cho, Hiroshima City, whose inside was completely burnt down. Next to this building is the old building of Fukuya Department Store = Photographed in mid-September 1945 by Eiichi Matsumoto

爆風によって破壊された車。後の建物は広島銀行集会場＝ 1945 年 9 月中旬、広島市大手町（撮影：松本栄一）
A car destroyed by the blast wave. Behind the car is the meeting hall of the Hiroshima Bank = Photographed in mid-September 1945 at Otemachi, Hiroshima City by Eiichi Matsumoto

爆心地から 1.21km。広島東警察の壁。時計は午前 8 時 10 分で停止している＝ 1945 年 9 月中旬、広島市下柳町（撮影：松本栄一）
1.21km from the ground zero. The wall of the Hiroshima East Police Station in Shimoyanagi-cho, Hiroshima City.
A clock, hang on the wall, stopped at 8:10 = Photographed in mid-September 1945 by Eiichi Matsumoto

爆風によって根元からなぎ倒された大きな松の木
＝1945年9月中旬、広島市（撮影：松本栄一）

A big pine tree blown down from its root by the blast wave = Photographed in Hiroshima City in mid-September 1945 by Eiichi Matsumoto

正面の木造の建物は粉々に壊れていた
＝1945年9月中旬、
広島市（撮影：松本栄一）

The wooden building in front was completely destroyed into pieces = Photographed in Hiroshima City in mid-September 1945 by Eiichi Matsumoto

広島城天守台から市街地を望む
＝1945年9月中旬（撮影：松本栄一）

View of the Hiroshima City from the main castle tower of the Hiroshima Castle = Photographed in mid-September 1945 by Eiichi Matsumoto

広島城の本丸と城北を結ぶ橋＝ 1945 年 9 月中旬、広島市基町（撮影：松本栄一）
The bridge connecting the main enclosure of the Hiroshima Castle and the Johoku (north of the castle) area of Hiroshima City
= Photographed in mid-September 1945 at Motomachi, Hitroshima City by Eiichi Matsumoto

広島城本丸から市街地を望む＝1945年9月中旬、広島市基町（撮影：松本栄一）
View of the Hiroshima City from the main enclosure of the Hiroshima Castle, Motomachi, Hiroshima City
= Photographed in mid-September 1945 by Eiichi Matsumoto

広島城天守閣から市街地を望む
＝ 1945年9月中旬、広島市基町
（撮影：松本栄一）

View of the Hiroshima City from the main castle tower of the Hiroshima Castle = Photographed in mid-September 1945 by Eiichi Matsumoto

美しかった樹林が倒れている
＝ 1945年9月中旬、広島市（撮影：松本栄一）

he trees of once beautiful forest were fallen down = Photographed in Hiroshima City in mid-September 1945 by Eiichi Matsumoto

爆心地から980m。広島県天守閣とお堀
＝ 1945年9月中旬、広島市基町
（撮影：松本栄一）

The main castle tower and moat of the Hiroshima Castle. 980m from the ground zero
= Photographed in mid-September 1945 at Motomachi, Hiroshima City by Eiichi Matsumoto

爆心地から790m。中国軍管区司令部の兵舎近くに作られていた防空壕＝1945年9月中旬、広島市西練兵場内（撮影：松本栄一）

The remains of a bomb shelter built near barracks of the Chugoku Army District HQ. 790m from the ground zero
= Photographed in mid-September 1945 at the West Military Drill Grounds by Eiichi Matsumoto

爆心地から1.5kmの広島赤十字病院1号館＝1945年9月中旬、広島市千田町（撮影：二瓶禎二）

No.1 building of Hiroshima Red Cross Hospital.
1.5km from the ground zero = Photographed in mid-September 1945
at Senda-machi, Hiroshima City by Teiji Nihei

爆心地から1.5kmの広島赤十字病院1号館＝1945年9月中旬、広島市千田町（撮影：二瓶禎二）

No.1 building of Hiroshima Red Cross Hospital.
1.5km from the ground zero = Photographed in mid-September 1945
at Senda-machi, Hiroshima City by Teiji Nihei

爆心地から 300m。爆風によって破壊された相生橋
= 1945 年 9 月中旬（撮影：二瓶禎二）

Aioi Bridge destroyed by the blast wave. 300m from the ground zero
= Photographed in mid-September 1945 by Teiji Nihei

爆心地から 300m の相生橋 = 1945 年 9 月中旬（撮影：二瓶禎二）

Aioi Bridge. 300m from the ground zero
= Photographed in mid-September 1945 by Teiji Nihei

広島市内の墓地の墓石 = 1945 年 9 月中旬、広島市（撮影：二瓶禎二）

The gravestone at a graveyard in Hiroshima City
= Photographed in Hiroshima City in mid-September 1945,
by Teiji Nihei

爆心地から 380m にあった日本銀行広島支店
= 1945 年 9 月中旬、広島市袋町（撮影：二瓶禎二）

The Bank of Japan Hiroshima Branch. 380m from the ground zero
= Photographed in mid-September 1945 at Fukuro-machi,
Hiroshima City by Teiji Nihei

広島商工会議所 = 1945 年 9 月 20 日頃、
爆心地より北西 200m（撮影：松本栄一）
Hiroshima Chamber of Commerce and Industry.
200m northwest of the ground zero.
= Photographed around September 20th 1945
by Eiichi Matsumoto

1945 年 9 月中旬、広島市
（撮影：文部省学術研究会議
原子爆弾災害調査研究特別委員会）
Somewhere in Hiroshima City in mid-September
1945. = Photographed by Special Committee for
the Investigation of A-bomb Damages

1945年9月中旬、広島市
(撮影:文部省学術研究会議
原子爆弾災害調査研究特別委員会)

Somewhere in Hiroshima City in mid-September 1945. = Photographed by Special Committee for the Investigation of A-bomb Damages

広島における放射温度と爆風圧の調査・研究班だったために、墓碑銘の削られた跡など細い所を発見して撮影している＝1945年9月中旬、広島市(撮影:文部省学術研究会議 原子爆弾災害調査研究特別委員会)

Since the team of the Special Committee for the Investigation of A-bomb Damages was assigned to study radiation temperature and pressure of blast wave, small details, such as the parts of gravestones carved away by the blast, were investigated and photographed
= Photographed in Hiroshima City in mid-September 1945 by Special Committee for the Investigation of A-bomb Damages

背中の熱傷。背中の丸みで熱傷の度合いが違っている＝1945年9月下旬、広島赤十字病院（撮影：松本栄一）

A victim's back burned. The degree of the burns varies with the curve of the back.
= Photographed at the end of September 1945 at Hiroshima Red Cross Hospital by Eiichi Matsumoto

相生橋東詰めにあった日本赤十字社広島支部から
広島県産業奨励館（原爆ドーム）を望む＝1945年9月下旬（撮影：松本栄一）

View of the Hiroshima Prefectural Industrial Promotion Hall (the Atomic Bomb Dome)
from the Hiroshima Branch of the Japanese Red Cross Society in east end of Aioi Bridge.
= Photographed at the end of September 1945 by Eiichi Matsumoto

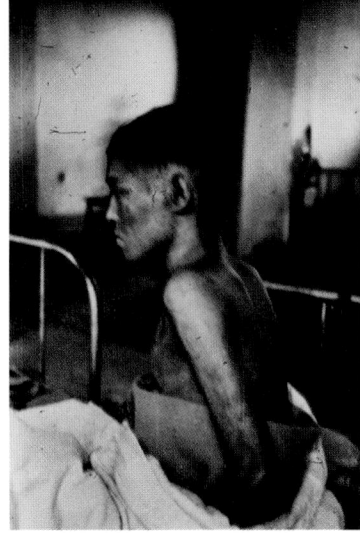

被爆した男性。広島赤十字病院で
＝1945年9月下旬、広島市千代田町
（撮影：松本栄一）

A radiation-exposed male. Photographed at the
Hiroshima Red Cross Hospital. = Chiyoda-cho,
Hiroshima City at the end of September 1945
by Eiichi Matsumoto

広島県産業奨励会館と広島の街＝1945年9月下旬、広島商工会議所の屋上から（撮影：松本栄一）
View of Hiroshima City with Hiroshima Prefectural Industrial Promotion Hall (the Atomic Bomb Dome),
from the rooftop of the Hiroshima Chamber of Commerce and Industry. = Photographed at the end of September 1945 by Eiichi Matsumoto

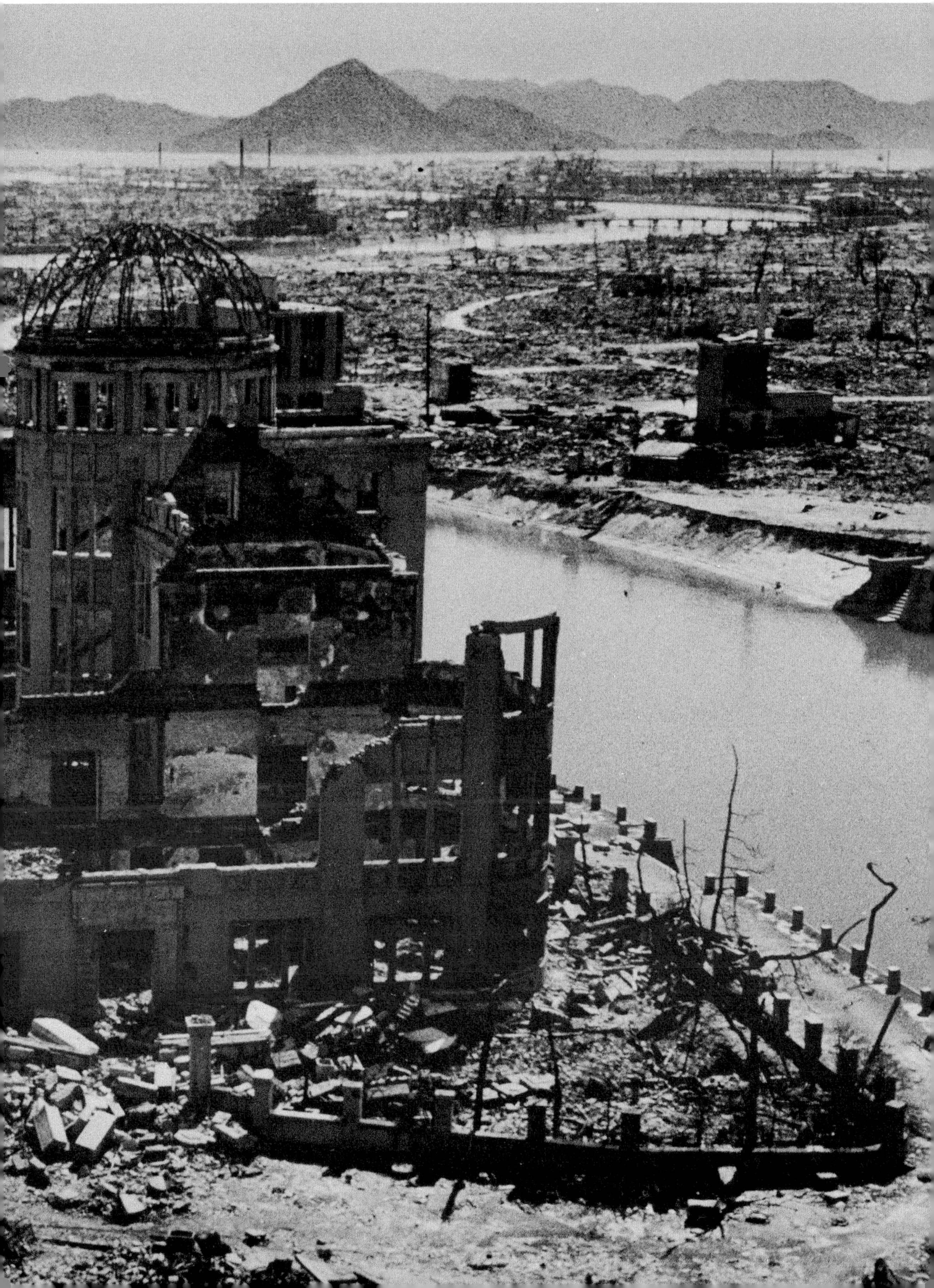

日本生命広島支店と銀行集会所＝1945年9月下旬、爆心地より南南東に150m（撮影：松本栄一）
Hiroshima Branch of Nippon Life and a assembly hall of the bank. 150m south-southeast of the ground zero.
= Photographed at the end of September 1945 by Eiichi Matsumoto

横にくずれ折れて、床下のようにみえるのが、つぶれた1階＝1945年9月中旬、広島市下村時計店（撮影：松本栄一）
Shimomura Clock Shop in Hiroshima City, collapsed sideways.
The remain that looks like an underfloor space is actually the destroyed first floor.
= Photographed at the end of September 1945 by Eiichi Matsumoto

1945年9月中旬、広島市下村時計店（撮影：松本栄一）
Shimomura Clock Shop in Hiroshima City. = Photographed in mid-September 1945 by Eiichi Matsumoto

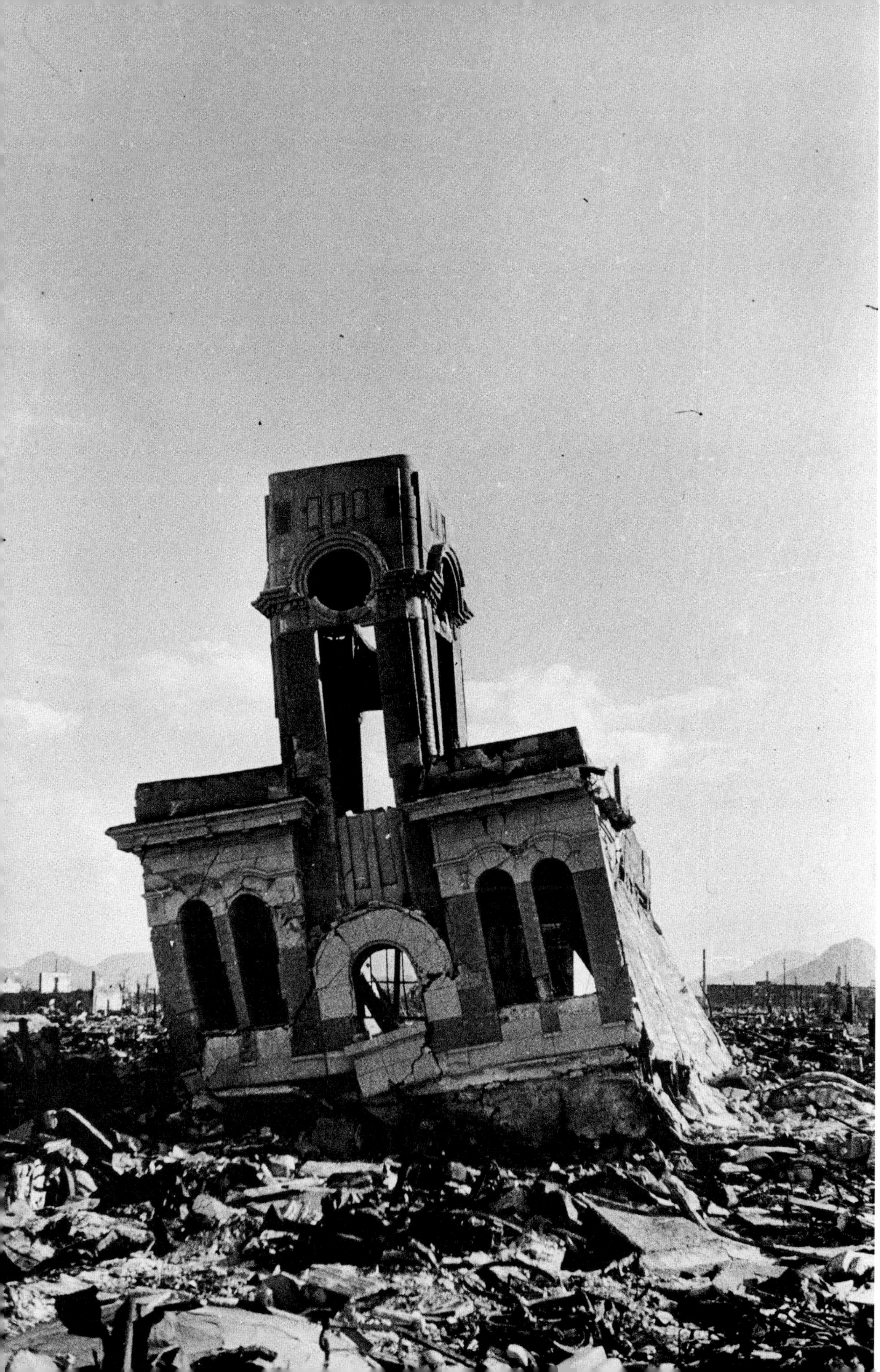

爆心地から東北東 1km の市電と自動車。電車は被爆時から移動させている＝1945 年 9 月下旬、広島市上幟町の流川メソジスト教会前（撮影：松本栄一）

The tram and automobile at 1km east-northeast of the ground zero. The tram has been transported here after the explosion. = Photographed at the end of September 1945 in front of Nagarekawa Methodist Church in Kaminobori-cho, Hiroshima City by Eiichi Matsumoto

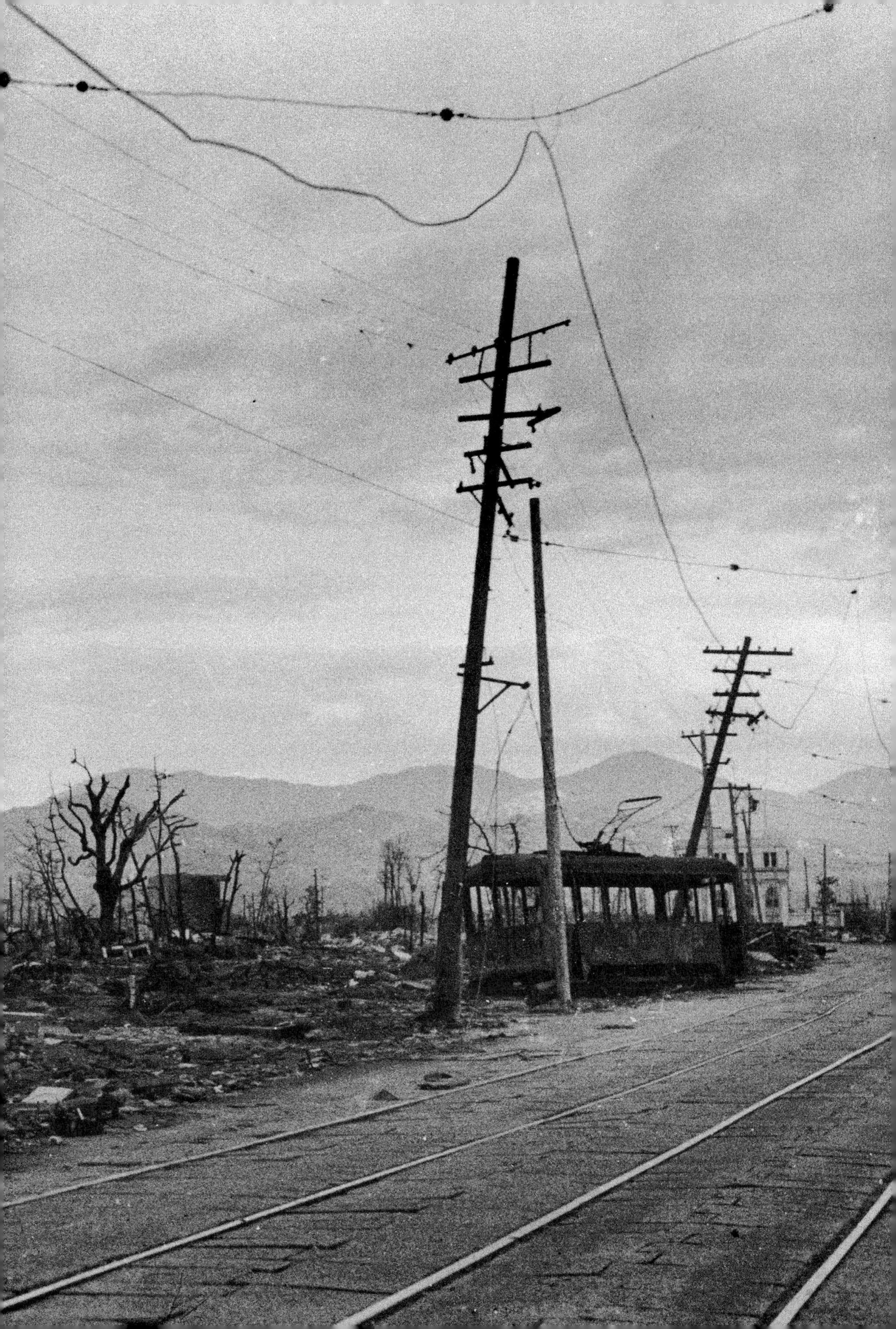

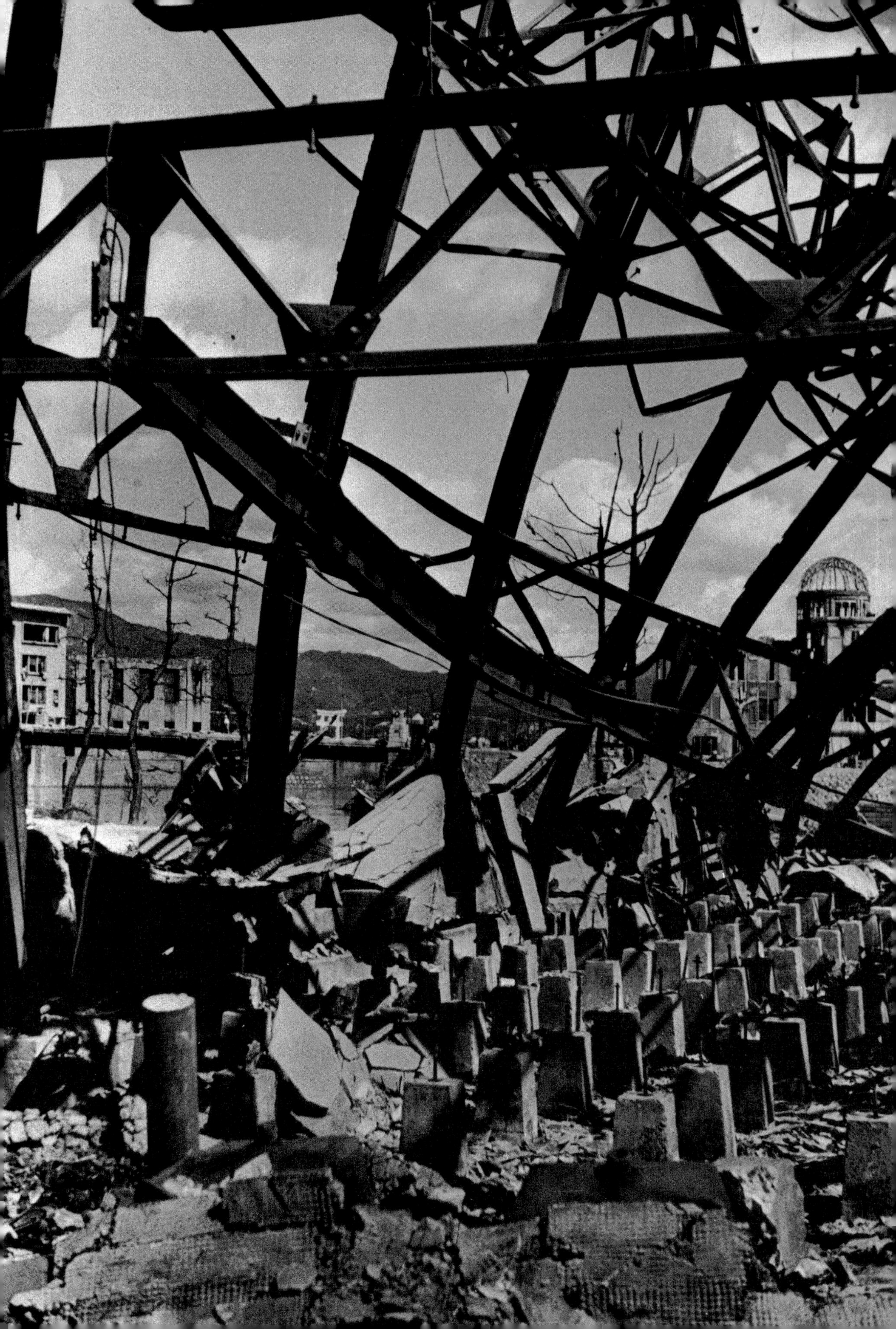

爆心地から約 1.5km にあった倒壊した中国軍管区関連施設の一部
= 1945 年 9 月下旬、広島市基町（撮影：松本栄一）

A part of the collapsed facility of the Chugoku Military District in Motomachi, Hiroshima City. Approximately 1.5km from the ground zero
= Photographed at the end of September 1945 by Eiichi Matsumoto

爆風のため壁面が凹んでいる。爆心から約 400 メートル
= 1945 年 9 月下旬、広島本川国民学校西校舎の東側（撮影：松本栄一）

The wall got dented due to the blast wave. Approximately 400m from the ground zero
= Photographed at the end of September 1945 on the east side of the west building of Hiroshima Honkawa Primary School by Eiichi Matsumoto

陸軍中国管区司令部周辺にあった小姓被服倉庫の全景
= 1945 年 9 月下旬、広島市基町（撮影：松本栄一）

A full view of Kosho-machi Hiroshima Army Clothing Depot in Motomachi, Hiroshima City, located near the Army HQ of the Chugoku Military District
= Photographed at the end of September 1945 by Eiichi Matsumoto

当時、基町におかれていた陸軍中国軍管区司令部の周りには
各種軍隊関係施設があった。
この建物、小姓町被服倉庫（爆心地より北北西約 800m）もそのひとつ。
2 階は崩壊、1 階は破壊と火災により奥まで見とおせるようになった
= 1945 年 9 月下旬、広島市基町（撮影：松本栄一）

There were several military facilities around the Army HQ of the Chugoku Military District located at Motomachi, Hiroshima City.
Kosho-machi Hiroshima Army Clothing Depot was one of them, located approximately 800m north-northwest of the ground zero.
The second floor was destroyed while the first floor was pierced through due to the demolition and fire
= Photographed at the end of September 1945 by Eiichi Matsumoto

爆心から西北西 350m にあった本川国民学校の講堂跡。鉄筋だけの不気味な姿に変わってしまった。
教師・児童あわせて判明しただけで 229 人が即死した = 1945 年 9 月下旬、広島本川国民学校（撮影：松本栄一）

The remains of the auditorium of Hiroshima Honkawa Primary School. 350m west-northeast of the ground zero.
Only reinforcing steel bars left. At least 229 students and teachers reportedly lost their lives
= Photographed at the end of September 1945 by Eiichi Matsumoto

天守閣は全部崩れ落ち石垣だけが残った＝1945年9月下旬、広島城（撮影：松本栄一）

The main castle tower of the Hiroshima Castle completely collapsed and only the stone walls remain
= photographed at the end of September 1945 by Eiichi Matsumoto

1945年9月下旬、広島城（撮影：松本栄一）

Hiroshima Castle. Photographed at the end of September 1945 by Eiichi Matsumoto

広島市紙屋町交差点あたりから福屋百貨店（右）と福屋旧館（左）を望む
＝ 1945 年 9 月下旬、爆心から東 250m（撮影：松本栄一）

View of Fukuya Department Store (right) and its old building (left)
from Kamiya-cho junction, Hiroshima City.　250m east of the ground zero
= Photographed at the end of September 1945 by Eiichi Matsumoto

死者は園内の小さな丘に埋められた。標札には、
左から、戦死者 5 名、38 名、21 名とある。大木の松は閃光に焼かれ、
爆風で枝や葉をもぎとられた＝ 1945 年 9 月下旬、広島市泉邸縮景園
（撮影：松本栄一）

Dead bodies were buried on a small hill inside the garden of the Sentei
(Shukukei-en). The sign board shows the number of dead. Five, thirty-eight,
and twenty-one (from the left). The flash of the atomic bomb burned this giant
pine tree, and its leaves and branches were ripped off by the blast wave
= Photographed at the end of September 1945 by Eiichi Matsumoto

爆心地より北北西約 800m の所にあった小姓町被服倉庫
＝ 1945 年 9 月下旬（撮影：松本栄一）

Kosho-machi Army Clothing Depot.
800m north-northeast of the ground zero = Photographed at
the end of September 1945 by Eiichi Matsumoto

名園として知られていた泉邸（縮景園）は恰好の避難場所であったが、死者が続出し、
火葬の火が敵機の目標になるというのでそのまま埋められていた。因みにこの写真から、去る1987年夏、発掘作業が行なわれ、
40数名の遺骨が発見され原爆供養塔に合祀された＝1945年9月下旬、泉邸縮景園（撮影：松本栄一）

Sentei (Shukukei-en), known as a masterpiece of garden, was the best site for people to evacuate. However, evacuees died in this evacuation center one after another. Their bodies were buried without being cremated because the fire and smoke from cremation could be a good target for enemy aircrafts. In summer 1987, an excavation project was conducted based on this photograph, and the bones of about 40 persons were discovered. They were later honored collectively in the Atomic Bomb Memorial Mound = Photographed at the end of September 1945 by Eiichi Matsumoto

広島護国神社正面全景 = 1945年9月下旬（撮影：松本栄一）
A full frontal view of the Hiroshima Gokoku Shrine, Hiroshima City
= Photographed at the end of September 1945 by Eiichi Matsumoto

広島護国神社本殿前、倒れた鳥居。爆心地より北北西300m
= 1945年9月下旬、広島市基町1番地（撮影：松本栄一）
The Collapsed Torii (entrance gate to the shrine) in front of the Main shrine of the Hiroshima Gokoku Shine at 1-banchi, Motomachi, Hiroshima City. 300m north-northwest of the ground zero
= Photographed at the end of September 1945 by Eiichi Matsumoto

1945年9月下旬、広島護国神社の参道（撮影：松本栄一）
The approach road to the Hiroshima Gokoku Shrine, Hiroshima City. Photographed at the end of September 1945 by Eiichi Matsumoto

石灯籠。爆心地より北北西に300m = 1945年9月下旬、広島護国神社（撮影：松本栄一）
The stone lantern of the Hiroshima Gokoku Shrine, Hiroshima City. 300m north-northwest of the ground zero
= Photographed at the end of September 1945 by Eiichi Matsumoto

饒津神社の参道＝1945年9月下旬、二葉の里
（撮影：松本栄一）

The approach road to the Nigitsu Shrine,
Futaba-no-sato, Hiroshima City
= Photographed at the end of September 1945
by Eiichi Matsumoto

爆心地から約1.7kmの饒津神社。
社殿が消滅した＝1945年9月下旬、二葉の里
（撮影：松本栄一）

Nigitsu Shrine in Hiroshima City. Approximately
1.7km from the ground zero. The Main shrine
building of this Shrine disappeared
= Photographed at the end of September 1945
by Eiichi Matsumoto

爆心地より北北東約1km。
兵士も焼かれ、木々も焼かれた
＝1945年9月下旬、陸軍歩兵第一補充部隊・
通称二部隊跡（撮影：松本栄一）

The remains of the Army Infantry First Supply
Convoy building (also known as the 2nd Unit).
Approximately 1km north-northeast of the ground
zero. Soldiers and trees were burned to death
= Photographed at the end of September 1945
by Eiichi Matsumoto

9月下旬、原子爆弾の被害地は、70年間にわたって不毛の地となるであろうとの外電が流れた。
だが、爆心地近くの瓦礫の間から、草花が息吹きはじめた。爆心地より北800mに咲いたカンナ＝1945年9月下旬、
陸軍歩兵第一補充部隊・通称二部隊跡（撮影：松本栄一）

Foreign news media reported that the area affected by the atomic bomb would be barren and deserted for the next seventy years. But in the beginning of September, plants started to grow through the gap in the rubble near the ground zero. At the site of the Army Infantry First Supply Convoy building (also known as the 2nd Unit), 800m north of the ground zero, Canna lily blooms = Photographed at the end of September 1945 by Eiichi Matsumoto

1945年9月下旬、広島市内の熱傷した木（撮影：松本栄一）

The burned tree in Hiroshima City. Photographed at the end of September 1945 by Eiichi Matsumoto

熱傷した木。雨に洗われたあと白いカビがはえていた。
広島市内のあちこちに、いまも焼けた幹のはだであの日の爆心の方向を示しながら、
木々は生きつづけている＝1945年9月下旬（撮影：松本栄一）

The burned tree in Hiroshima City. White mold grew on the tree after it was being washed by the rain.
Trees damaged by the atomic bomb are still alive everywhere in Hiroshima City,
with the side of their burned skin indicating the direction of the ground zero
= Photographed at the end of September 1945 by Eiichi Matsumoto

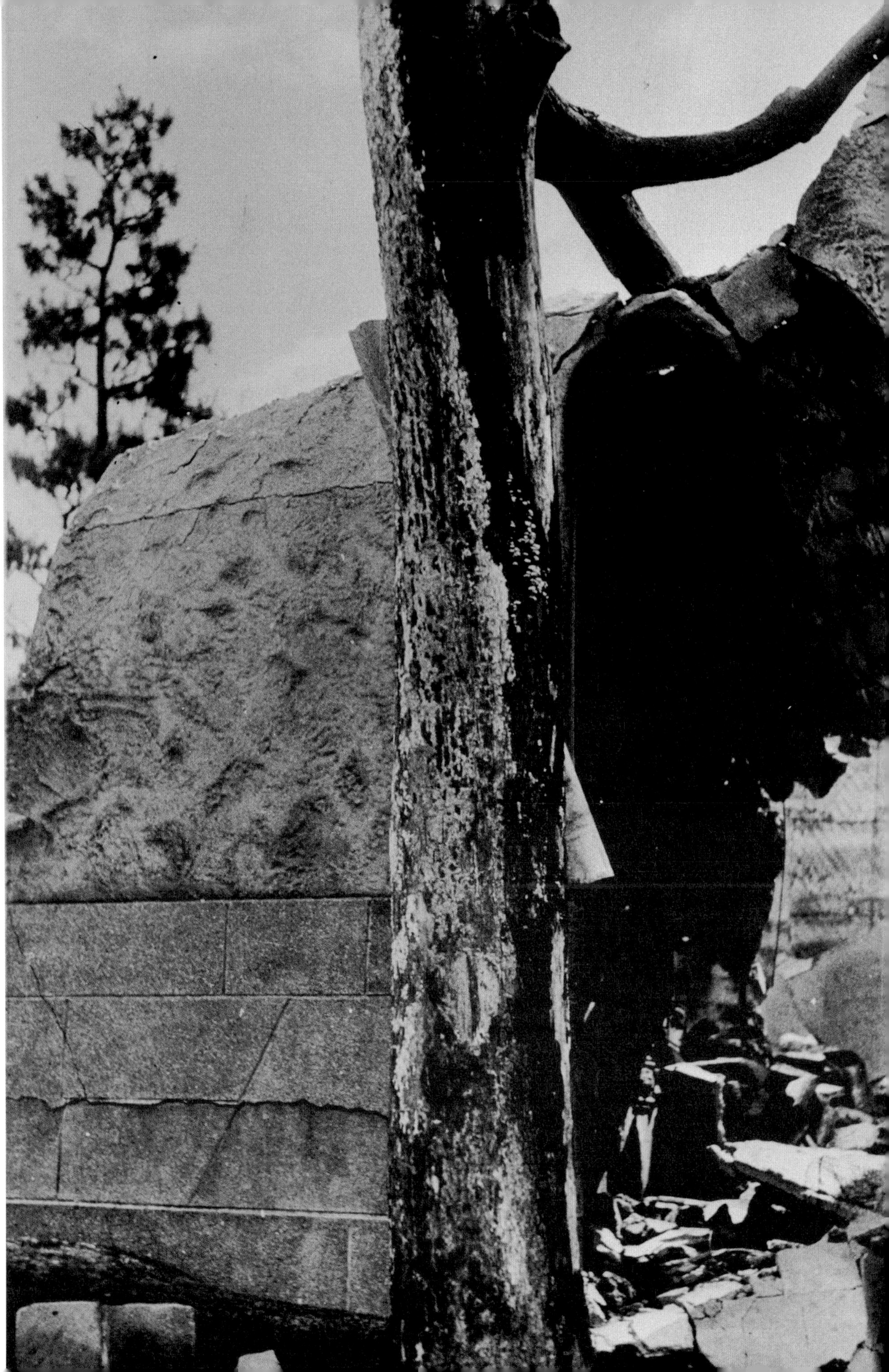

爆風で張り出した待合室は倒壊。本体の屋根は押し下げられ変形破損した。その後、広島駅舎は全焼、多数の死傷者を出したが、
翌7日には宇品線、8日には広島・横川間、9月山陽本線、芸備線が開通、10日には駅事務所がバラックに急造され、
救護隊の入市や被災者の脱出の助けになった＝ 1945年10月頃、南から北北東に向って（撮影：川本俊雄）

The stretched waiting room of the Hiroshima Station collapsed completely by the blast wave. The roof of the main building has been pushed down, deformed and destroyed. Later, the station burnt to the grounds leaving large number of casualties. But on 7th August Ujina-line, on 8th Hiroshima - Yokogawa Line, and by September Sanyo Main Line and Geibi Line reopened. On 10th August, construction of the barracks for the train station offices completed, allowing rescuers to enter the city and victims to evacuate. = Photographed in October 1945 facing north- northeast from south by Toshio Kawamoto

大きな時計台を乗せた鉄筋コンクリート造り2階建てのハイカラな建物は小さいながらも遠くからもよく見えランドマークにもなった。
爆風によって1階は完全に押しつぶされアーチ窓の2階と時計台の残骸が残った。
写真右爆心地側からの爆風は、かろうじて残った建物全体を左側に傾かせた＝ 1945年10月頃、広島市下村時計店（正面）（撮影：川本俊雄）

View of the Shimomura Clock Shop, facing south from north. The small stylish 2 stories building of high reinforced concrete, with a huge clock tower on top, can be seen from afar. It was a landmark. The blast wave crushed the first floor, leaving only the second floor with the arched window and the destroyed clocktower. On the right is the building barely standing, tilted to the left due to the blast wave from the ground zero, which was on the right hand side. = Photographed around October 1945 by Toshio Kawamoto

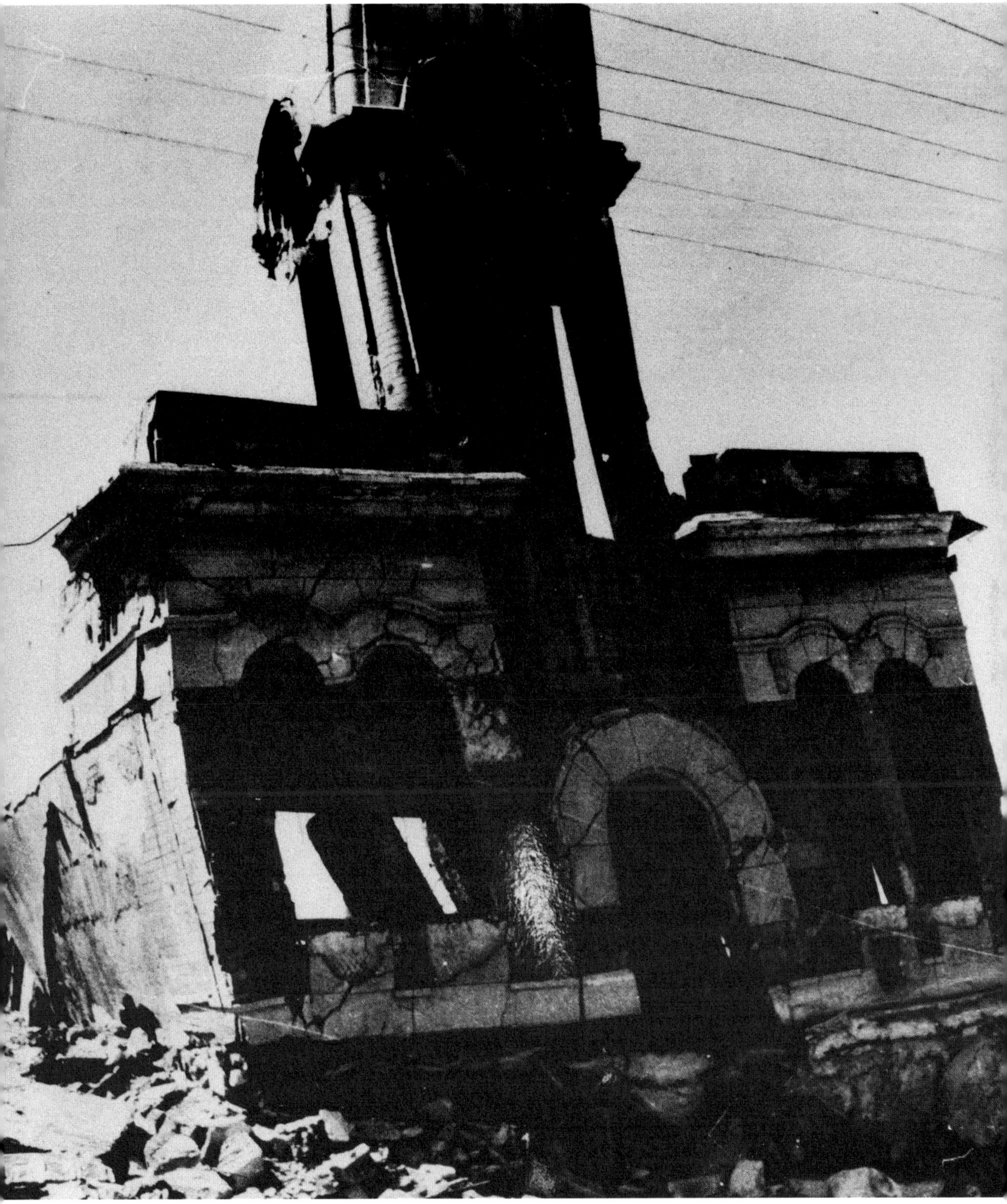

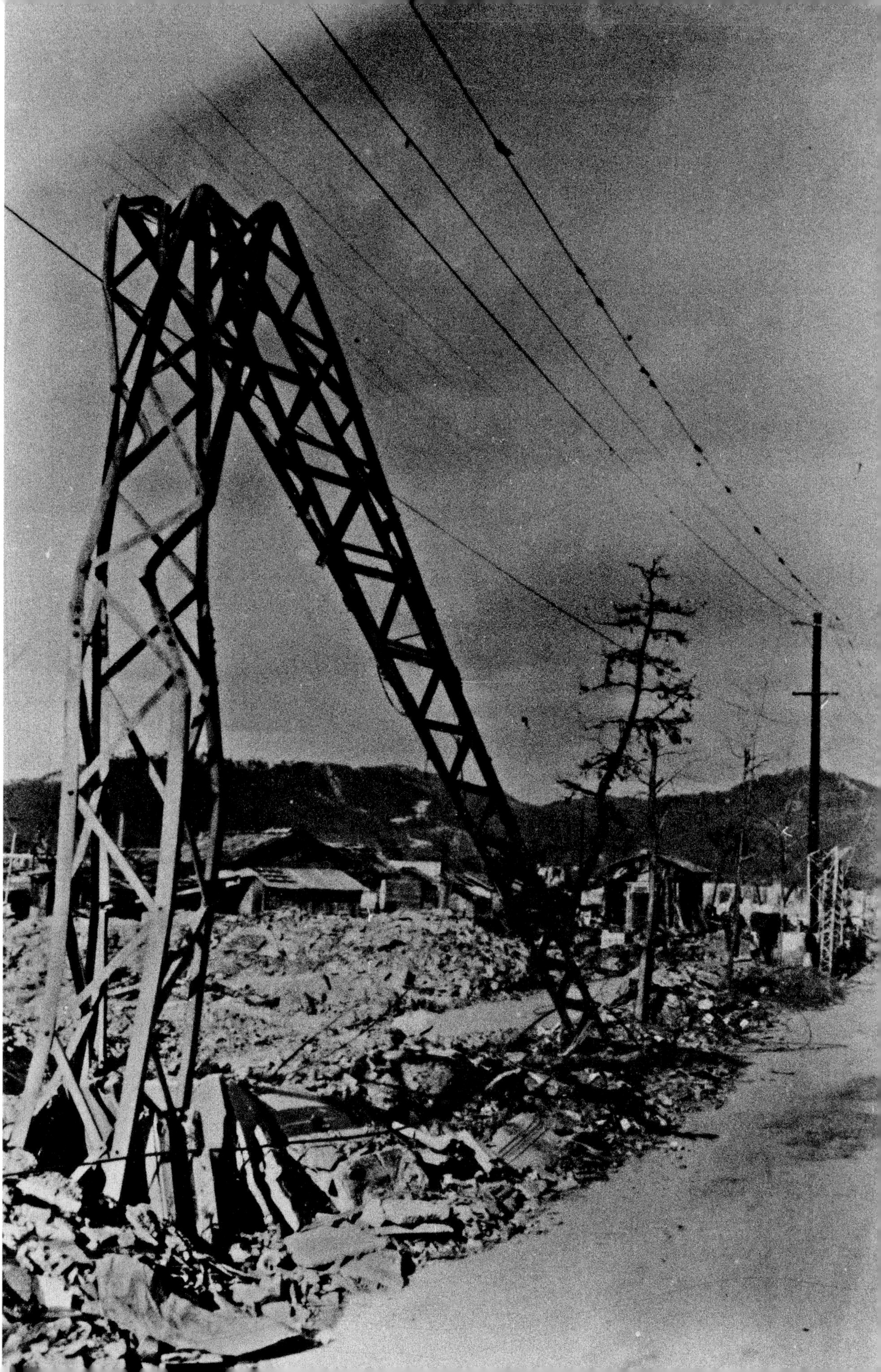

爆心方向のため橋の笠石が横にずれている。
中国配電 KK の記録用として
監督の指示により撮影す。
爆心地からもっとも近い地点で爆風が
垂直のため橋の笠石が左右にずれる。
左の建物は燃料会館、
中央は日本簡易火災保険広島支店
＝ 1945 年 10 月～ 11 月、
爆心地付近の元安橋（撮影：岸本吉太）

Motoyasu Bridge near the ground zero. The capping stone of the bridge shifted sideways by the blast wave. This photograph was taken on orders of the Chugoku Power Supply Co. for its internal records. Due to the closeness to the ground zero, the blast wave attacked the bridge vertically and the capping stone moved sideways. The building on the left is the Nenryo Kaikan (Fuel Hall). In the center is the Hiroshima Branch of the Nippon Kan'i Kasai Hoken Company. = Photographed in October or November 1945 by Yoshita Kishimoto

爆心地より南南東に 3.9km ＝ 1945 年 10 月 1 日、広島第一陸軍病院宇品分院正門（撮影：菊池俊吉）
3.9km south-southeast of the ground zero.
= Photographed on 1st October 1945 at the main gate of Ujina Branch of the Hiroshima First Army Hospital by Shunkichi Kikuchi

中国配電の記録用として監督の指示により撮影す。
爆心地から北西 900m の広瀬中町付近にバラックが建ちだす＝ 1945 年 10 月～ 11 月、広島市広瀬中町付近道路（撮影：岸本吉太）

This photograph was taken on orders of the Chugoku Power Supply Co. for its internal records.
Barracks were started to be built near Hirose-Nakamachi, Hiroshima City. 900m northwest of the ground zero.
= Photographed in October or November 1945 by Yoshita Kishimoto

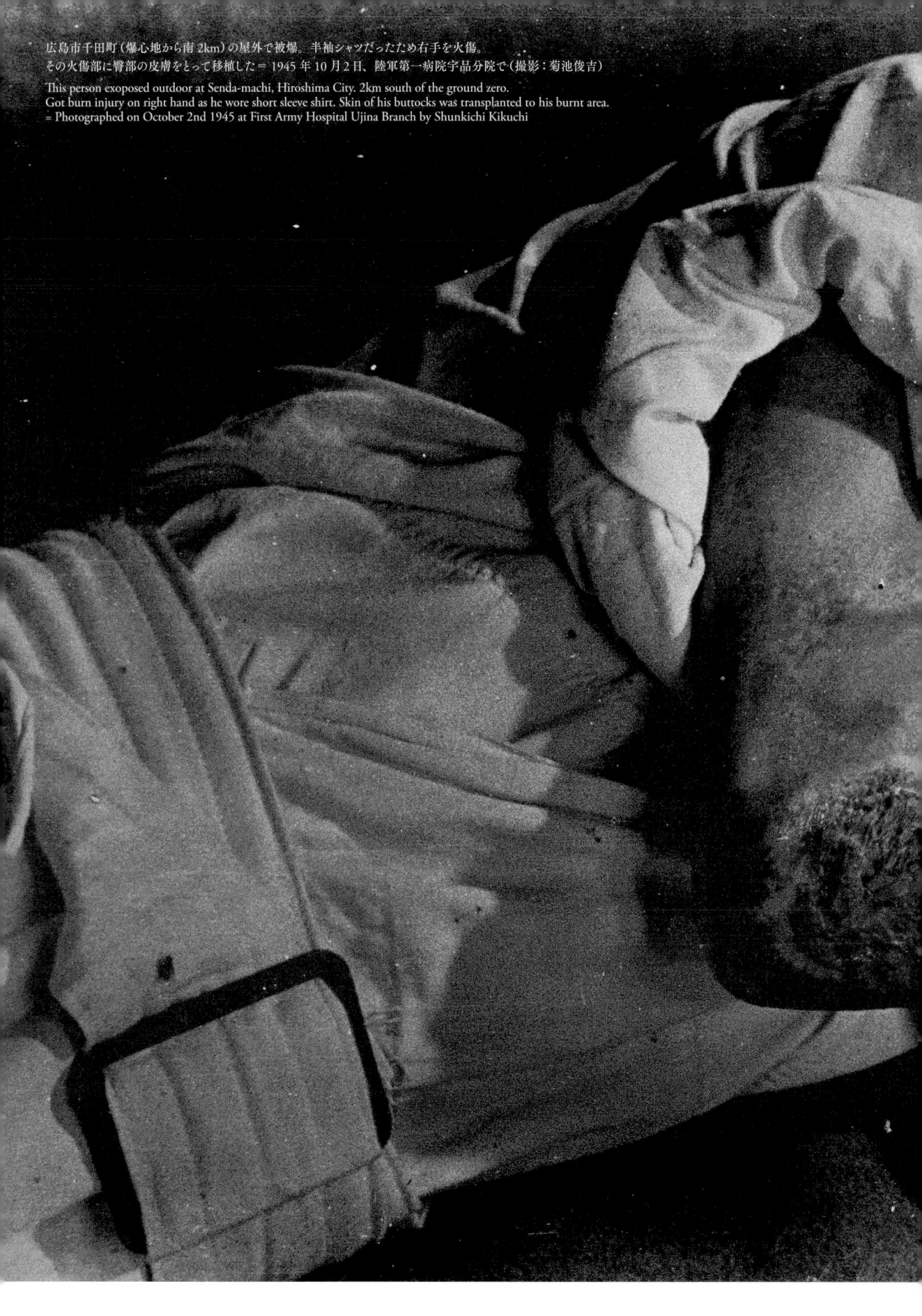

広島市千田町（爆心地から南2km）の屋外で被爆。半袖シャツだったため右手を火傷。
その火傷部に臀部の皮膚をとって移植した＝1945年10月2日、陸軍第一病院宇品分院で（撮影：菊池俊吉）

This person exoposed outdoor at Senda-machi, Hiroshima City. 2km south of the ground zero.
Got burn injury on right hand as he wore short sleeve shirt. Skin of his buttocks was transplanted to his burnt area.
= Photographed on October 2nd 1945 at First Army Hospital Ujina Branch by Shunkichi Kikuchi

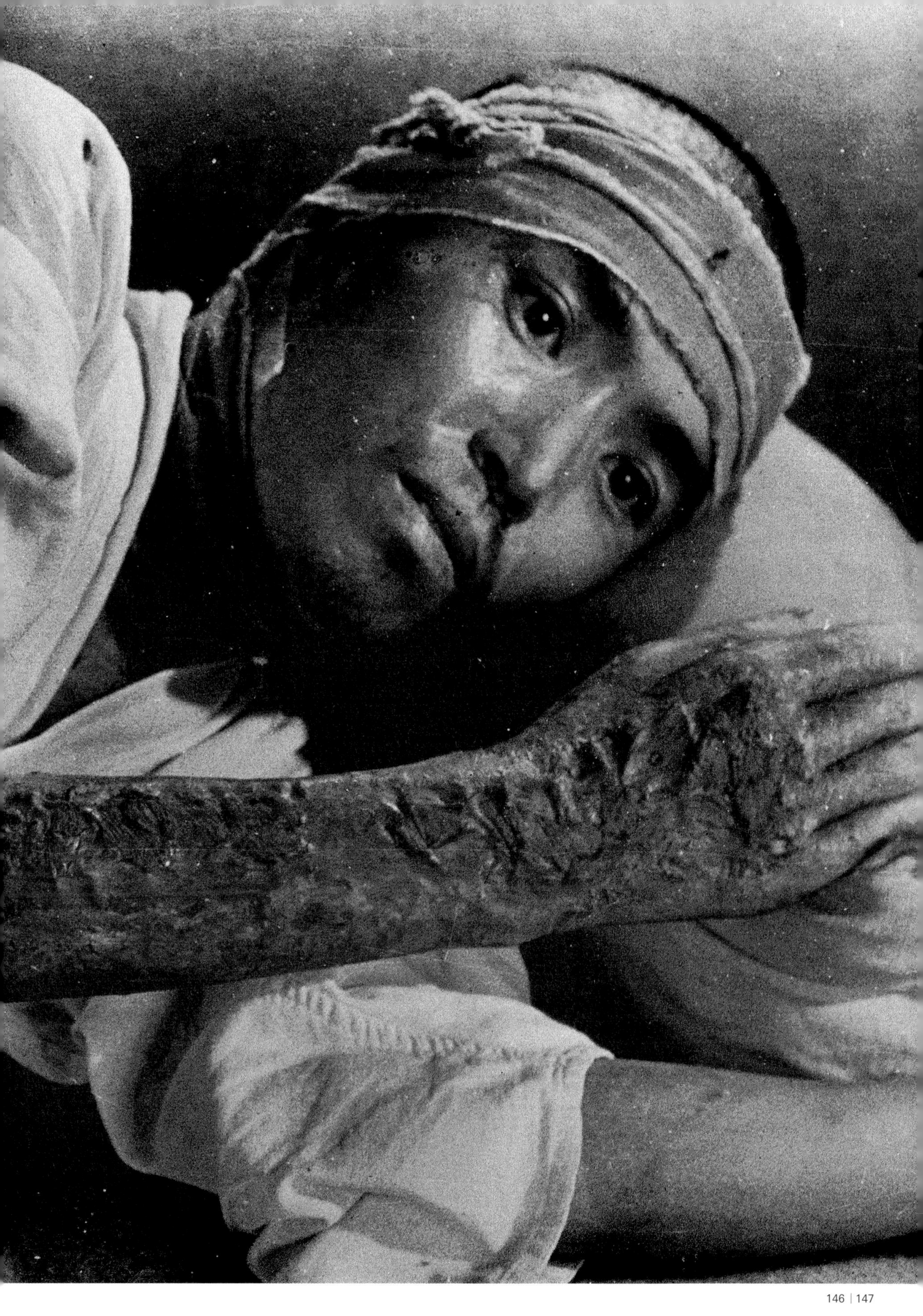

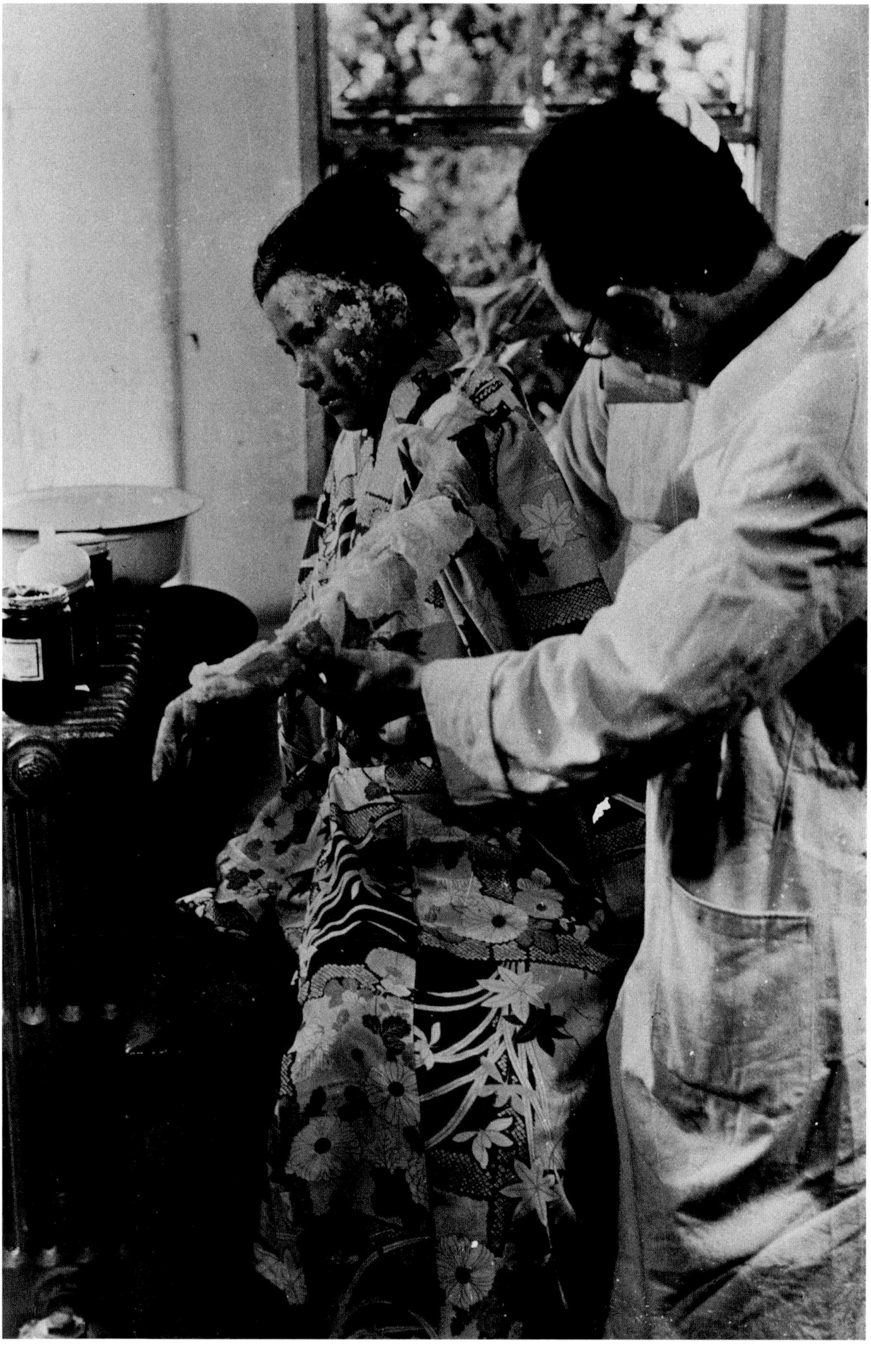

瓦礫のなかを若い婦人が荷車に乗って通院してきた＝1945年10月4日、日本赤十字社広島病院前（撮影：菊池俊吉）
In front of Japanese Red Cross Society Hiroshima Hospital. A young lady came by cart, getting through the road with a lot of rubble and debris
= Photographed on October 4th 1945 by Shunkichi Kikuchi

日本赤十字社広島病院の外来患者治療室で＝1945年10月4日（撮影：菊池俊吉）
In an outpatient treatment room at Japanese Red Cross Hiroshima Hospital. = Photographed on October 4th 1945 by Shunkichi Kikuchi.

爆心地から南約 600m という至近距離にあった国泰寺では数多くの墓石が、メチャメチャな倒壊のしかたをしていた。
爆風が複雑な流れ方をしたためと思われるが、由緒ある寺の、古い墓石もひとたまりもなかった。
左の大木は国宝に指定されていた古い大楠木（樹齢 400 年）だったが、1 株は根元から爆風で引き裂かれて倒された
＝ 1945 年 10 月 4 日、国泰寺（撮影：菊池俊吉）

In Kokutai Temple. About 600 meters south of the ground zero. Many gravestones collapsed randomly. Because of the complex patterns of the blast wave, the old gravestones in this traditional temple were completely destroyed. The big tree on the left side was the old camphor (aged 400 years) .
It was designated as a National Treasure but destroyed by the blast wave ＝ Photographed on October 4th 1945 by Shunkichi Kikuchi

この上空 570m で原爆は炸裂した。
町民は全滅、一面の瓦礫のなかに焼けた電柱が鉛筆の芯をけずったようにとがって立ち、
四角の鉄筋コンクリート造りの防火用水は、四方にはじけたように壊れ、
その底もこなごなに砕けて、原爆の強烈な炸裂のさまを示していた
＝ 1945 年 10 月 4 日、爆心直下、広島市細工町（大手町 1 丁目）の島病院入口（撮影：菊池俊吉）

An atomic bomb was exploded at 570 meters above in the air. The people living here were all dead.
A burnt electric pole stood among rubble and debris like a sharpened pencil.
A square-shaped fire prevention water tank made of reinforced concrete was torn apart into four directions.
Its bottom was also destroyed, implying the power of the bomb
= Photographed in front of Shima Hospital, ground zero in Saiku-machi (currently 1cho-me Otemachi),
Hiroshima City on October 4th 1945 by Shunkichi Kikuchi

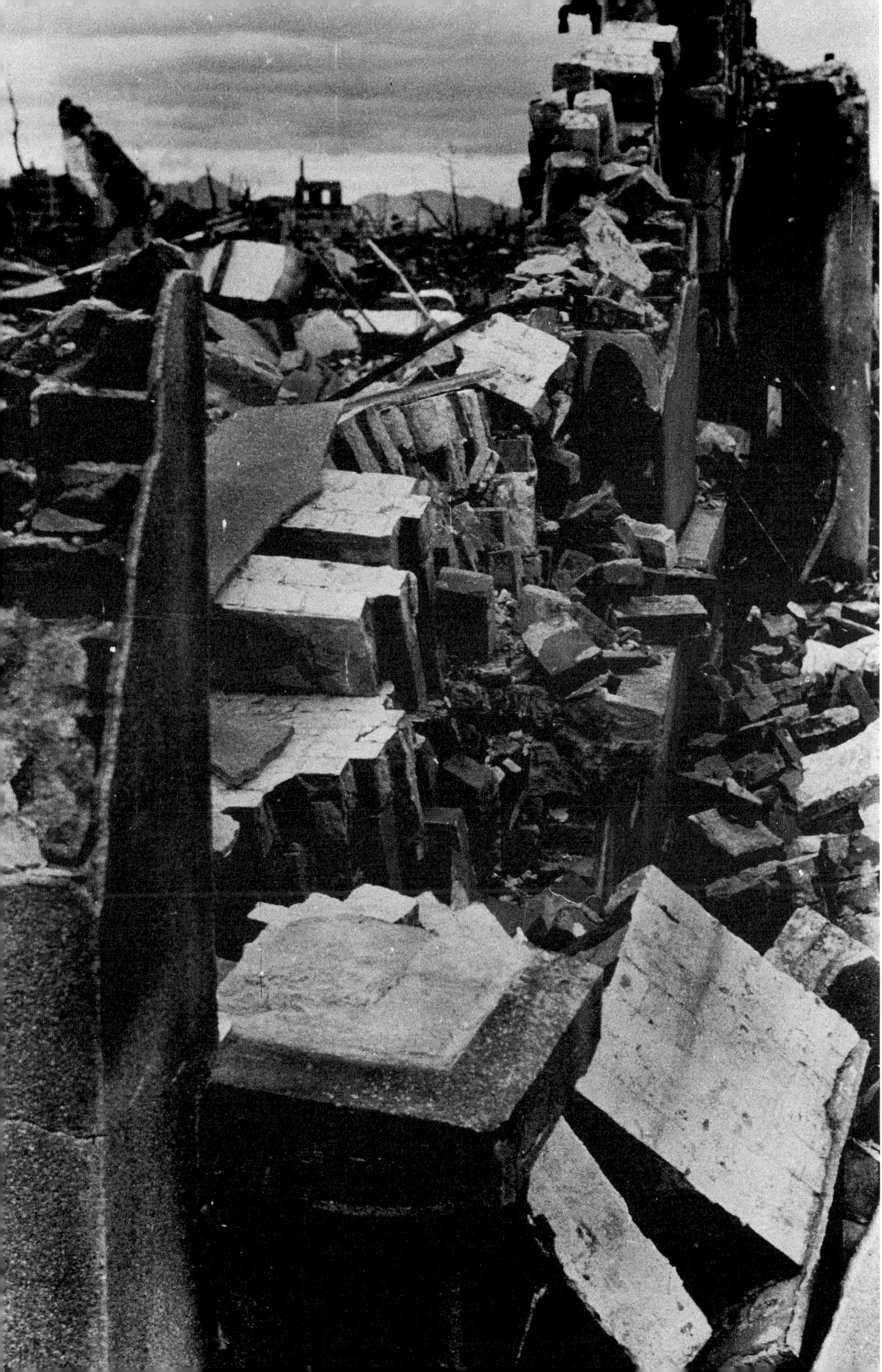

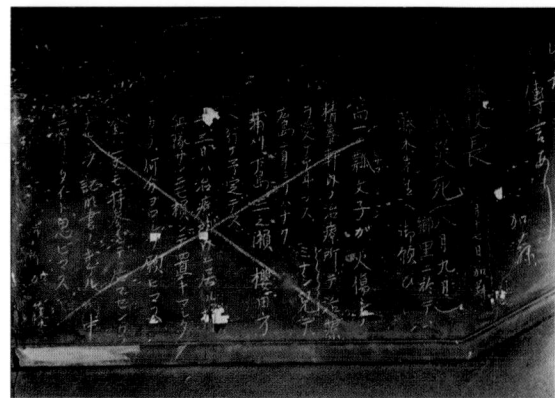

袋町国民学校（爆心地から南東500m）の階段の壁に、
白墨で書かれていた伝言。子どもの死を生徒に伝える父親のことば、
校長先生の死を知らせるもの、やけどの教え子を伝えようとする
先生の伝言などが書かれている＝1945年10月6日、
袋町国民学校（撮影：菊池俊吉）
Messages written with chalks on the wall of stairs at Fukuromachi Primary School.
500m southeast of the ground zero. One message from a father tells students
of his child's death, another tells the death of the school principal.
Teachers write about burn injury of their students.
= Photographed on October 6th 1945 by Shunkichi Kikuchi

左奥で治療する大田薮江医師＝1945年10月6日、袋町国民学校臨時救護所（撮影：菊池俊吉）
In the left back, Dr. Ota treats patients at the temporary first-aid station at Fukuromachi Primary School.
= Photographed on October 6th 1945 by Shunkichi Kikuchi

1945年10月6日、袋町国民学校臨時救護所（撮影：菊池俊吉）
Photographed on October 6th 1945 at the temporary first-aid station set up at Fukuromachi Primary School by Shunkichi Kikuchi

爆心地より南東 500m ＝ 1945 年 10 月 6 日、袋町国民学校臨時救護所（撮影：菊池俊吉）

500m southeast of the ground zero. = Photographed on October 6th 1945 at the temporary first-aid station set up at Fukuromachi Primary School, by Shunkichi Kikuchi

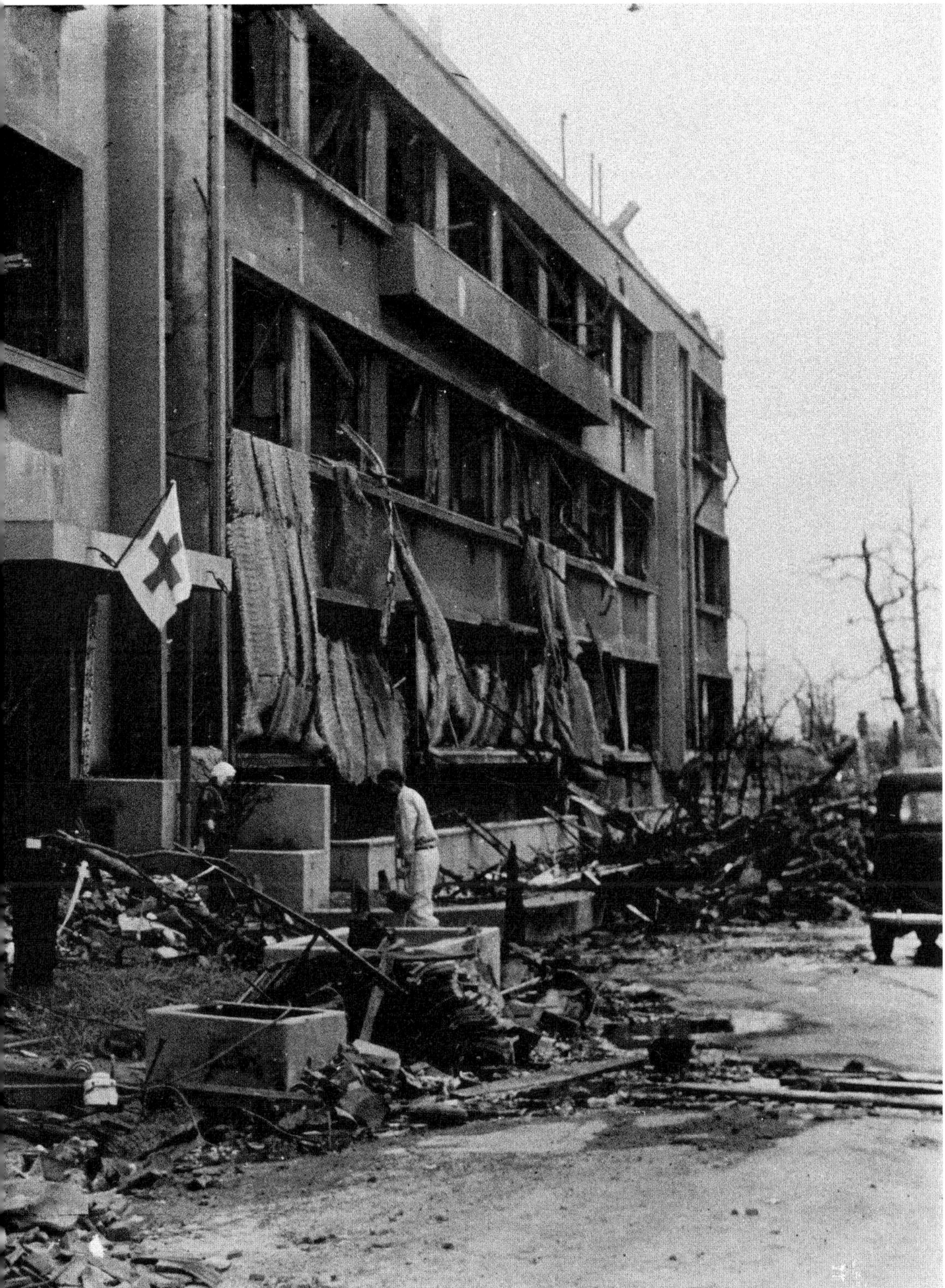

爆心地より南東 500m にあった袋町国民学校
＝ 1945 年 10 月 6 日（撮影：菊池俊吉）

Fukuromachi Primary School at 500m southeast
of the ground zero. = Photographed on October 6th
1945 by Shunkichi Kikuchi

1945 年 10 月 8 日、広島の広島逓信病院（撮影：菊池俊吉）

Photographed on October 8th 1945
at Hiroshima Teishin Hospital by Shunkichi Kikuchi

広島逓信病院（爆心地より北東 1.3km）の被害もひどかった。
だが、火災をまぬがれたので、当日の夕方には被災者が治療を求めて押し寄せた。
重傷者は院内のあらゆる場所を埋め、軽傷者は長い列をつくった。こうした状態が 9 月いっぱい続いた
＝ 1945 年 10 月 8 日、広島市基町 6 番地（撮影：菊池俊吉）

There were severe damages at the Hiroshima Teishin Hospital. 1.3km northeast of the ground zero.
The hospital was able to escape the fire and on the evening of that day, victims rushed in for the treatment.
Severely injured victims filled every space inside the hospital and mildly injured victims made a long line.
Such situation remains until the end of September.
= Photographed on October 8th 1945 at 6-banchi, Motomachi, Hiroshima City by Shunkichi Kikuchi

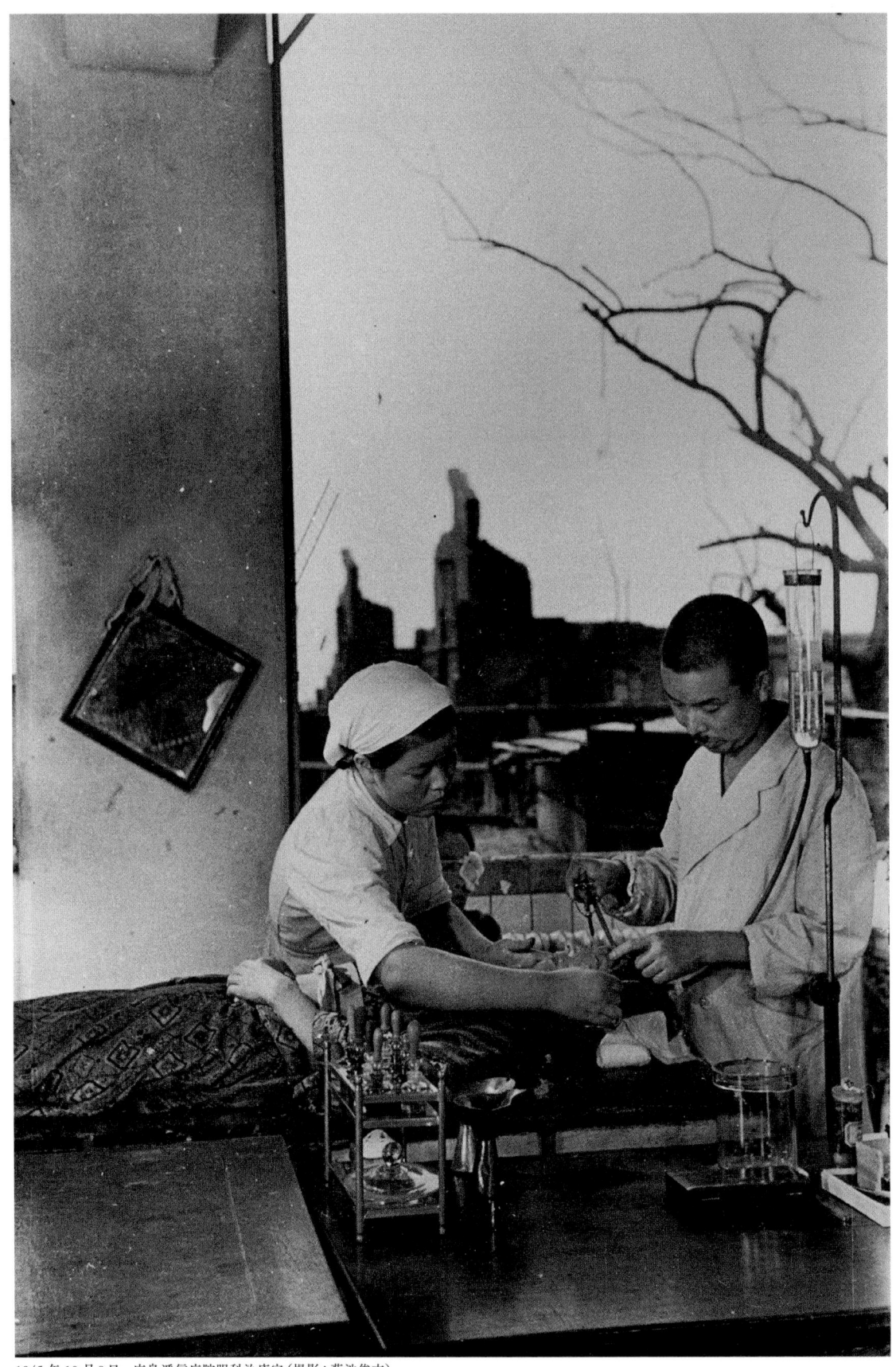

1945年10月8日、広島逓信病院眼科治療室（撮影：菊池俊吉）
Photographed on October 8th 1945 at Hiroshima Teishin Hospital Ophthalmology treatment room by Shunkichi Kikuchi

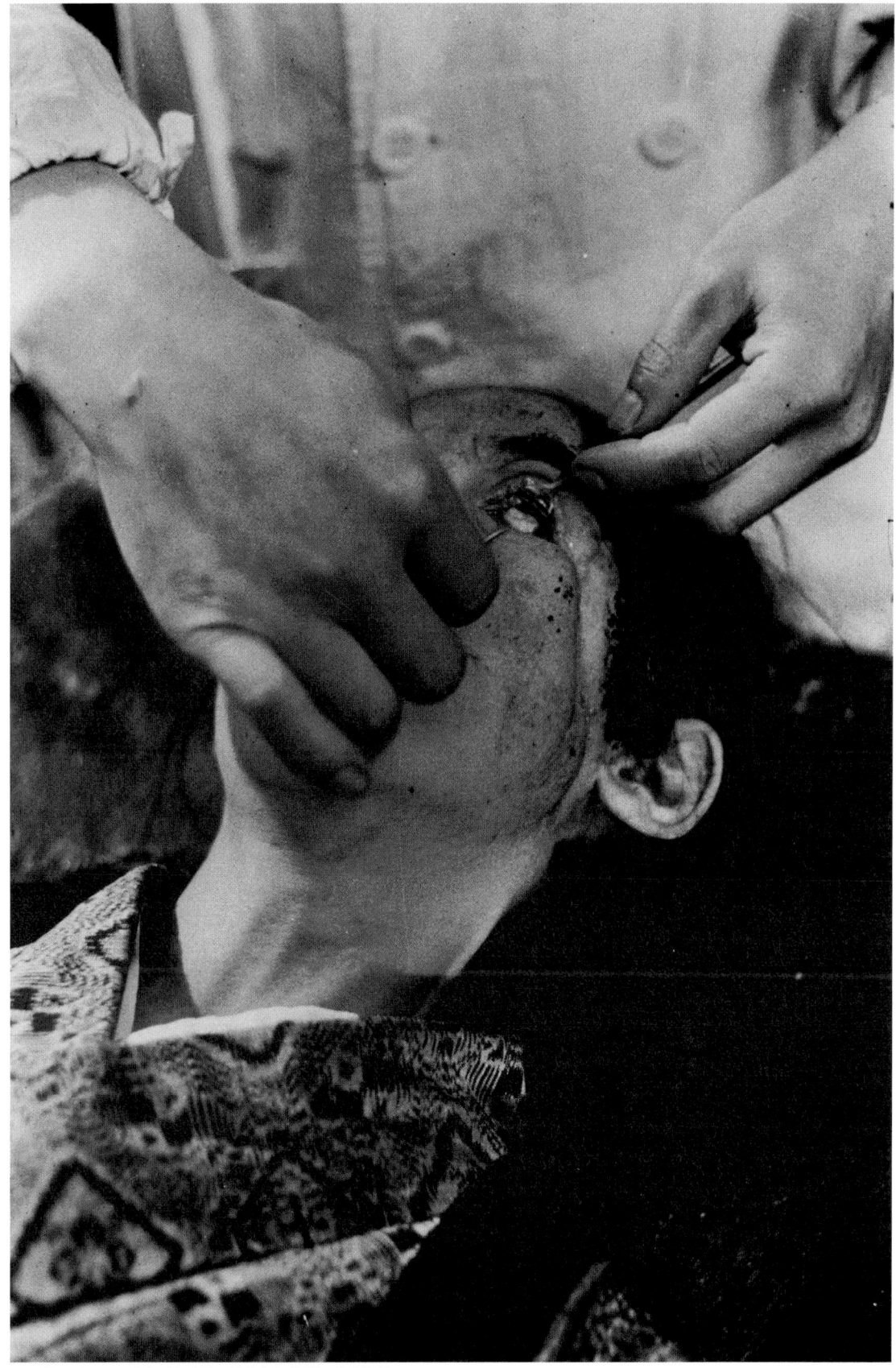

1945年10月8日、広島逓信病院眼科治療室(撮影:菊池俊吉)
Photographed on October 8th 1945 at Hiroshima Teishin Hospital Ophthalmology treatment room by Shunkichi Kikuchi

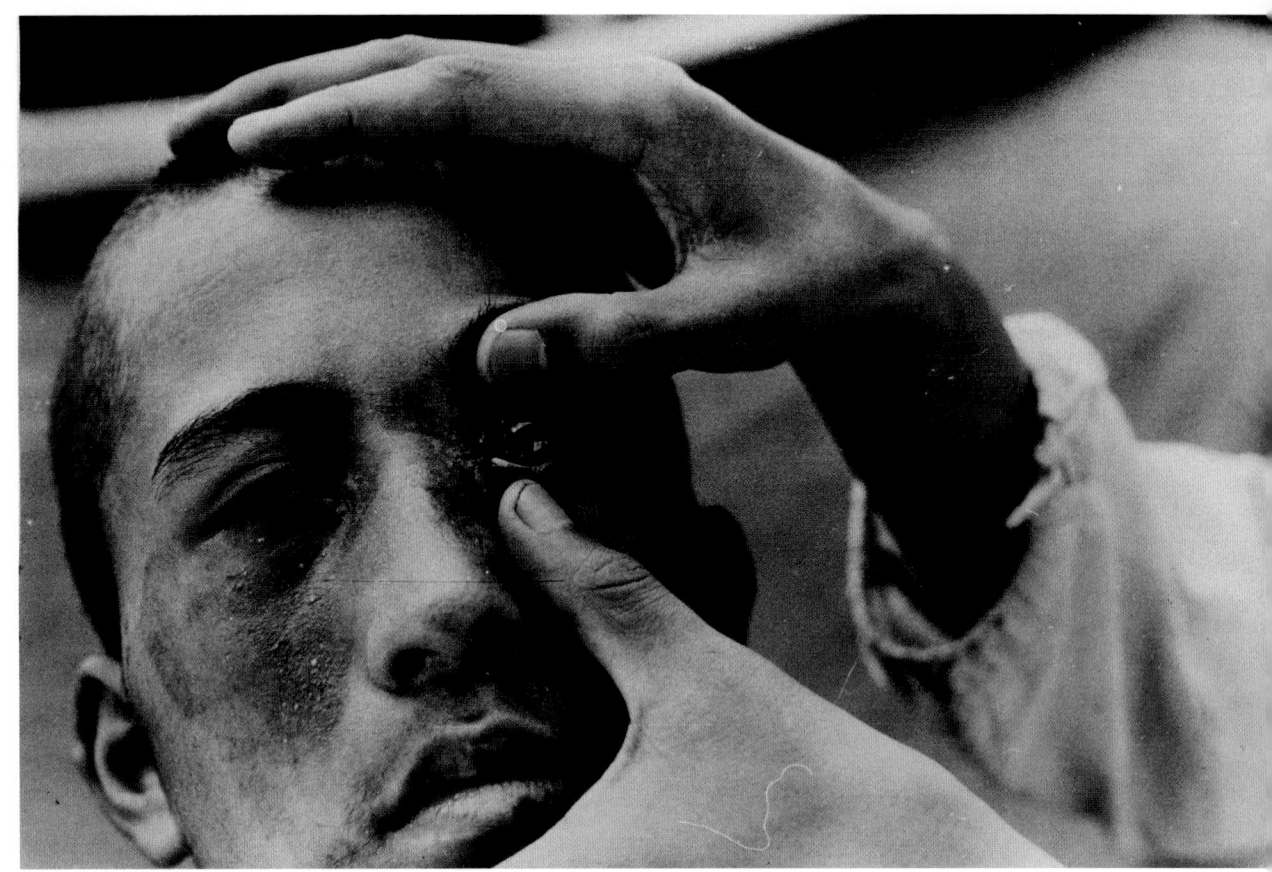

爆心地より 2 km 離れた地で軍服姿でかけ足中に左前より光線を受けた。
両眼に浅い角膜炎＝ 1945 年 10 月上旬、広島市陸軍病院宇品分院（撮影：菊池俊吉）

Front left side of this person's body was exposed while running in army uniform at the site 2km away from the ground zero.
Got slight cornea inflammation on both eyes. = Photographed at the beginning of October 1945 at First Army Hospital Ujina Branch by Shunkichi Kikuchi

爆心地より北東 1.3km の広島逓信病院＝ 1945 年 10 月 8 日、
広島市基町 6 番地（撮影：菊池俊吉）

Hiroshima Teishin Hospital. 1.3km northeast of the ground zero.
= Photographed on October 8th 1945 at 6-banchi, Motomoachi, Hiroshima City by Shunkichi Kikuchi

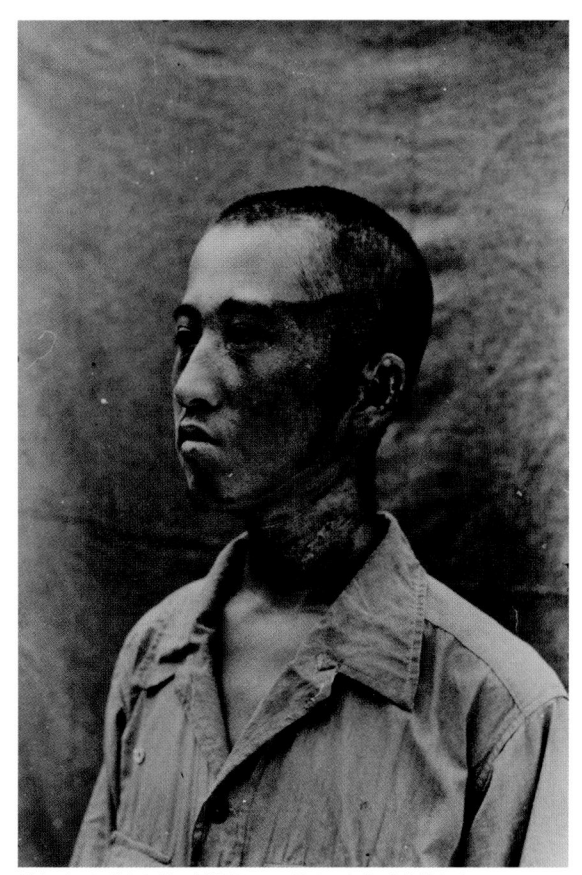

爆心より2km離れた地。軍服姿でかけ足中に左前より光線を受ける。
帽子を脱ぐとその跡がはっきりわかった。両眼に浅い角膜炎
＝1945年10月上旬、広島市陸軍病院宇品分院（撮影：菊池俊吉）
Front left side of this person's body was exposed while running in army uniform at the site 2km away from the ground zero. The trace was clearly visible once he took off his hat. Got slight cornea infllamation on both eyes.
= Photographed at the beginning of October 1945
at First Army Hospital Ujina Branch by Shunkichi Kikuchi

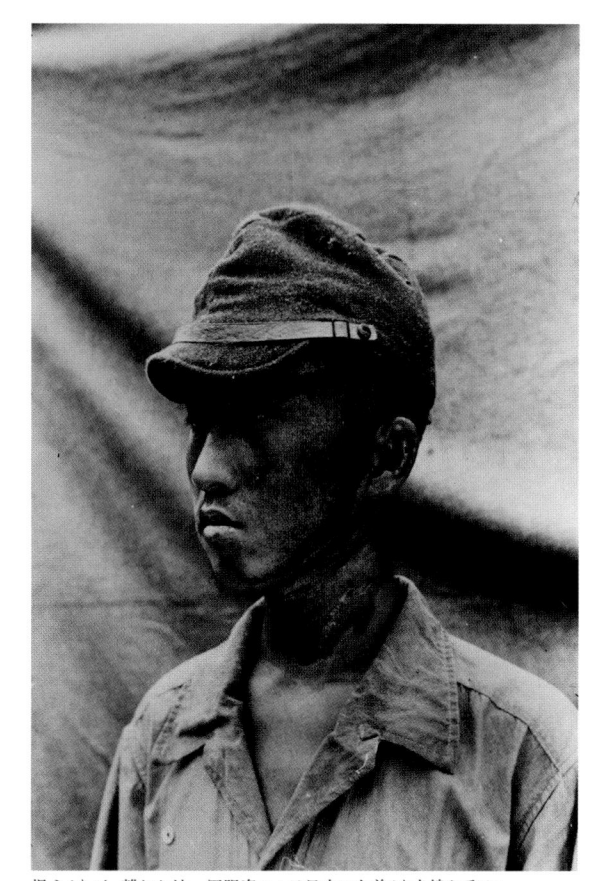

爆心より2km離れた地。軍服姿でかけ足中に左前より光線を受ける。
帽子を脱ぐとその跡がはっきりわかった。両眼に浅い角膜炎
＝1945年10月上旬、広島市陸軍病院宇品分院（撮影：菊池俊吉）
Front left side of this person's body was exposed while running in army uniform at the site 2km away from the ground zero. The trace was clearly visible once he took off his hat. Got slight cornea infllamation on both eyes.
= Photographed at the beginning of October 1945
at First Army Hospital Ujina Branch by Shunkichi Kikuchi

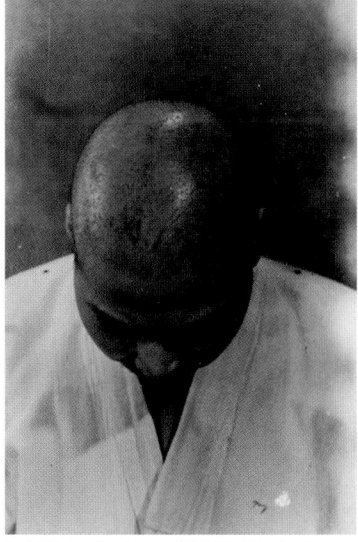

1945年10月上旬、広島市陸軍第一病院
宇品分院で（撮影：菊池俊吉）
Photographed at the beginning of October 1945 at First Army Hospital Ujina branch by Shunkichi Kikuchi

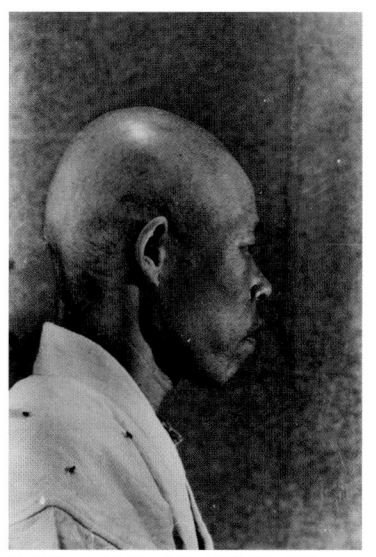

1945年10月上旬、広島市陸軍第一病院
宇品分院で（撮影：菊池俊吉）
Photographed at the beginning of October 1945 at First Army Hospital Ujina branch by Shunkichi Kikuchi

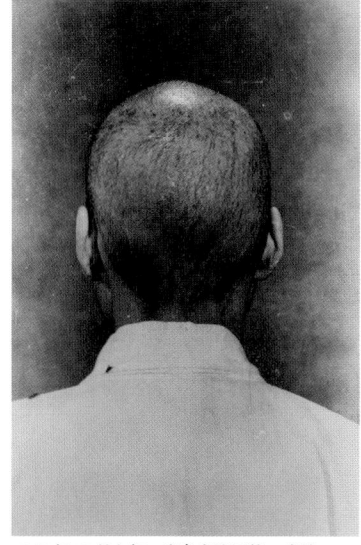

1945年10月上旬、広島市陸軍第一病院
宇品分院で（撮影：菊池俊吉）
Photographed at the beginning of October 1945 at First Army Hospital Ujina branch by Shunkichi Kikuchi

被害は大きかったが、原爆が投下された
8月6日の午後から医療活動に入った
日本赤十字社広島病院＝1945年10月上旬
（撮影：菊池俊吉）

Despite the severe damage, Japanese Red Cross Hiroshima Hospital started medical service in the afternoon of August 6th, the day the bomb exploded. = Photographed at the beginning of October 1945 by Shunkichi Kikuchi

職員・建物にかなりの被害があったが、
その日、8月6日午後から医療活動に入っている
＝1945年10月上旬、日本赤十字社広島病院
（撮影：菊池俊吉）

Japanese Red Cross Hiroshima Hospital. Both the building and the staff suffered severe damages on October 6th, but the Hospital restarted medical services in the afternoon of that day.
= Photographed at the beginning of October 1945 by Shunkichi Kikuchi

1945年10月上旬、日本赤十字社広島病院
（撮影：菊池俊吉）

Photographed at the beginning of October 1945 at Japanese Red Cross Hiroshima Hospital by Shunkichi Kikuchi

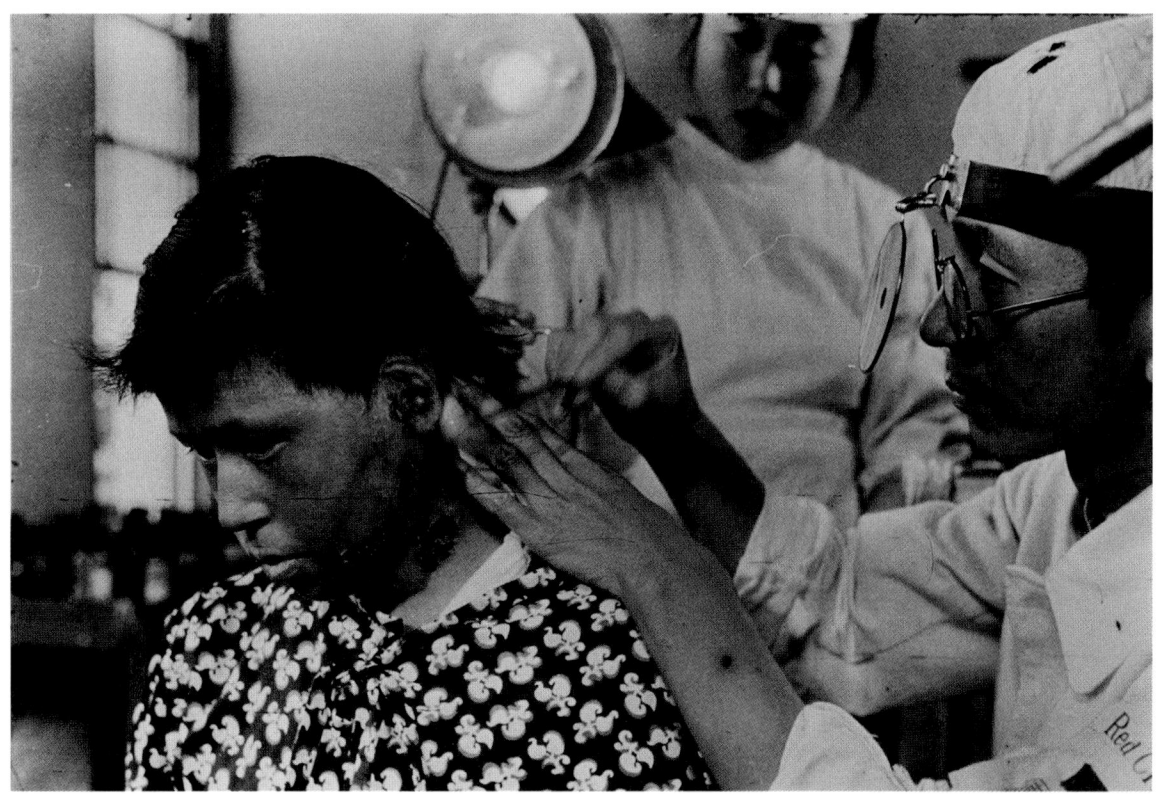

治療を受ける被爆者＝1945年10月上旬、日本赤十字社病院広島病院耳鼻科（撮影：菊池俊吉）
Bomb victims being treated. = Photographed at the beginning of October 1945 at Japanese Red Cross Hiroshima Hospital Otolaryngology treatment room by Shunkichi Kikuchi

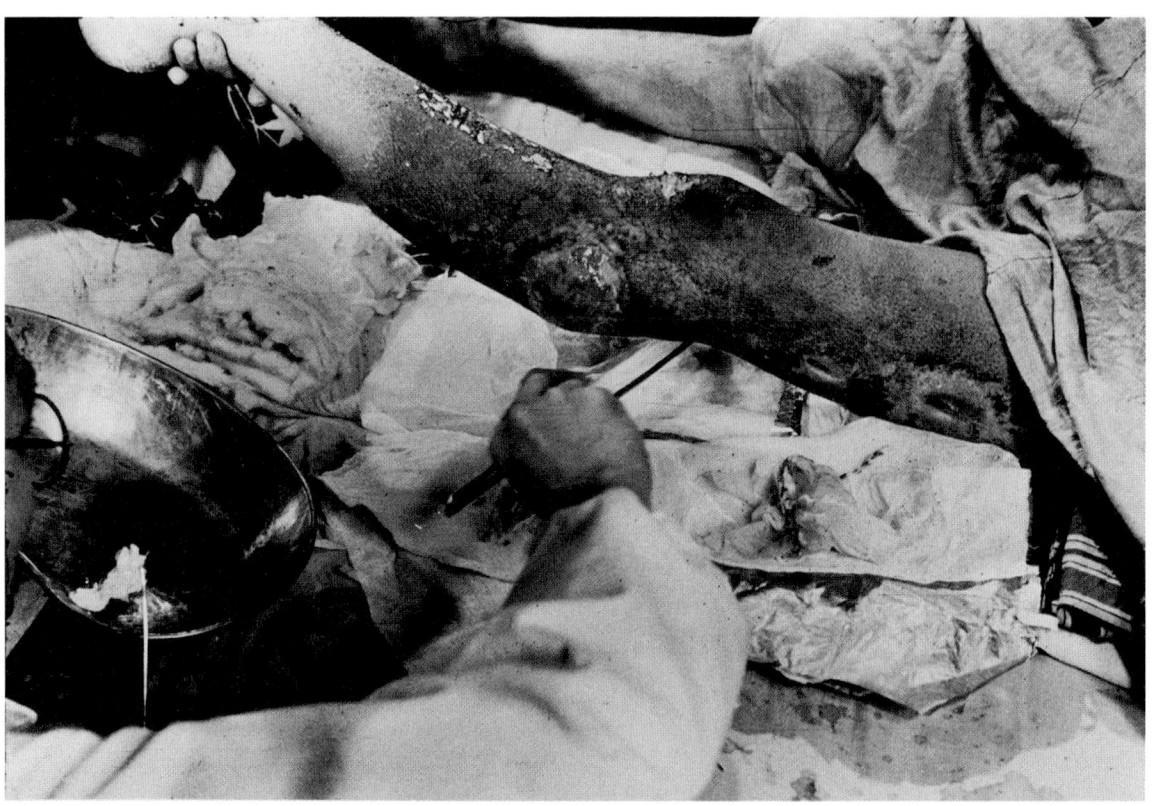

1945年10月上旬、日本赤十字社広島病院（撮影：菊池俊吉）
Photographed at the beginning of October 1945 at Japanese Red Cross Hiroshima Hospital by Shunkichi Kikuchi.

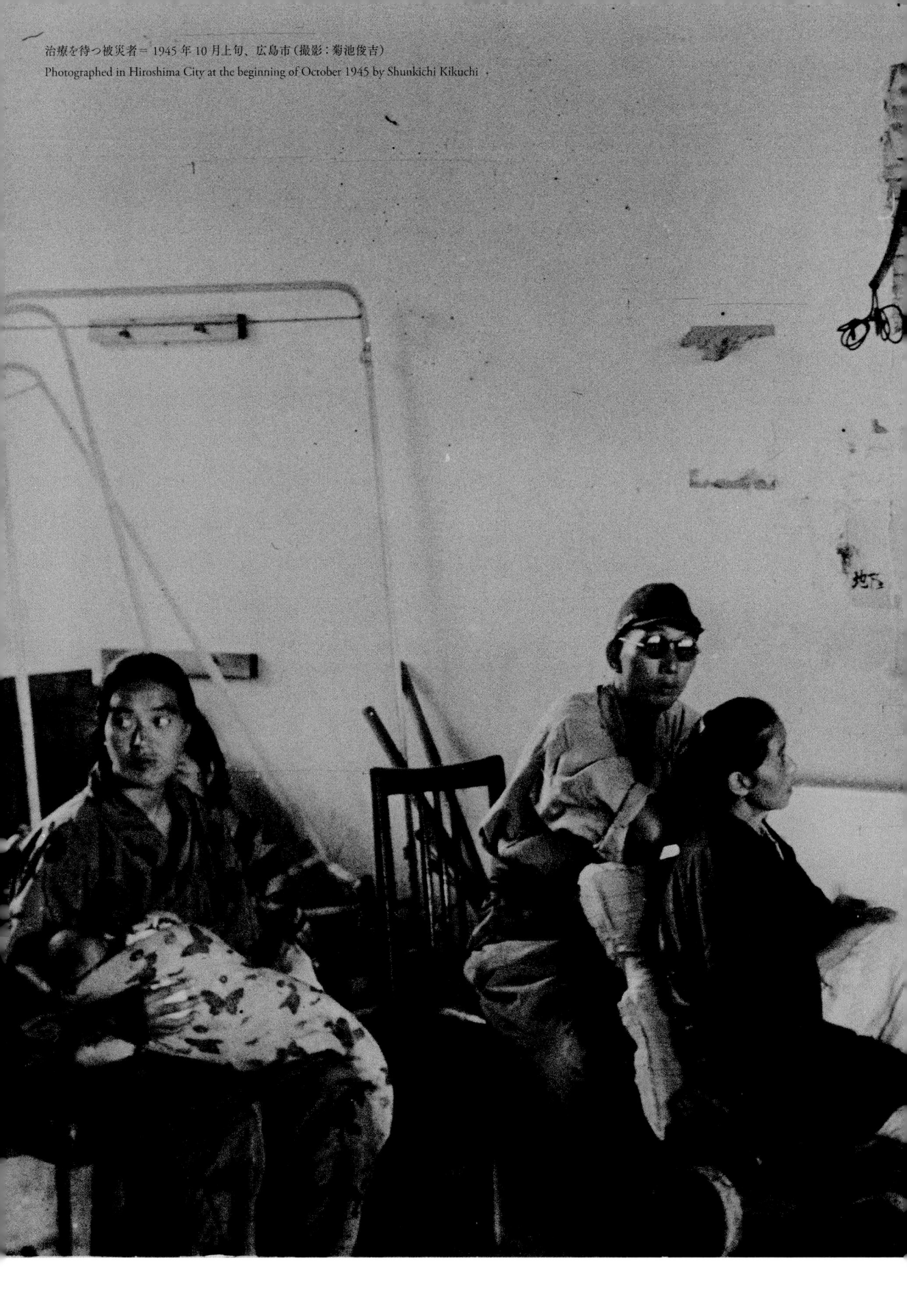

治療を待つ被災者＝1945年10月上旬、広島市（撮影：菊池俊吉）
Photographed in Hiroshima City at the beginning of October 1945 by Shunkichi Kikuchi

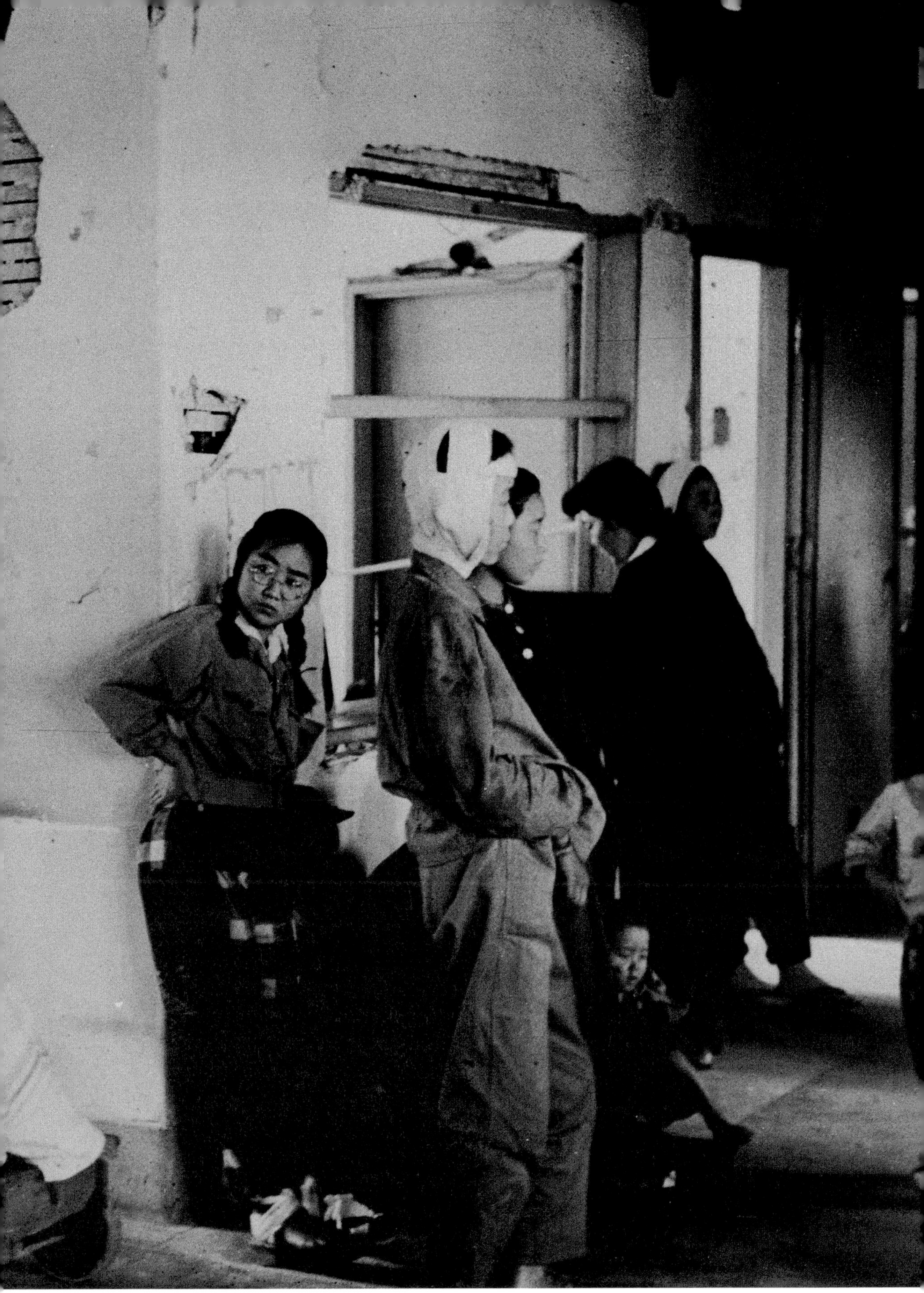

頭髪が抜けた姉弟。被爆後2カ月後から頭髪が抜け始め弟は1949年死亡。
姉は1965年に原爆後障害で死亡した＝1945年10月上旬、広島市（撮影：菊池俊吉）

Siblings who lost their hair. The brother's hair started falling out 2 months after the bomb and he died in 1949.
The sister died of bomb's aftereffects in 1965. = Photographed at the beginning of October 1945 by Shunkichi Kikuchi

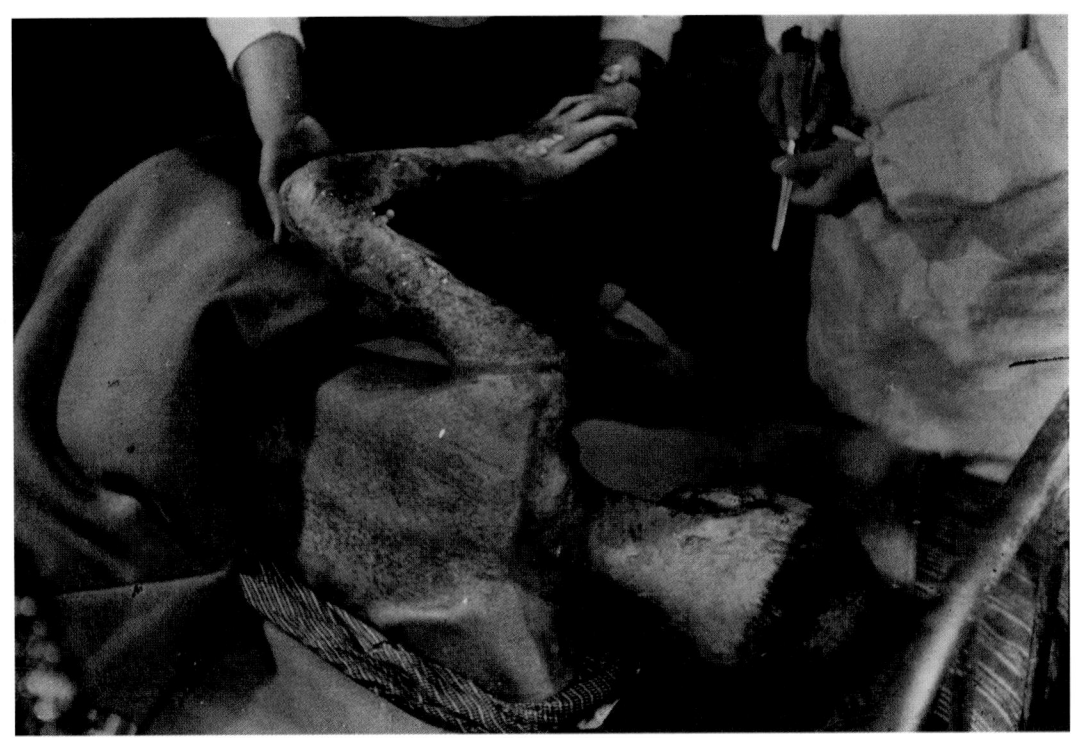

爆心地近くの中国軍官区兵器庫で受傷した26歳の男性。脱毛、下痢、発熱40度、火傷2度広範にわたり、あまりに痛々しく写すのが申し訳なく思った＝1945年10月上旬（撮影：菊池俊吉）

Severely injured 26 years old male who was at the Chugoku District Army armory near the ground zero. He suffered from hair loss, diarrhea, fever of 40 degrees Celsius and second degree burns all over the body. It looked so painful that I felt terribly sorry to take a photograph.
= Photographed at the beginning of October 1945 by Shunkichi Kikuchi

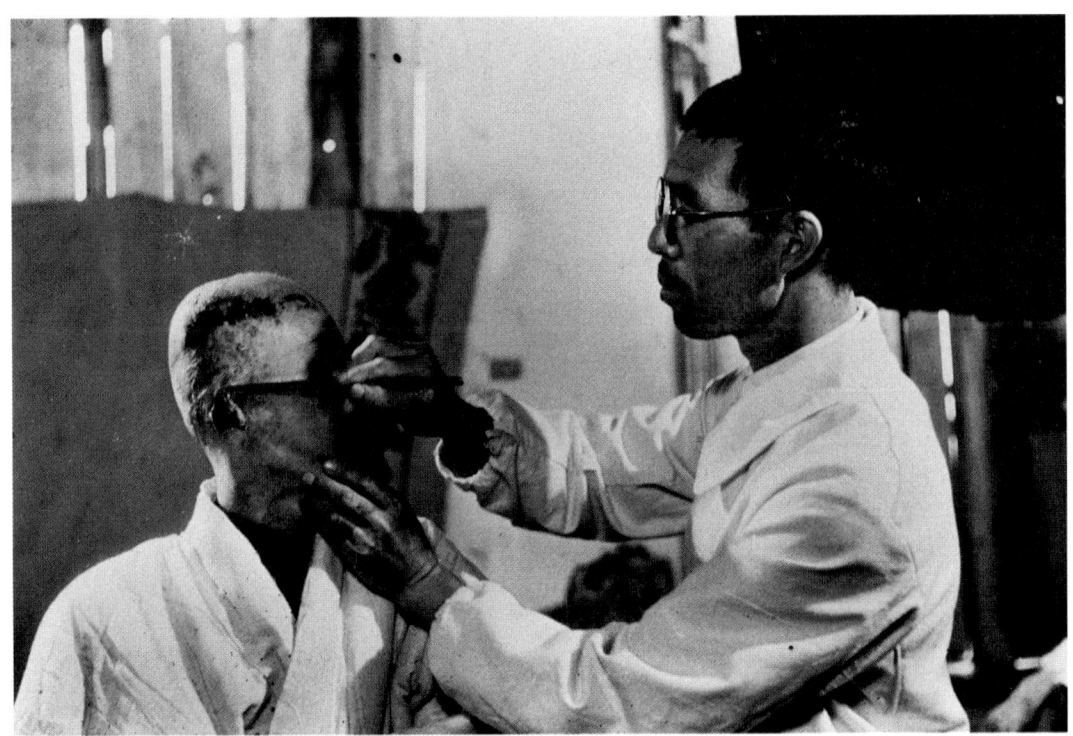

入院中の衛生兵・23歳　朝礼の集合中に後方より被爆。熱傷と放射能障害。
「奇跡的生還」の一人である由＝1945年10月上旬、日本赤十字社広島病院（撮影：菊池俊吉）

Hospitalized 23 years old army medic who exposed from behind during morning gathering. He sufferd from heat burns and radiation sickness. Known as one of the people who survived miraculously.
= Photographed at the beginning of October 1945 at Japanese Red Cross Hiroshima Hospital by Shunkichi Kikuchi

1945年10月上旬、日本赤十字社広島病院（撮影：菊池俊吉）
Photographed at the beginning of October 1945 at Japanese Red Cross Hiroshima Hospital by Shunkichi Kikuchi

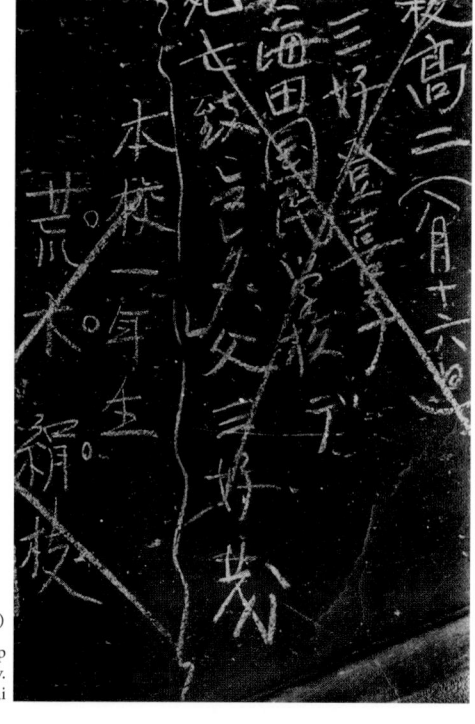

壁に書かれた伝言＝1945年10月上旬、広島袋町国民学校臨時救護所（撮影：菊池俊吉）
Messages written on the wall of the temporary first-aid station set up at Hiroshima Fukuro-machi Primary School in Hiroshima City.
= Photographed at the beginning of October 1945 by Shunkichi Kikuchi

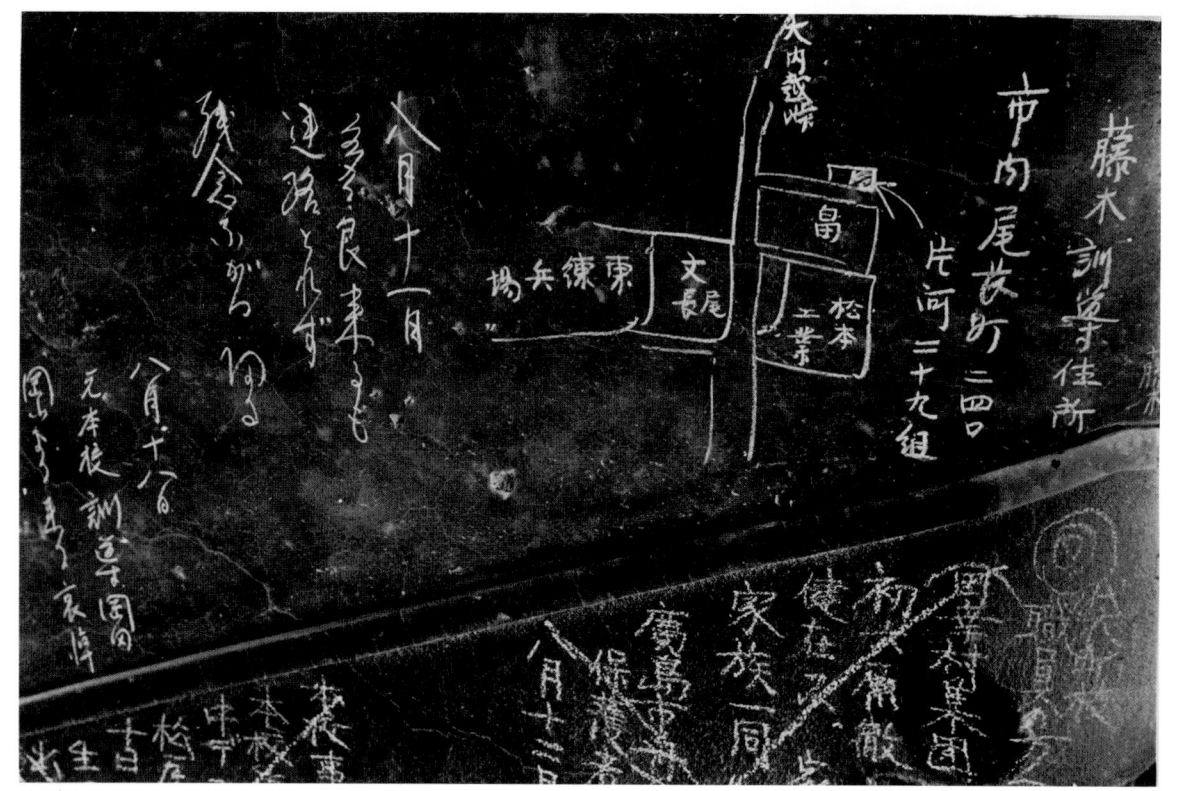

壁に書かれた伝言＝1945年10月上旬、広島袋町国民学校臨時救護所（撮影：菊池俊吉）
Messages written on the wall of the temporary first-aid station set up at Hiroshima Fukuro-machi Primary School in Hiroshima City.
= Photographed at the beginning of October 1945 by Shunkichi Kikuchi

壁に書かれた伝言＝ 1945 年 10 月上旬、広島袋町国民学校臨時救護所（撮影：菊池俊吉）
Messages written on the wall of the temporary first-aid station set up at Hiroshima Fukuro-machi Primary School in Hiroshima City.
= Photographed at the beginning of October 1945 by Shunkichi Kikuchi

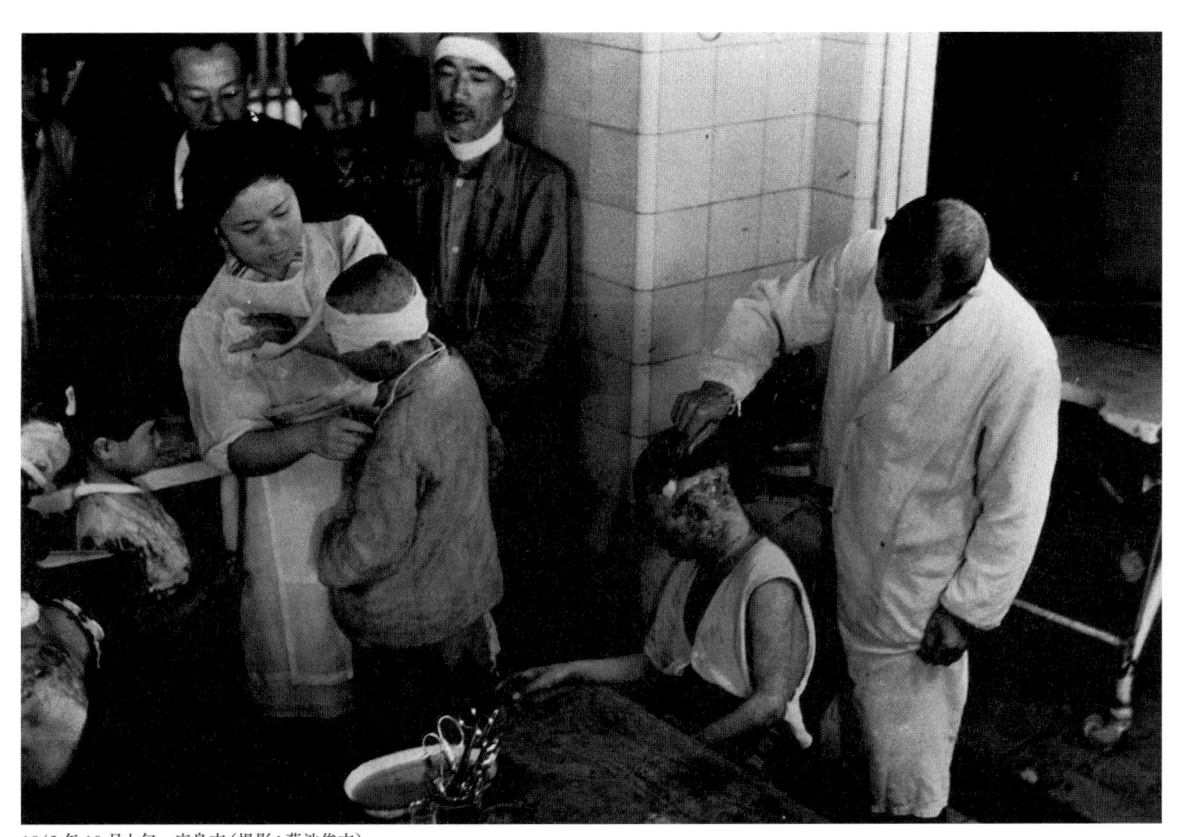

1945 年 10 月上旬、広島市（撮影：菊池俊吉）
Photographed in Hiroshima City at the beginning of October 1945 by Shunkichi Kikuchi

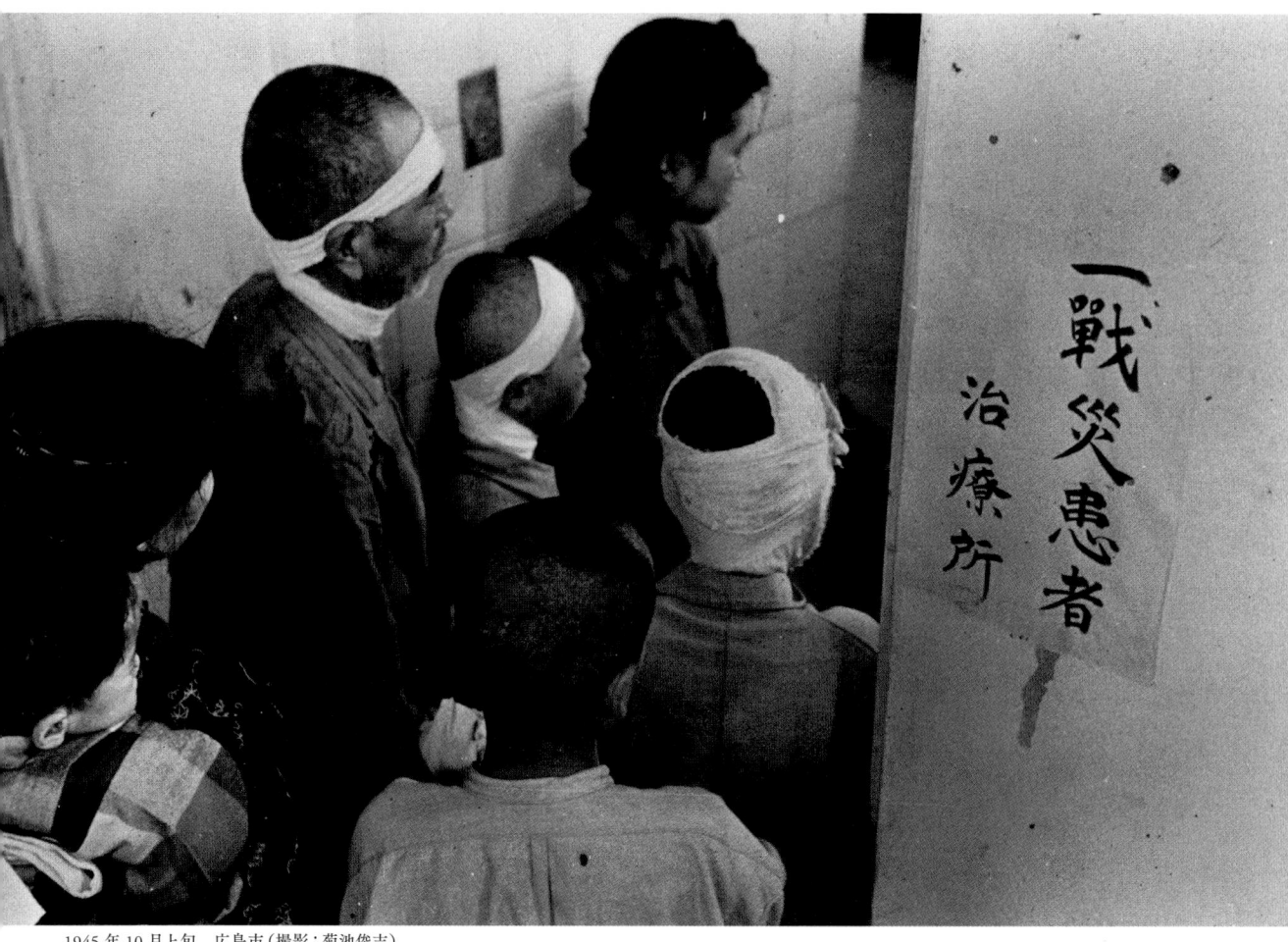

1945年10月上旬、広島市（撮影：菊池俊吉）
Photographed in Hiroshima City at the beginning of October 1945 by Shunkichi Kikuchi

1945 年 10 月上旬、広島市（撮影：菊池俊吉）

Photographed in Hiroshima City
at the beginning of October 1945
by Shunkichi Kikuchi

1945 年 10 月上旬、広島市（撮影：菊池俊吉）

Photographed in Hiroshima City
at the beginning of October 1945
by Shunkichi Kikuchi

1945年10月上旬、広島市（撮影：菊池俊吉）

Photographed in Hiroshima City at the beginning of October 1945 by Shunkichi Kikuchi

爆心地から北北西へ250mにある広島護国神社の狛犬の台座。
御影石の台座に熱線の影がくっきりとできていた＝1945年10月上旬、
広島市基町1番地（撮影：菊池俊吉）

Basement of Komainu (stone curved guardian dog)
in Hiroshima Gokoku Shrine, 1-banchi, Motomachi, Hiroshima City.
250 meters north – northwest of the ground zero.
The heat ray left clear shadows on the Granite basement
= Photographed at the beginning of October 1945 by Shunkichi Kikuchi

広島護国神社の狛犬の台座。爆心地より北北西に250m。
御影石の台座に熱線の影がくっきりできている。熱線をうけた面は
磨きたてのように、白くきれいになっていた＝1945年10月上旬、
広島市基町1番地（撮影：菊池俊吉）

Basement of Komainu (stone curved guardian dog)
in Hiroshima Gokoku Shrine, 1-banchi, Motomachi, Hiroshima City.
250 meters north – northwest of the ground zero. The heat ray left
clear shadows on the Granite basement. The side attacked by the heat ray
became white and smooth just as being polished
= Photographed at the beginning of October 1945 by Shunkichi Kikuchi

広島護国神社の大鳥居周辺＝1945年10月上旬（撮影：菊池俊吉）

Around the big Torii (entrance gate to the shrine)
in Hiroshima Gokoku Shrine
= Photographed at the beginning of October 1945 by Shunkichi Kikuchi

爆心地より東南 120m。
本通りをはさんで左に第一銀行、右に三和銀行
＝ 1945 年 10 月上旬（撮影：菊池俊吉）

120 meters southeast of the ground zero.
The First Bank on the left, and Sanwa Bank on the right across the Hondori street, Hiroshima City
= Photographed at the beginning of October 1945 by Shunkichi Kikuchi

崩壊した大同生命ビルから東方、
福屋百貨店方面をみる。
爆心地より東に 290m
＝ 1945 年 10 月上旬、広島市紙屋町交差点（撮影：菊池俊吉）

Eastward view of the Fukuya Department Store from collapsed Daido-Seimei building. 290 meters east of the ground zero = Photographed at the beginning of October 1945 at the Intersection in Kamiya-cho, Hiroshima City by Shunkichi Kikuchi

爆心地より 2000m。
爆風と火災により駅内部はがらんどう
＝ 1945 年 10 月上旬、広島駅（撮影：菊池俊吉）

Hiroshima Station. 2000 meters east of the ground zero. There is nothing left in this building because of the blast wave and fire
= Photographed at the beginning of October 1945 by Shunkichi Kikuchi

1945年10月上旬、広島駅本館構内（撮影：菊池俊吉）
Inside the main building of Hiroshima Station.
Photographed at the beginning of October 1945
by Shunkichi Kikuchi

1945年10月上旬、広島駅につくられた仮設の改札口（撮影：菊池俊吉）
A temporary ticket gate of Hiroshima Station. Photographed at the beginning of October 1945 by Shunkichi Kikuchi

爆心側の北東面は全壊したが西・南面は崩壊をまぬがれた。
左から日本銀行広島支店、広島瓦斯本社、中国配電本社
＝1945年10月上旬、広島瓦斯本社を北西側から見る
（撮影：林重男）

While the northeast side of the ground zero was completely collapsed, the west and south escaped the ravage. The Bank of Japan Hiroshima Branch (left), HQ of the Hiroshima Gas (center), and HQ of the Chugoku Haiden (right) = Photographed from northwest at the beginning of October 1945 by Shigeo Hayashi

爆心に面した北東側は全壊したが
2階バルコニーを丸柱で支えた玄関は残った。
玄関前左右が大手町通り＝1945年10月上旬、
広島瓦斯本社を北東側から見る（撮影：林重男）

View of the Hiroshima Gas HQ from northeast side. While the northeast part facing the ground zero was completely collapsed, the entrance with the second-floor balcony supported by columns remained. The road in front of the entrance is Otemachi Street, Hiroshima City = Photographed at the beginning of October 1945 by Shigeo Hayashi

左から広島瓦斯本社、広島県産業奨励館。
大手町通りに面した玄関部分。
中央部の玄関は崩壊を免れたが、爆心側の北面は全壊、
南側壁面も含め三階部分は吹き飛ばされた
＝1945年10月上旬、広島瓦斯本社を東南東から見る
（撮影：林重男）

HQ of Hiroshima Gas (left) and the Hiroshima Prefectural Industrial Promotion Hall (the Atomic Bomb Dome) (right). Those entrance face Otemachi Street, Hiroshima City. While the entrance avoided collapse, the north part facing the ground zero was completely collapsed, and the third floor was blown away with the south-side walls = Photographed from east-southeast at the beginning of October 1945 by Shigeo Hayashi

左から福屋百貨店、広島電鉄市内電車軌道、奥に広島県商工経済会、福屋旧館、全壊の広電市内電車（421or430型）、
電車軌道にそらせて放置された＝1945年10月上旬、広島市鉄砲町から広電電車通りを西に向って（撮影：林重男）
Hiroden Tram Street viewed westward from Teppo-cho, Hiroshima City. (From left to right) Fukuya Department Store,
tramway of the Hiroshima Electric Railway Co., Ltd., the Hiroshima Chamber of Commerce and Industry,
the old building of Fukuya Department Store and debris of a tram car (type 421 or 430) which went off the track
= Photographed at the beginning of October 1945 by Shigeo Hayashi

左下広島電鉄市内電車軌道付近を運行中の木炭バス。
左中央部には全壊した広島電鉄市内電車が放置。
電車軌道右の石垣は広島城外堀跡、左から中国憲兵隊司令部、
市水道部基町庁舎作業場、西練兵場、偕行社
＝1945年10月上旬、商工組合中央金庫広島支所屋上（4階）から
北西に向って（撮影：林重男）

Northwest view from the rooftop (4th floor) of Shoko Chukin Bank Hiroshima Branch, Hiroshima City. At lower left, a charcoal powered bus run along the tramway of Hiroshima Electric Railway Co., Ltd. A collapsed tram car abandoned. The stone wall at right side of the tramway is the remains of the moat of Hiroshima Castle. From left to right, Chugoku HQ of Military Police, Motomachi working station of the Hiroshima City Municipal Office Water Department, Nishi Military Exercise Ground and Kaiko-sha clubhouse = Photographed at the beginning of October 1945 by Shigeo Hayashi

左から比治山、金輪島、広島瓦斯広島工場、多田小児科、
キリンビヤホール、江田島。商工組合中央金庫広島支所屋上南側の
欄干は爆風で崩落した＝1945年10月上旬、
商工組合中央金庫広島支所屋上（4階）から南東に向って
（撮影：林重男）

Southeast view from the rooftop (4th floor) of Shoko Chukin Bank Hiroshima Branch, Hiroshima City. From left to right, Mt. Hiji, Kanawa Island, Hiroshima Gas Co.,Ltd. Hiroshima factory, Tada Pediatrics Clinic, Kirin Beer Garden and Eta-jima. The parapet located in the south side of rooftop of The Shoko Chukin Bank Hiroshima Branch was collapsed by the blast wave = Photographed at the beginning of October 1945 by Shigeo Hayashi

広島市立町東北角から北西に向って。市水道部基町庁舎作業場は、
爆心方向からの強い爆風のため鉄骨がはげしくかしぎ全焼全壊した。
基町庁舎作業場左端石垣は広島城外堀跡。
手前は火災のため全焼した広島電鉄市内電車、
路線確保のため車輌は脇へよけられた＝1945年10月上旬、
市水道部基町庁舎作業場（撮影：林重男）

View of the Motomachi working station of the Hiroshima City Municipal Office Water Department from the northeast corner of Tatemachi, Hiroshima City to the northwest. This working station was completely burnt down and its steel frame was severely inclining because of the strong blast wave from the ground zero. The stone wall at the left side of the working station was the remains of the moat of Hiroshima Castle. A completely burnt tram car of Hiroshima Electric Railway Co.,Ltd. was removed from the rail in order to ensure the tram operation
= Photographed at the beginning of October 1945 by Shigeo Hayashi

広島市基町広島城跡外堀から北に向って。市水道部基町庁舎作業場は、
爆心方向からの強い爆風のため、鉄骨がはげしくかしぎ全焼全壊した。
左側の石垣は広島城外堀跡＝1945年10月上旬、
市水道部基町庁舎作業場（撮影：林重男）

Northward View from the outer moat of Hiroshima Castle, Motomachi, Hiroshima City. Motomachi working station of the Hiroshima City Municipal Office Water Department was completely burnt down and its steel frame was severely inclining because of strong blast wave from the ground zero. The stone wall at the left side of the working station was the remains of the moat
= Photogrtaphed at the beginning of October 1945 by Shigeo Hayashi

広島市内の宇田家の吹き飛ばされた雨戸に付着した泥雨（黒い雨）を
調べる学術調査団員＝1945年10月上旬（撮影：林重男）

Member of science research group investigating water drops of
muddy rain (Black Rain) on a storm sash of a house owned by a person
named Uda = Photographed at the beginning of October 1945
by Shigeo Hayashi

被爆変形したヒイラギ＝1945年10月上旬、
広島文理科大学構内（撮影：林重男）

he shape of a holly leaf was changed because of radiation exposure
= Photographed at the beginning of October 1945
at Hiroshima Imperial University Teachers College by Shigeo Hayashi

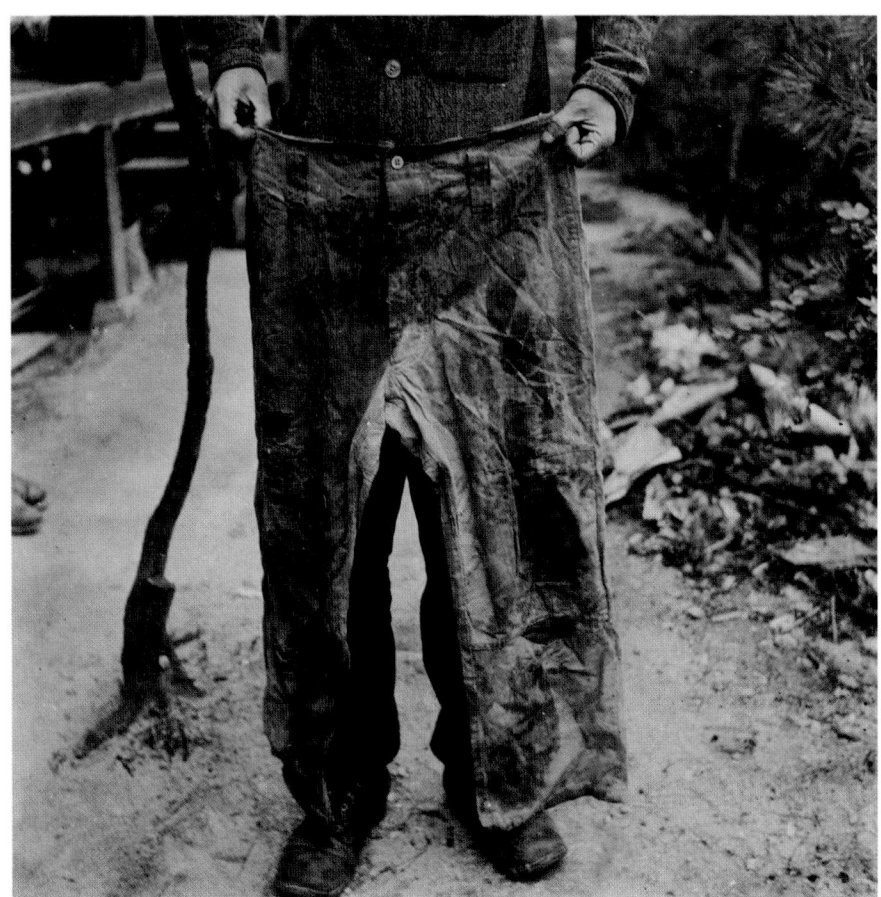

黒い雨に汚染された
ズボンを手にする学術調査団員
＝1945年10月上旬、広島市
（撮影：林重男）

Member of science research group
having a pair of trousers contaminated
by Black Rain = Photographed at the
beginning of October 1945
by Shigeo Hayashi

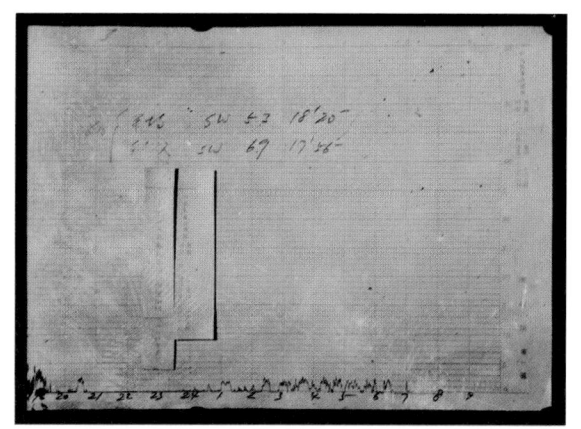

ダインズ式自記風圧器記録紙。
1945（昭和20）年8月6日の風圧を記録した
広島地方気象台の観測記録。
午前8時過ぎから午前9時の間は記録されていない
＝1945年10月上旬（撮影：林重男）

Recorded papers of Dines automatic wind barometer, showing wind pressures taken at Hiroshima Regional Meteorological Office on August 6th, 1945. The data from 8 to 9 am were not recorded
= Photographed at the beginning of October 1945 by Shigeo Hayashi

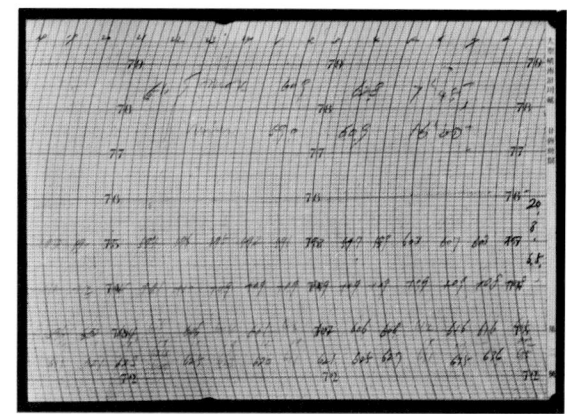

大型晴雨計記録紙。
1945（昭和20）年8月6日の気圧を記録した広島地方気象台の観測記録。
午前8時15分過ぎの海面気圧は763.6mmHg
（現在のヘクトパスカルと同じ）＝1945年10月上旬（撮影：林重男）

This large barometer recording paper shows atmospheric pressure taken at Hiroshima Regional Meteorological Office on August 6th, 1945.
The pressure at sea level recorded at 8.15am was 763.6 mmHg (same as hPa)
= Photographed at the beginning of October 1945 by Shigeo Hayashi

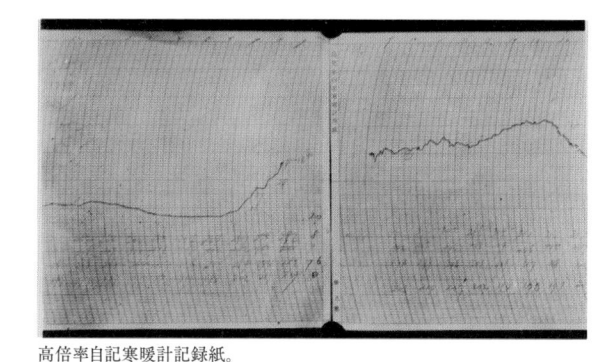

高倍率自記寒暖計記録紙。
右側は8月5日午前9時から午後4時まで、
左側は8月7日午前零時から9時までの気温を記録した
広島地方気象台の観測記録紙。
8月6日午前8時15分前後の記録はこの記録紙にはない
＝1945年10月上旬（撮影：林重男）

High magnification automatic thermometer recording paper showing temperatures from 9 am to 4 pm on August 5th (right)
and from 12 midnight to 9 am on August 7th (left).
These records were taken at Hiroshima Regional Meteorological Office.
There was no records before and after 8:15 am on August 6th
= Photographed at the beginning of October 1945 by Shigeo Hayashi

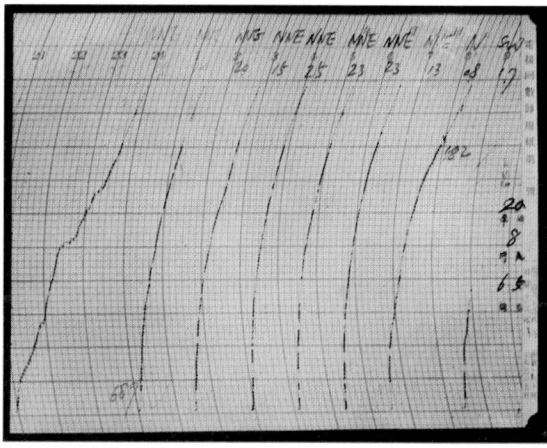

自記電接計数器記録紙。
1945（昭和20）年8月6日の風速を記した広島地方気象台の観測記録。
午前8時の風速は北0.8m、午前9時南西1.7mであった
＝1945年10月上旬（撮影：林重男）

Totalizing chronograph recording paper showing records of wind speed taken at Hiroshima Regional Meteorological Office on August 6th 1945.
The wind speed at 8 am was 0.8 meters (north) and
at 9 am 1.7 meters (southwest)
= Photographed at the beginning of October 1945 by Shigeo Hayashi

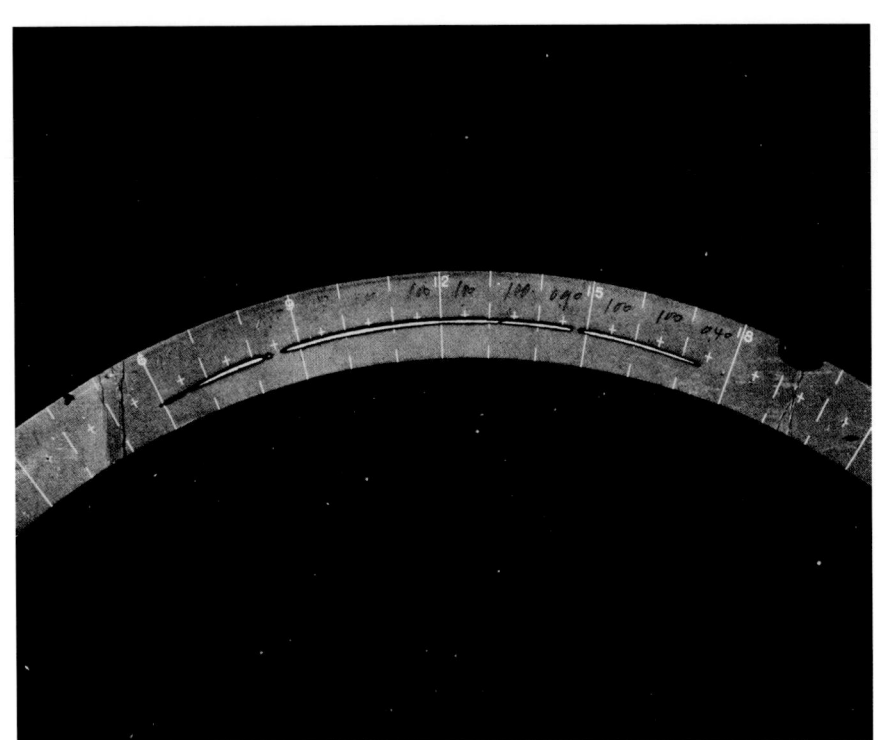

1945年8月6日の日照を記録した広島地方気象台の記録紙＝1945年10月上旬（撮影／林重男）

Recorded papers of sunlight taken at Hiroshima Regional Meteorological Office on August 6th 1945 = Photographed at the beginning of October 1945 by Shigeo Hayashi

北から南に向って（正面側）。爆心側からの強い爆風を受け東（左）に向って倒れ込み、1階部分は押しつぶされ平建てのように見える。建物の座屈した前左右が広島の本通り（旧山陽道、西国街道）＝1945年10月上旬、下村時計店（撮影：林重男）

Front View (from north to south) of the Shimomura Clock Shop, Hiroshima City. The building was collapsed toward the east (left) direction. The first floor was pressured into flat by the strong blast wave from the ground zero and the store now looks like a single-story house. The street in front is the Hondori Street (former Sanyo-do and Saigoku-Kaido)
= Photographed at the beginning of October 1945 by Shigeo Hayashi

中央の道が本通り（旧山陽道、西国街道）。左から下村時計店、安田銀行広島支店。本通り奥に帝国銀行広島支店、三和銀行広島支店、安田生命広島支店。右に大林組広島支店、住友銀行広島支店、芸備銀行本店。1階が押しつぶされた下村時計店は、爆風の影響で塔屋も南へ倒れ込んだ。この頃になると市民生活も少しづつ回復し、町に人々の姿が目立ち始めた＝1945年10月上旬、本通り（キリンビヤホール付近）東から西に向って（撮影：林重男）

View from east to west of the Hondori Street (former Sanyo-do and Saigoku-Kaido) near Kirin Beer Garden. (From left to right) Shimomura Clock Shop, Yasuda Bank Hiroshima Branch. Teikoku Bank Hiroshima Branch, Sanwa Bank Hiroshima Branch and Yasuda Life Insurance Company Hiroshima Branch are on the left side of Hondori. Obayashi-Gumi Hiroshima Branch, Sumitomo Bank Hiroshima Branch and Geibi Bank HQ are on the right side. Shimomura Clock Shop, whose first floor was pressured flat, was collapsed with its penthouse to the south direction by the blast wave. People's daily lives were gradually recovered at this time, and people seen on the street is increasing
= Photographed at the beginning of October 1945 by Shigeo Hayashi

広島護国神社大鳥居前で入市初日のミーティング中の
広島・長崎学術調査団。大鳥居裏(北側)の扁額は強い爆風で
飛ばされ落下したが、爆心側の扁額は正面からの爆風に
押し付けられたのか落下しなかった。左後の広島護国神社社殿は
木造建物のため基壇を残して全焼全壊した。境内を取り囲んでいた
御影石の玉垣、灯籠、狛犬、鳥居などに強い熱線の跡が残り
原爆の炸裂した高さや爆心地の決定に役立った＝ 1945 年 10 月上旬、
広島護国神社（撮影：林重男）

Hiroshima and Nagasaki Academic Survey Team having a meeting in front of the big Torii (entrance to the shrine) in Hiroshima Gokoku Shrine on the first day of their arrival at Hiroshima City. While the Hengaku (signboard) behind the Torii (entrance gate to the shrine) (north side) was blown away by blast wave, the one facing the ground zero was not dropped probably because of being pressed by the wave from the front. The wooden Main shrine of Hiroshima Gokoku Shrine was completely burnt down except its podium. The altitude of the explosion and the whereabouts of the ground zero were defined based on the lines, made by heat wave, on fences of Mikage stones around the shrine, on stone lanterns, on Komainu (stone-curved guardian dogs) and also on Torii = Photographed at the beginning of October 1945 by Shigeo Hayashi

全壊した小田政商店。左から広島逓信局、缶詰工場、小田政商店。
右奥に広島中央放送局、広島流川教会、右端に中国新聞社新館。
手前から、流川町、堀川町、胡町。左煙突付近は八丁堀。
後の山は阿武山、牛田山など＝ 1945 年 10 月上旬、
広島市流川町から北に向って（撮影：林重男）

View from Nagarekawa-cho, Hiroshima City to the north. From left to right, Hiroshima Teishin-kyoku (Communications and Transportation Center), a canning factory and wholely collapsed Odamasa Store. At right back, Hiroshima Central Broadcasting Station and Hiroshima Nagarekawa Church. New building of the Chugoku Shimbunsha is in front. From front to back, Nagarekawa-cho, Horikawa-machi and Ebisu-cho. Hacho-bori was in the left side near the chimney. Mountains such as Mt. Abu and Mt. Ushita are far behind = Photographed at the beginning of October 1945 by Shigeo Hayashi

広島護国神社大鳥居前でミーティング中の調査団。
西北西に向って＝ 1945 年 10 月上旬、広島護国神社（撮影：林重男）

Hiroshima and Nagasaki Academic Survey Team having a meeting in front of the big Torii (entrance gate to the shrine) in Hiroshima Gokoku Shrine = Photographed at the beginning of October 1945 by Shigeo Hayashi

東から北西に向って。大鳥居裏（北）側の扁額は、強い爆風で
飛ばされ落下したが、爆心側の扁額は正面からの爆風に
押し付けられたのか落下しなかった。後の広島護国神社社殿は
木造建物のため基壇を残して全焼全壊した。境内を取り囲んでいた
御影石の玉垣、灯籠、狛犬、鳥居などに強い熱線の跡が残り
原爆の炸裂した高さや爆心地の決定に役立った＝ 1945 年 10 月上旬、
広島護国神社大鳥居（撮影：林重男）

Hiroshima and Nagasaki Academic Survey Team having a meeting in front of the big Torii (entrance to the shrine) in Hiroshima Gokoku Shrine on the first day of their arrival at Hiroshima City. While the Hengaku (signboard) behind the Torii (entrance gate to the shrine) (north side) was blown away by blast wave, the one facing the ground zero was not dropped probably because of being pressed by the wave from the front. The wooden Main shrine of Hiroshima Gokoku Shrine was completely burnt down except its podium. The altitude of the explosion and the whereabouts of the ground zero were defined based on the lines, made by heat wave, on fences of Mikage stones around the shrine, on stone lanterns, on Komainu (stone-curved guardian dogs) and also on Torii = Photographed at the beginning of October 1945 by Shigeo Hayashi

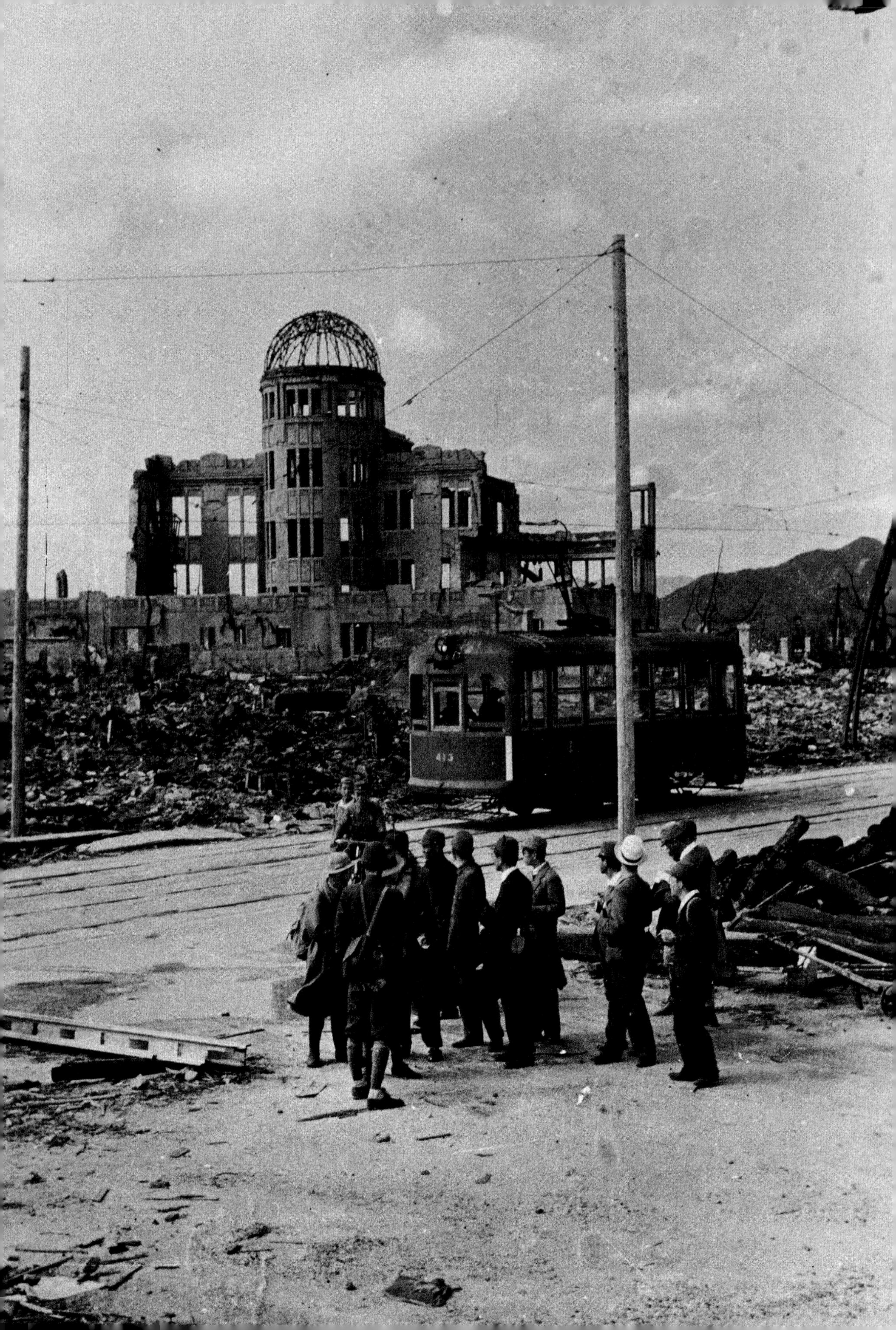
413

全壊した基町の軍施設跡。左に広島護国神社参道。
右に第五師団司令部 1 号庁舎、広島陸軍第一病院第一分院。
広島陸軍第一病院第一分院西側の破壊された側溝と
火災の被害をうけた樹木＝ 1945 年 10 月上旬、
広島護国神社参道大鳥居東側から北に向って（撮影：林重男）

Northward view of a collapsed military facility in Motomachi, Hiroshima City from the east side of the big Torii (entrance gate to the shrine) of Hiroshima Gokoku Shrine. The approach road to the Shrine is on the left. The No. 1 building of the HQ of Army 5th Division and the No.1 branch of Hiroshima Daiichi Army Hospital are on the right. You can see the collapsed gutter cover in the west part of the Hospital and trees damaged by fire
= Photographed at the beginning of October 1945 by Shigeo Hayashi

広島県商工経済会。中央の柳は爆風で枝をもぎ取られた。
左から全焼全壊した日本赤十字社広島支部、広島県商工経済会、
本川の基町護岸にいち早く建った被爆者のバラック住宅 2 棟
＝ 1945 年 10 月上旬、広島護国神社参道大鳥居北方西側から
南西に向って（撮影：林重男）

View of Hiroshima Chamber of Commerce and Industry building from the northwest side of the big Torii (entrance gate to the shrine) of Hiroshima Gokoku Shrine to the southwest direction. The branches of a willow were blown away by the blast wave. From left to right, Japanese Red Cross Society Hiroshima Office, Hiroshima Chamber of Commerce and Industry and two barracks for atomic bomb survivors built in a protected shore of Honkawa River, Hiroshima City
= Photographed at the beginning of October 1945 by Shigeo Hayashi

左奥に本川国民学校、中央部に広島護国神社拝殿、
右奥に広島護国神社本殿。爆心地のほぼ真北 330m の所に
東に向って立っていた鳥居は西に向って倒壊、灯籠や狛犬、鳥居、
玉垣など石造物の多くも爆風のため倒壊したが右の社号標は
倒れなかった。又多くの石造物は熱線の跡を残し爆点、
爆心地決定の礎になった＝ 1945 年 10 月上旬、
広島護国神社拝殿前から西南西に向って（撮影：林重男）

View toward the west south-west direction of the Honkawa Primary School (left back) , Front shrine (center) and Main shrine (right back) of the Hiroshima Gokoku Shrine. Torii (entrance gste to the shrine), facing east at 330 meters north of the ground zero, collapsed toward the west. Stoneworks such as lanterns, komainu (guardian dogs), Toriil and tamagaki (fence) were destroyed by blast wave, while the Hengaku (signboard) was not blown away. The whereabouts of the ground zero were defined based on the lines made by heat wave on those stoneworks
= Photographed at the beginning of October 1945 by Shigeo Hayashi

左上隅は広島県商工経済会、上中央に戦後いち早く建てられた
被災者のバラック住宅、右上に本川国民学校。爆心地の真北にあたる
拝殿前の御影石の灯籠と鳥居は、それぞれ北と西に向って倒れた。
強い爆風と爆圧により一瞬真空状態が起こり、風はツムジ風のように
方向を定めず吹いた＝ 1945 年 10 月上旬、
広島護国神社拝殿前北東隅から西南に向って（撮影：林重男）

View from the northeast corner of the Front shrine of Hiroshima Gokoku Shrine toward the southwest direction, of the Hiroshima Prefecture Commerce, Industry and Business Association (upper left), barrack houses for the victims, consructed soon after the war (upper middle) and Honkawa Primary School (upper right). A lantern and Torii (entrance gate to the shrine), both made of Mikage stone, located in front of the Front shrine, just in the north of the ground zero, were collapsed to the north and west respectively. Vacuum state was generated instantly by the strong blast wave and pressure, and wind blew in every direction just like a whirlwind
= Photographed at the beginning of October 1945 by Shigeo Hayashi

宿舎の海田日本製鋼所からトラックで広島入市初日の佐々木忠義氏、相原秀雄氏ら約 10 名の広島・長崎学術調査団。
広島県産業奨励館前を紙屋町方面に右側運行中の（413 型）広島電鉄市内電車。
この付近（左官町・八丁堀間）の電車軌道の復旧は 1945（昭和 20）年 9 月 7 日＝広島護国神社大鳥居前から南西に向って（撮影：林重男）

Hiroshima and Nagasaki Academic Survey Team consisted of 10 members including Tadayoshi Sasaki and Hideo Aihara, on the way to enter Hiroshima City by truck from the factory of the Kaida Steel Works, Ltd. , where they stayed. In front of the Hiroshima Prefectural Industrial Promotion Hall (the Atomic Bomb Dome), a tram car of Hiroshima Electric Railway Co.,Ltd. (Type 413) running toward right to Kamiyac-ho. Restoration of the tramway from Sakan-cho to Hacho-bori was completed on September 7th 1945 = Photographed in front of the Hiroshima Gokoku Shrine to the southwest direction by Shigeo Hayashi

左上隅広島県商工経済会、上中央に戦後いち早く建てられた
被災者のバラック住宅、右上に本川国民学校。爆心地の真北にあたる
拝殿前の御影石の灯籠と鳥居は、それぞれ北と西に向って倒れた。
強い爆風と爆圧により一瞬真空状態が起こり、風はツムジ風のように
方向を定めず吹いた＝1945年10月上旬、
広島護国神社拝殿前北東隅から西南に向って（撮影：林重男）

View from the northeast corner of the Front shrine of Hiroshima Gokoku Shrine toward the southwest direction, of the Hiroshima Prefecture Commerce, Industry and Business Association (upper left), barrack houses for the victims, consructed soon after the war (upper middle) and Honkawa Primary School (upper right). A lantern and Torii (entrance gate to the shrine), both made of Mikage stone, located in front of the Front shrine, just in the north of the ground zero, were collapsed to the north and west respectively. Vacuum state was generated instantly by the strong blast wave and pressure, and wind blew in every direction just like a whirlwind
= Photographed at the beginning of October 1945 by Shigeo Hayashi

拝殿前参道南側にあった手水舎の御影石製の手水鉢は、
一度空中に浮き上がり90度回転して落下したようである。
左上には被爆後いち早く建てた被災者のバラック住宅、
本川国民学校＝1945年10月上旬、
広島護国神社拝殿前から西南西に向って（撮影：林重男）

View from the Front shrine of Hiroshima Gokoku Shrine to the west-southwest direction. The washbasin made of Mikage stone in the chozuya (water ablution pavilion) located in the south side of the approach road in front of the Front shrine, floated in the air by the blast wave, was rotated by 90 degree and dropped to the ground. Barrack houses for the victims, consructed soon after the war, and Honkawa Primary School are in upper left
= Photographed at the beginning of October 1945 by Shigeo Hayashi

拝殿前南側の倒壊した手水舎と灯籠。手水舎の御影石製の手水鉢は、一度空中に浮き上がり90度回転して落下したようである。
拝殿前倒壊した鳥居の左右にあった灯籠は両方とも爆風により北側に向って倒れた。参道沿いの木々も強い爆風で引きちぎられ枝を飛ばされた。
上方の焼け跡は広島陸軍第一病院第一分院＝1945年10月上旬、広島護国神社拝殿前南側広場から東北東に向って（撮影：林重男）

View from the South Open Space of the Front shrine of Hiroshima Gokoku Shrine to the east-northeast direction. A collapsed Chozuya (water ablution pavilion) and lanterns at the south side of the Front shrine. The washbasin made of Mikage stone in the chozuya (water ablution pavilion) located in the south side of the approach road in front of the Front shrine, floated in the air by the blast wave, was rotated by 90 degree and dropped to the ground.
Lanterns at both sides of the destroyed Torii (entrance gate to the shrine) in front of the Front shrine were collapsed to the north by the blast wave. Branches of the trees along the approach road were blown away. The ruins by fire (in upper side) are that of the No.1 branch of Hiroshima Daiichi Army Hospital
= Photographed at the beginning of October 1945 by Shigeo Hayashi

手前に爆風により西に向って倒壊した鳥居。左上方には爆心の反対側に倒壊した灯籠、中央には倒れなかった社号標、
強い爆風と爆圧により一瞬真空状態が起こり風はツムジ風のように方向を定めず吹いた。上方の広島城跡、軍関係施設は跡形もなく、
わずかに枯木が残るのみである＝1945年10月上旬、広島護国神社拝殿前から東北東に向って（撮影：林重男）

View from the Front shrine of Hiroshima Gokoku Shrine to the east-northeast direction. Torii (entrance gate to the shrine) collapsed to the west by blast wave. A lantern collapsed to the opposite side of the ground zero. Hengaku (signboard) was not blown away. Vacuum state was generated instantly by strong blast wave and wind blew in every direction just like a whirlwind. There remains only few dead trees at the site of Hiroshima Castle and army-related facilities
= Photographed at the beginning of October 1945 by Shigeo Hayashi

広島護国神社大鳥居前の灯篭の影を調べる調査団。
向って左（西）側の灯籠の北東隅を北西側から見る。折り尺しで
熱線の焼きついた影の位置を示す広島・長崎学術調査団の
物理学班員＝1945年10月上旬、広島護国神社大鳥居前（南）参道
（撮影：林重男）

Hiroshima and Nagasaki Academic Survey Team investigating the shadow
on a lantern located in front of the big Torii (entrance gate to the shrine)
of Hiroshima Gokoku Shrine. Viewed from the northwest to the northeast
corner of the lantern (right) (west) . A physical scientist of the Team shows
the shadow of heat ray using a folding ruler = Photographed east-northeast
direction at the (south) approach in front of the big Torii of Hiroshima
Gokoku Shrine, in the beginning of October 1945 by Shigeo Hayashi

広島護国神社大鳥居前の灯篭。
灯籠の台座に焼きついた熱線による影
＝1945年10月上旬、広島護国神社大鳥居前
（撮影：林重男）

A lantern located in front of the big Torii (entrance gate to the shrine) of
Hiroshima Gokoku Shrine. A shadow burnt into the pedestal of the lantern
by the heat ray = Photographed in the beginning of October 1945
by Shigeo Hayashi

爆心直下の西向寺墓地の墓石は移動や倒壊し爆風のはげしさを見せつけた
＝1945年10月上旬、西向寺墓地（撮影：林重男）

Gravestones in the cemetery of Saiko Temple, just near the ground zero,
were moved or collapsed, indicating the powerful force of the blast wave
= Photographed in the beginning of October 1945 by Shigeo Hayashi

爆心直下の西向寺墓地の墓石は移動や倒壊し爆風のはげしさを
見せつけた＝ 1945 年 10 月上旬、西向寺墓地（撮影：林重男）

Gravestones in the cemetery of Saiko Temple, just near the ground zero, were moved or collapsed, indicating the powerful force of the blast wave = Photographed at the beginning of October 1945 by Shigeo Hayashi

北から南に向って。島病院前の南北の通りから完全壊滅した
玄関付近の様子。世界初の原子爆弾は島病院上空約 580m の所で
爆発した＝ 1945 年 10 月上旬、爆心地・島病院正面（撮影：林重男）

Northward view from the south of the road in front of Shima Hospital. The entrance of the Hospital collapsed completely. The explosion of world's first atomic bomb attack occured at an altitude of approximately 580 meters over this Hospital = Photographed at the beginning of October 1945 by Shigeo Hayashi

広島県産業奨励館を中心に左に清病院の壁、西蓮寺墓地、
日本赤十字社広島支部。
手前石柱にくくりつけた消息を尋ねる伝言板＝ 1945 年 10 月上旬、
東南東から北北西に向って（撮影：林重男）

View from the east-southeast to the north-northwest of Hiroshima Prefectural Industrial Promotion Hall(the Atomic Bomb Dome) (center). From left to right, the wall of Kiyoshi Hospital, the cemetery of the Sairen Temple, and Japanese Red Cross Society Hiroshima Branch, a message board seeking for missing persons, hanged on a stone pillar = Photographed at the beginning of October 1945, viewed by Shigeo Hayashi

島病院北から南に向って。爆心直下のレンガ造り 2 階建ての病院は
基礎と玄関の丸柱、円窓を残して全壊。約 75 名の患者、
看護婦など病院関係者は建物とともに全滅した。
中央に島病院玄関の残骸、その奥が似島、右端に広島郵便電信局
＝ 1945 年 10 月上旬、爆心地・島病院北面（撮影：林重男）

View from the north side of Shima Hospital to the south. The two-story hospital made of bricks, located directly under the ground zero, was completely collapsed except its foundation, columns and round windows. The collapse of the building killed about 75 people including patients and the hospital workers such as nurses. Behind the ruins of the entrance, Ninoshima Island can be seen. Hiroshima Post and Telegraph Office is at the right corner = Photographed at the beginning of October 1945 by Shigeo Hayashi

左から千代田生命広島支店、芸備銀行本店、住田銀行広島支店、安田生命広島支店、農林中央金庫広島支所、三和銀行広島支店。
手前爆心地島病院部分
＝1945年10月上旬、爆心地から
広島市大手町通り紙屋町付近の銀行街西から
東に向かって（撮影：林重男）

Eastward view from the ground zero toward the "bank street" on Otemachi street near Kamiya-cho, Hiroshima City. From left to right: Chiyoda Mutual Life Insurance Hiroshima branch, Geibi Bank HQ, Sumida Bank Hiroshima branch, Yasuda Life Insurance Hiroshima branch, Norin-chukin Bank Hiroshima branch office, Sanwa Bank Hiroshima branch. The ground zero is in the front (at the Shima Hospital) ＝ Photographed at the beginning of October 1945 by Shigeo Hayashi

中央奥の玉垣に囲まれた所が
広島護国神社拝殿北の中津宮。
左側が爆心側で、強い爆風により石造りの鳥居や灯籠は北に向かって倒壊した。
左上方の灯籠は爆風で浮き上がった瞬間
芯の鉄棒が抜け、斜に持ち上がった
＝1945年10月上旬、西に向かって（撮影：林重男）

Westward view of the Nakatsumiya of Hiroshima Gokoku Shrine (in the center back). Located on the north of the Front shrine of Hiroshima Gokoku Shrine, surrounded by Tamagaki (shrine fence). As the left side was closer to the ground zero, the stone-made Torii (entrance gate to the shrine) and garden lanterns collapsed towards the north. An iron bar in the core of the left upper side of the lantern fell out when it was blown off by the blast wave. The lantern was lifted up obliquely ＝ Photographed at the beginning of October 1945 by Shigeo Hayashi

左側が爆心側で強い爆風により
左側の灯籠は移動し、
右の灯籠は爆風で浮き上がった瞬間
芯の鉄棒が抜け斜に持ち上がった
＝1945年10月上旬、
広島護国神社拝殿に向かう中央参道北側の灯籠
（撮影：林重男）

View of garden lanterns located on the north side of the main approach road to the Front shrine of the Hiroshima Gokoku Shrine. As the left side was closer to the ground zero, the iron bar in the core of the lantern fell out when the lantern was lifted up by the blast wave ＝ Photographed at the beginning of October 1945 by Shigeo Hayashi

右の傘石と左右の灯籠の台座は、
爆心側に強い熱線の影響を受けひび割れ
剥離した。
左（南）側の灯籠は爆風による火袋の
北への移動も見られる。
後右端一段高い所が本殿跡、手前が拝殿跡
＝ 1945 年 10 月上旬、広島護国神社拝殿に向う
中央参道南側の灯籠（撮影：林重男）

View of the garden lanterns located on the south side of the main approach road to the Front shrine of the Hiroshima Gokoku Shrine. The top stone of the lantern on the right, and the foundation stones of both lanterns were cracked and fell off on their ground zero side by strong heat rays. The fire box of the lantern on the left (the south side) was moved toward the north due to the blast wave. The high-elevated place behind is where the Main shrine located and in front of this, the Front shrine located ＝ Photographed at the beginning of October 1945 by Shigeo Hayashi

爆心側からの爆風により移動。下から二段目と三段目の台石の間に
爆風によって引き千切られた小枝がはさまった。後の段の上、
左端白い部分が本殿跡の一部＝ 1945 年 10 月上旬、
広島護国神社拝殿に向う中央参道の北側の灯籠（撮影：林重男）

View of a garden lantern located on the north side of the main approach road to the Front shrine of the Hiroshima Gokoku Shrine. The lantern was moved by the blast wave from the ground zero. A small branch torn by the wave stuck between the 2nd and the 3rd foundation stones from the bottom. The white part on the left end of the step behind was the site where the Main shrine located ＝ Photographed at the beginning of October 1945 by Shigeo Hayashi

灯籠の左、爆心側は強い熱線の影響を受け傘石・台座共に
ヒビ割れし剥離した。灯籠の火袋の後の一段高い所が本殿跡、
手前が拝殿跡＝ 1945 年 10 月上旬、
広島護国神社拝殿に向う中央参道南側の灯籠（撮影：林重男）

View of a garden lantern located on the south side of the main approach road to the Front shrine of the Hiroshima Gokoku Shrine. As the left side (the ground zero side) of the lantern received strong heat rays, both stones of top and foundation were cracked and fell off. The high-elevated place behind is where the Main shrine located and in front of this, the Front shrine located ＝ Photographed at the beginning of October 1945 by Shigeo Hayashi

倒壊した鳥居の基部を調査中の調査員 = 1945年10月上旬、広島護国神社拝殿前（撮影：林重男）

A resercher is investigating the foundation of the Torii (entrance gate to the shrine) in front of the Front shrine of the collapsed Hiroshima Gokoku Shrine
= Photographed at the beginning of October 1945 by Shigeo Hayashi

爆風によって相生橋北側の車道と歩道の間に30cmから140cmのずれを生じた。相生橋から西に向って
= 1945年10月上旬、広島市（撮影：林重男）

30-140 cm of fissures occurred by the blast wave between the carriage way and the sidewalk in the north of Aioi bridge.
= Photographed westward from Aioi bridge at the beginning of October 1945 by Shigeo Hayashi

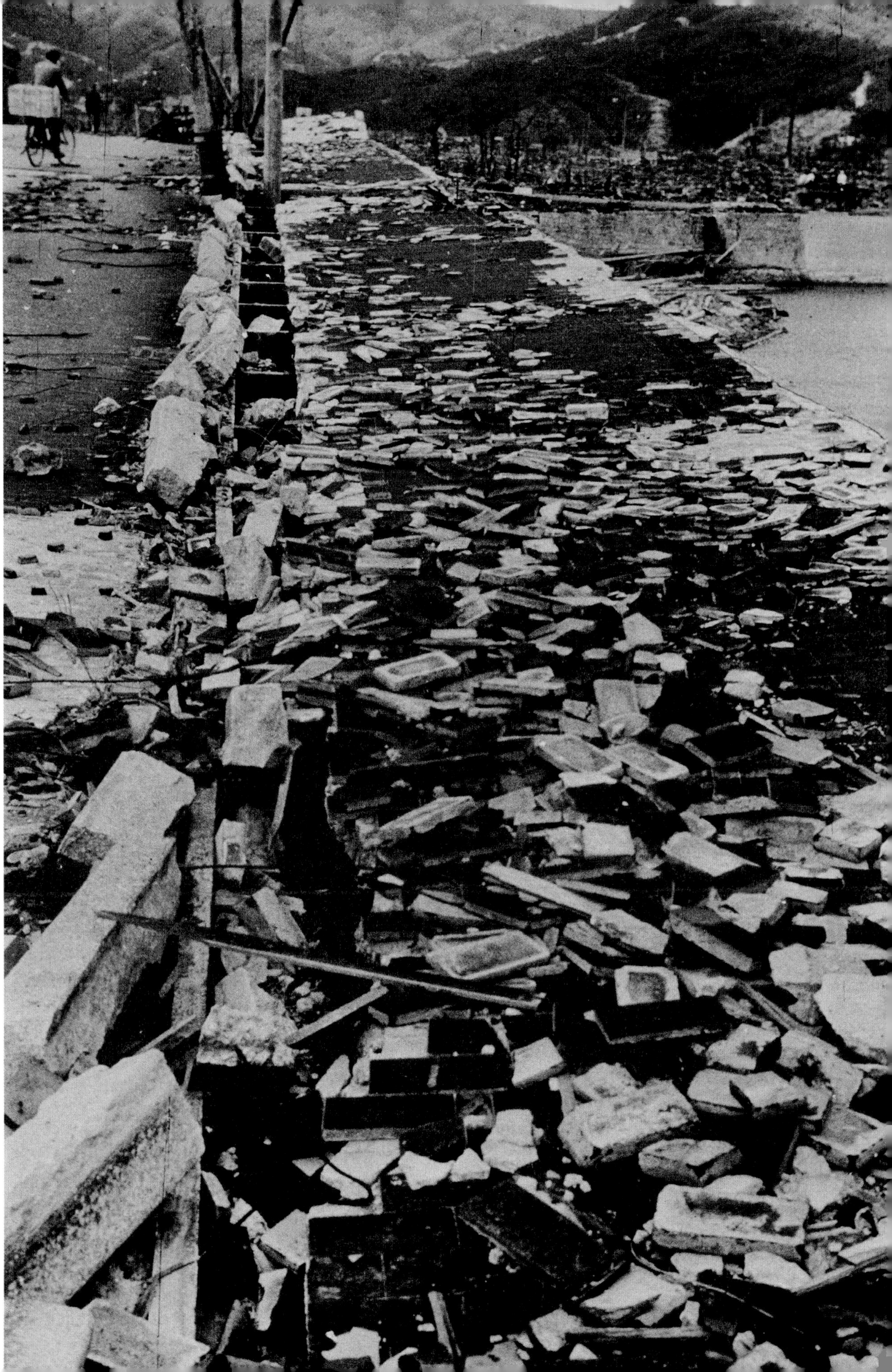

手前は相生橋。左から広島県産業奨励館、日本銀行広島支店、広島瓦斯本社、元安橋、中国配電本社、
燃料会館、広島市役所。相生橋の欄干は爆風の影響でほとんどが破壊された。
被災者や近郊からの救援の人々の姿にも落着きが感じられる＝1945年10月上旬、相生橋中央部付近から南南東に向って（撮影：林重男）

View from the center of Aioi bridge toward the south-southeast. Aioi bridge is in front. From left to right, the Hiroshima Prefectural Industrial Promotion Hall (the Atomic Bomb Dome), the Bank of Japan Hiroshima branch, Hiroshima Gas HQ, Motoyasu bridge, Chugoku Haiden HQ, Nenryo Kaikan (Fuel Center), Hiroshima City Municipal Office. The most part of the parapets of Aioi bridge collapsed by the blast wave.
Calmness on the faces of victims and rescues who came from the suburbs = Photographed at the beginning of October 1945 by Shigeo Hayashi

奥左から日赤赤十字社広島支部、広島県産業奨励館（原爆ドーム）、日本銀行広島支店、元安橋。
爆風の影響で歩道と車道の間には最大1.4mもの隙間ができた＝1945年10月上旬、相生橋西詰北側親柱付近から東南東に向って（撮影：林重男）

View from the newel post in the north of the west end of Aioi Bridge toward east south-east direction. From left to right in the back:
Japanese Red Cross Hiroshima office, the Hiroshima Prefectural Industrial Promotion Hall (the Atomic Bomb Dome),
the Bank of Japan Hiroshima branch, Motoyasu bridge. At most1.4 meters of fissures occurred between the carriage way and the sidewalk by the blast wave
= Photographed at the beginning of October 1945 by Shigeo Hayashi

正面左に、広島県商工経済会、右に日本赤十字社広島支部。
爆風の影響で歩道と車道の間には最大1.4mもの隙間ができ
電柱も左右にたおれ込んだ＝1945年10月上旬、
相生橋西詰北側親柱付近から東に向って（撮影：林重男）

Eastward View from the newel post in the north of the west end of Aioi Bridge. The front left is the Hiroshima Prefecture Commerce, Industry, and Business Association Building. The front right is the Japanese Red Cross Society Hiroshima Office. At most 1.4 meters of fissures occurred between the carriage way and the sidewalk by the blast wave. Utility poles also collapsed to right and left
= Photographed at the beginning of October 1945 by Shigeo Hayashi

左から広島県商工経済会、手前土手に広島電鉄櫓下変電所、相生橋、
原爆ドーム中央部のドーム。本川に架る相生橋は原爆投下目標となった
T字型の特徴的な橋である。橋は欄干も路床も爆風により破壊され、
上流側のトラスの外板もはがれた。手前木材溜りは9月17日の
枕崎台風で上流から流れ着いたものである＝1945年10月上旬、
相生橋西詰上流河岸から東に向って（撮影：林重男）

Eastward view from the west end of Aioi bridge. Hiroshima Prefecture Commerce, Industry, and Business Association Building in the left back. Yagurashita Electrical Substation of Hiroshima Electric Railway, Aioi bridge, the Hiroshima Prefectural Industrial Promotion Hall (the Atomic Bomb Dome) are in front. Aioi bridge, a characteristic bridge with t-shape on the Hongawa river was a target to drop the atomic bomb. Its parapets and roadbed collapsed by the blast wave and outer panels of the truss in the upstream side came off. You can see the pile of woods in front, drifted from upstream by Makurazaki Typhoon on September 17th
= Photographed at the beginning of October 1945 by Shigeo Hayashi

爆風の影響を受けた広島電鉄市内電車軌道はズレを生じ、
応急に復旧工事が行われた。右上方に広島県商工経済会建物の一部。
上部中央の人は応急復旧工事の人。
手前レール脇に白く残る被災者の遺骨＝1945年10月上旬、
相生橋西詰南側親柱付近から東北東に向って（撮影：林重男）

View from the newel pole in the south of the west end of Aioi bridge toward the east-northeast. Urgent repair done for gaps by the blast wave on the tramway of Hiroshima Electric Railway. The upper right is a part of the building of Hiroshima Prefecture Commerce, Industry, and Business Association. People in upper center are workers for the urgent repair works. Whitish human bones can be seen near the rail in front
= Photographed at the beginning of October 1945 by Shigeo Hayashi

左から日本赤十字社広島支部、相生橋西詰め南側親柱、
広島県産業奨励館。市内電車用コンクリート製角電柱に
「中島熊吉氏方・横山直蔵外一同」と書かれた被災者の伝言メモ。
相生橋西詰め付近は爆風の影響で軌道敷にズレを生じ、
応急復旧工事が行われた。親柱のたもとには、軌道敷石や、
斜路のレールなどが仮置きされている。手前レール脇に白く残る
被災者の遺骨＝1945年10月上旬、相生橋西詰南側親柱付近から
東に向って（撮影：林重男）

Eastward view from the newel pole in the south of the west end of Aioi bridge. From left to right : the Japanese Red Cross Society Hiroshima Office, the newel pole, Hiroshima Prefectural Industrial Promotion Hall (the Atomic Bomb Dome). There is a message from victims on a concrete utility pole for the tram: "Naozo Yokoyama and others are staying at Kumakichi Nakajima's house". Urgent repair done for gaps on the tramway of Hiroshima Electric Railway. Near the newel pole, paving stones and rails are temporarily stored. Whitish human bones can be seen near the rail in front
= Photographed at the beginning of October 1945 by Shigeo Hayashi

左から広島県商工経済会、相生橋、日本赤十字社広島支部、
相生橋奥に福屋百貨店。爆心付近に架かる相生橋は爆風の影響で
最大1.4mの隙間ができ、水面から反射した爆風は歩道の一部を
山形に持ち上げた＝1945年10月上旬、
相生橋北歩道西よりから東に向って（撮影：林重男）

Eastward view from the west side of the north sidewalk of the Aioi bridge. From left to right, the Hiroshima Prefectural Industrial Promotion Hall (the Atomic Bomb Dome), Aioi bridge, Japanese Red Cross Society Hiroshima Office. Fukuya Department Store is behind the Aioi bridge. Due to the blast wave, at most 1.4 m of fissures occurred on the Aioi bridge, located near the ground zero. The blast wave thrown back from the river surface lifted up part of the sidewalk and made it into mountain shape
= Photographed at the beginning of October 1945 by Shigeo Hayashi

手前の雨水枡は、水面に反射した爆風により歩道から飛び出した。北側車道と歩道の間は爆風の影響で最大1.4mもズレを生じた。
広島電鉄市内電車は、相生橋西詰め軌道復旧工事も終え、市内電車の運行がみうけられる＝1945年10月上旬、
相生橋中央部北側歩道付近から西に向って。（撮影：林重男）

Westward view from the north side of the sidewalk in the middle of Aioi bridge. A rainwater catch basin in the front stuck out from the sidewalk by the blast wave thrown back from the river surface. At most 1.4 meters of fissures occurred between the carriage way and the sidewalk by the blast wave.
You can see the tram of the Hiroshima Electric Railway in operation after rail repair works completed near the newel pole of the west end of Aioi bridge
= Photographed at the beginning of October 1945 by Shigeo Hayashi

南から北に向って。御影石の玉垣は爆風で吹き飛ばされたが、
強い熱線は地覆石に熱線の方向と高さを示す黒い三角形の影を残した
＝ 1945 年 10 月上旬、広島護国神社拝殿前玉垣（撮影：林重男）
View from south to north at Tamagaki (stone fence) in front of the Front shrine of the Hiroshima Gokoku Shrine. The granite fence was blown away by the blast wave and the strong heat ray left a black triangle shadow on the foundation stones. The shadow shows the direction of the heat ray
= Photographed at the beginning of October 1945 by Shigeo Hayashi

東から西に向って。御影石の玉垣は爆風で吹き飛ばされたが、
強い熱線は地覆石に熱線の方向と高さを示す黒い三角形の影を残した
＝ 1945 年 10 月上旬、広島護国神社拝殿前玉垣（撮影：林重男）
View from east to west at Tamagaki (stone fence) in front of the Front shrine of the Hiroshima Gokoku Shrine. The granite fence was blown away by the blast wave and the strong heat ray left a black triangle shadow on the foundation stones. The shadow shows the direction of the heat ray
= Photographed in the beginning of October 1945 by Shigeo Hayashi

広島護国神社拝殿北側本社の玉垣の影。
左が中津宮、東西の玉垣、西から東に向って。
右側が爆心側で玉垣の影が石垣の上に残る＝ 1945 年 10 月上旬、
広島護国神社拝殿北側中津宮付近（撮影：林重男）
View from the Nakatsumiya in the north of the front shrine of Hiroshima Gokoku Shrine. The shadows of Tamagaki (stone fence) made by the strong heat ray remains on the stone walls. The ground zero is in the right
= Photographed at the beginning of October 1945 by Shigeo Hayashi

西に向って。中央奥の玉垣に囲まれた所が広島護国神社拝殿北の
中津宮。写真左（南）側が爆心方向で、強い爆風により
石造りの鳥居や灯籠は北に向かって倒壊した＝ 1945 年 10 月上旬、
広島護国神社拝殿北側の本社（撮影：林重男）
Westward view from the Main shrine of the Hiroshima Gokoku Shrine. The place surrounded by Tamagaki (stone fence) in the center back is Nakatsumiya located in the north of the Front shrine. The ground zero is to the left (south) and The stone-made Torii (entrance gate to the shrine) and garden lanterns collapsed toward the north
= Photographed at the beginning of October 1945 by Shigeo Hayashi

地中の残留放射能を測定中の物理班の池田政男氏、理化学研究所の宮崎友喜雄氏＝1945年10月上旬、爆心地島病院中央部南側（撮影：林重男）

Masao Ikeda of physical scientist group and Yukio Miyazaki of Riken are measuring residual radioactivity in the soil
= Photographed at the beginning of October 1945 at the Shima Hospital located at the ground zero by Shigeo Hayashi

左には日本映画社の撮影スタッフ、中央に地中の残溜放射能を測定中の物理班の池田正雄氏と理化学研究所の宮崎友喜雄氏
＝ 1945 年 10 月上旬、爆心地島病院を南側から見る（撮影：林重男）
View from the south of the Shima Hospital located at the ground zero. On the left is film staff of Nippon Eiga-sha (Japan Film Corporation).
Seen in the center are Masao Ikeda of physical scientist group and Yukio Miyazaki of Riken, measuring residual radioactivity in the soil
= Photographed at the beginning of October 1945 by Shigeo Hayashi

爆心地・放射能測定。地中の残溜放射能を測定中の物理班の池田正雄氏と理化学研究所の宮崎友喜雄氏
＝ 1945 年 10 月上旬、爆心地島病院中央部南側（撮影：林重男）
Masao Ikeda of physical scientist group and Yukio Miyazaki of Riken, measuring residual radioactivity in the soil at the south side of the Shima Hospital located
at the ground zero = Photographed at the beginning of October 1945 by Shigeo Hayashi

爆心地のミミズを採取する生物学科会班大渕真龍調査員
＝ 1945 年 10 月上旬（撮影：林重男）

Shinryu Obuchi of the biological research team collecting earthworms at the ground zero = Photographed at the beginning of October 1945
by Shigeo Hayashi

左から藤井商事、日本簡易火災広島支店、元安橋南側親柱、
三井生命広島支店。右一帯は中島本町、右下に元安川。
爆心直下の元安橋は、ほぼ真上からの爆風を受け、
欄干は元安川に落下し、親柱の火袋はずれた＝ 1945 年 10 月上旬、
元安橋東側上流側から西（中島地区）に向って（撮影：林重男）

Westward view from the upstream side of the east end of Motoyasu Bridge. From left to right, Fujii Trading Company, Nippon Kan'i Kasai Insurance Hiroshima Branch, newel posts on the south side of Motoyasu Bridge, Mitsui Life Insurance Hiroshima Branch. Area on the right is Nakajima-Honmachi, Hiroshima City. Motoyasu River is seen at the bottom right. Motoyasu Bridge, located at the ground zero, received the blast wave from almost directly above. Parapets dropped into the river and the firebox parts of the newel posts were shoved by the blast wave
= Photographed at the beginning of October 1945 by Shigeo Hayashi

左から千代田生命広島支店、芸備銀行本店、農林中央金庫広島支所、
住友銀行広島支店、三井物産広島出張所、三和銀行広島支店、
帝国銀行広島支店、橋の向こうは細工町。上空に飛行機が見える。
爆心直下の元安橋は、ほぼ真上からの爆風を受け、
欄干は元安川に落下し、親柱の火袋はずれた＝ 1945 年 10 月上旬、
元安橋西側中央から東に向って（撮影：林重男）

Eastward view from the center of the Motoyasu Bridge. From left to right, Chiyoda Mutual Life Insurance Hiroshima Branch, Geibi Bank Central Branch, Norin-chukin Bank Hiroshima Branch, Sumitomo Bank Hiroshima Branch, Mitsui Bussan Hiroshima Branch, Sanwa Bank Hiroshima Branch, Teikoku Bank Hiroshima Branch. Beyond the bridge lies Saiku-machi area Hiroshima City. An airplane is seen in the sky. Motoyasu Bridge, located at the gound zero, received the blast wave from almost directly above. Parapets dropped into the river and the fire box parts of the newel posts were shoved by the blast wave = Photographed at the beginning of October 1945
by Shigeo Hayashi

正面左川向こうに爆心地島病院。中央に千代田生命広島支店。
右に芸備銀行本店、農林中央金庫広島支所、住友銀行広島支店。
後の山は右から二葉山、尾長山、呉娑々宇山など。爆心直下の元安橋は、
ほぼ真上からの爆風を受け、上流側の欄干は上流側の川へ、
下流側の欄干は下流側の川へ全て落下し、親柱の火袋も
それぞれ左右にずれたり落下した。左手前（中島町・右岸）の親柱は
基礎石以外は西に倒れた＝ 1945 年 10 月上旬、
元安橋西詰（中島本町）から東に向って（撮影：林重男）

Eastward view from the west end of the Motoyasu Bridge, Nakajima-Honmachi, Hiroshima City. Across the river, on the left is the Shima Hospital at the ground zero. Chiyoda Mutual Life Insurance Hiroshima Branch is seen in the center. On the right are Geibi Bank Central Branch, Norin-chukin Bank Hiroshima Branch, Sumitomo Bank Hiroshima Branch.
The background mountains are (from right to left) Mt. Futaba, Mt. Onaga and Mt. Gosaso. Motoyasu Bridge, located at the ground zero, received the blast wave from almost directly above. Parapets of the upstream side all dropped into the upper stream of the river, and those of the downstream side into the lower stream. The fire box parts of the newel posts of each side shoved right and left respectively, or dropped off. In the left foreground (Nakajima-cho, the right bank area), the newel poles fell over to the west leaving the foundation stones behind = Photographed at the beginning of October 1945
by Shigeo Hayashi

南（元安川東側道路）から北北西に向って。南から玄関部分を見る。
奥に相生橋、日本赤十字広島支部。爆風は南翼の2階以上の
レンガ壁を西側に吹き飛ばし、川岸道路を埋めつくした。
玄関部分の屋上西側の欄干は10月10日の阿久根台風で
落下した＝1945年10月上旬、広島県産業奨励館（原爆ドーム）
南から（撮影：林重男）

View of the entrance of the Hiroshima Prefectural Industrial Promotion Hall (the Atomic Bomb Dome), toward the north north-wast from the south (street along the east side of Motoyasu River). Behind is Aioi Bridge and Japan Red Cross Hospital Hiroshima Branch. Brick walls of the Dome's second floor and above of the south wing were blown off to the west. The collapsed bricks filled the riverside street. Parapets of the west side of the entrance rooftop dropped off due to Akune Typhoon on 10th October = Photographed at the beginning of October 1945 by Shigeo Hayashi

手前が元安川下流。正面に燃料会館、右に藤商事、
日本簡易火災広島店。元安橋から西に向かう通は
中島通り（旧山陽道・西国街道）。燃料会館左（南）側焼け跡は、
中島本町の原田外科付近。爆心直下の元安橋はほぼ真上からの
爆風を受け欄干は落下、親柱は火袋がずれた。燃料会館の
東面南寄りの欄干は破壊され落下した＝1945年10月上旬、
元安橋東側下流側から西（中島本町）に向って（撮影：林重男）

Westward view from the downstream side of the Motoyasu Bridge. Seen in the foreground is the lower stream of Motoyasu River. Nenryo Kaikan (Fuel Hall) at the front, Fujii Trading Company and Nippon Kan'i Kasai Hiroshima Branch on the right. Nakajima Street (the old Sanyo-Do and Saigoku-Kaido) runs from Motoyasu Bridge to the west. The burnt ruins on the left (south) side of the Nenryo Kaikan is where the building of Harada Surgery Clinic was standing (Nakajima-Honmachi, Hiroshima City). Motoyasu Bridge, located at the ground zero, received the blast wave from almost directly above. Parapets dropped into the river and the fire box parts of the newel posts were shoved by the blast. Parapets of the southerly area of the east side of the Nenryo Kaikan were collapsed and dropped off = Photographed at the beginning of October 1945 by Shigeo Hayashi

放射線の影響で斑が入ったフジバカマ＝1945年10月上旬、
広島城跡旧大本営跡付近（撮影：林重男）

Leaves of boneset mottled by radiation = Photographed at the beginning of October 1945 near the ruins of the former Imperial HQ at Hiroshima Castle by Shigeo Hayashi

橋の向こう左から千代田生命広島支店、右農林中央金庫広島支所、住友銀行広島支所、三井物産広島出張所、三和銀行広島支店、下に元安川。
爆心直下の元安橋は、ほぼ真上から爆風を受け、上流側の欄干は上流側の川へ、下流側の欄干は下流側の川へ落下し、
親柱の火袋もそれぞれ左右にずれたり落下した。
細工町元安橋左岸下流の更科ソバの店と野田印刷物の間の裏木戸の石段だけが無残な姿で残っている。
裏木戸の上り口あたりに焼けた庭木の大木＝1945年10月上旬、元安橋中央部下流側から東に向って（撮影：林重男）

Eastward view from the central part of the Motoyasu Bridge. Across the bridge, from left to right, Chiyoda Mutual Life Insurance Hiroshima Branch, Norin-chukin Bank Hiroshima Branch, Sumitomo Bank Hiroshima Branch, Mitsui Bussan Hiroshima Branch, Sanwa Bank Hiroshima Branch. Running below is Motoyasu River. Motoyasu Bridge, located at the ground zero, received the blast wave from almost directly above. Parapets of the upstream side all dropped into the upper stream of the river, and those of the downstream side into the lower stream. The fire box parts of the newel posts of each side shoved right and left respectively, or dropped off. The Sarashina Soba restaurant and Noda print shop that were located at the downstream, left side of the Motoyasu Bridge (Saiku-machi, Hiroshima City) were collapsed.
Only the stone steps of the wooden postern between the two buildings are left. A burnt big garden tree remains at the foot of the steps
= Photographed at the beginning of October 1945 by Shigeo Hayashi

放射線影響で斑が入ったフジバカマ＝1945年10月上旬、
広島城跡旧大本営跡付近（撮影：林重男）

Leaves of boneset mottled by radiation = Photographed at the beginning of October 1945 near the ruins of the former Imperial HQ in Hiroshima Castle by Shigeo Hayashi

爆風で折れた松。爆風で樹の根元から2mくらいの所で折れ、
北（爆心地の反対側）に向って倒れた皇太子殿下（昭和天皇）御手植松
＝1945年10月上旬、広島城跡本丸南御殿跡付近（撮影：林重男）

Pine tree planted by Prince Royal (later Showa Emperor) at the site of Hiroshima Castle's main compound South Palace.
It was broken by the blast wave at the height of 2 meters and fell down toward the north (opposite the ground zero)
= Photographed at the beginning of October 1945 by Shigeo Hayashi

放射線の影響で斑が入ったヤマゴボウ＝1945年10月上旬、
広島城跡旧大本営跡付近（撮影：林重男）

Leaves of pokeweeds mottled by radiation at the site of the former Imperial HQ in Hiroshima Castle = Photographed at the beginning of October 1945 by Shigeo Hayashi

放射線影響で斑が入ったフジバカマ＝1945年10月上旬、
広島城跡旧大本営跡付近（撮影：林重男）

Leaves of boneset mottled by radiation = Photographed at the beginning of October 1945 near the ruins of the former Imperial HQ in Hiroshima Castle by Shigeo Hayashi

爆心地から北北東1km。爆風にやられた広島城天守閣北側の木立ち＝1945年10月上旬（撮影：林重男）

Trees on the northern side of the tower of Hiroshima Castle, 1 km north-northeast of the hypocenter
= Early October 1945 (Photo: Shigeo Hayashi)

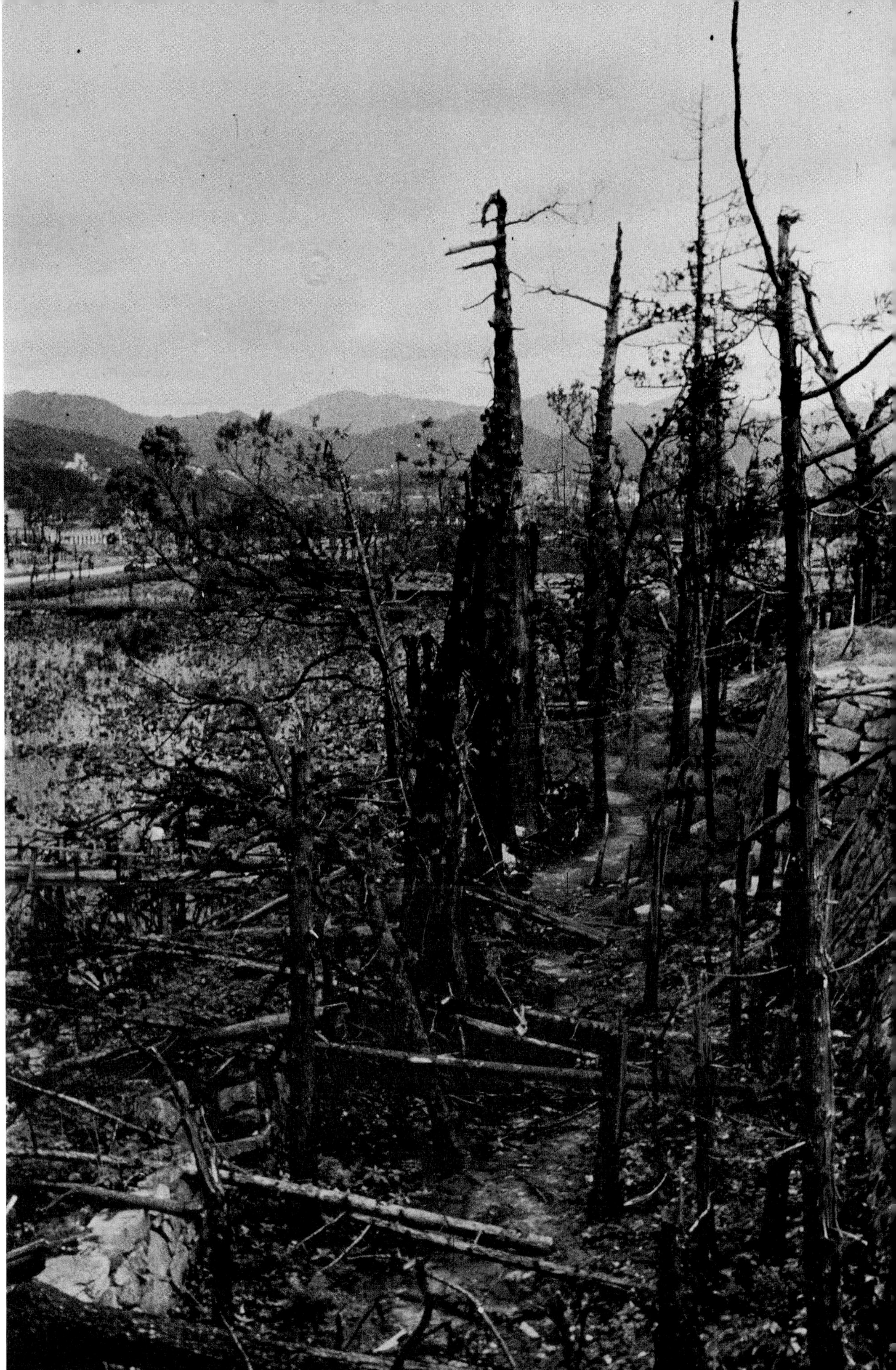

木造天守閣は爆風で全壊したが火災は発生しなかった
＝ 1945 年 10 月上旬、広島城跡本丸御殿付近東から北西に向って
（撮影：林重男）

Main tower of the Hiroshima Castle, made of wood, was totally collapsed by the blast wave, but no fire occurred = Photographed at the beginning of October 1945 toward northwest from the east side of Hiroshima Castle's main compound by Shigeo Hayashi

広島城御殿跡に建てられた旧大本営は、
木造建物のため爆風で全壊したが火災は起こらなかった。
現在は基段が残る＝ 1945 年 10 月上旬、
旧大本営跡を南東側から西に向って（撮影：林重男）

Westward view of the former Imperial HQ, built on the site of the ruins of a palace of Hiroshima Castle. The wooden building was totally collapsed by the blast wave, but no fire occurred. The foundation steps now remain
= Photographed at the beginning of October 1945 by Shigeo Hayashi

木造天守閣は全壊したが火災は発生しなかった
＝ 1945 年 10 月上旬、広島城跡天守台、
本丸御殿付近東から北西に向って（撮影：林重男）

Main tower of the Hiroshima Castle, made of wood, was totally collapsed by the blast wave, but no fire occurred = Photographed at the beginning of October 1945 toward northwest from the east side of Hiroshima Castle's main compound by Shigeo Hayashi

広島城内堀北面、広島陸軍幼年学校、奥に牛田山
＝ 1945 年 10 月上旬、広島城跡本丸跡から北に向って（撮影：林重男）

North side of the inner moat of Hiroshima Castle and the Hiroshima Army Cadet School. Mt. Ushida is seen in the back = Photographed at the beginning of October 1945, looking north from the ruins of Hiroshima Castle's main compound, by Shigeo Hayashi

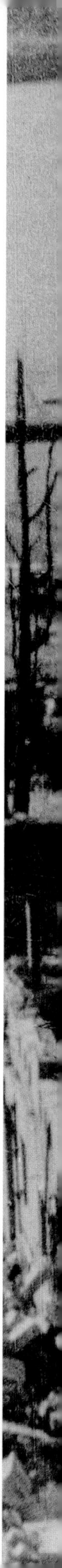

広島県産業奨励館（原爆ドーム）から元安川に架かる相生橋を望む＝ 1945 年 10 月上旬（撮影：林重男）

Aioi Bridge over Motoyasu River, viewed from Hiroshima Prefectural Industrial Promotion Hall (the Atomic Bomb Dome)
= Photographed at the beginning of October 1945 by Shigeo Hayashi

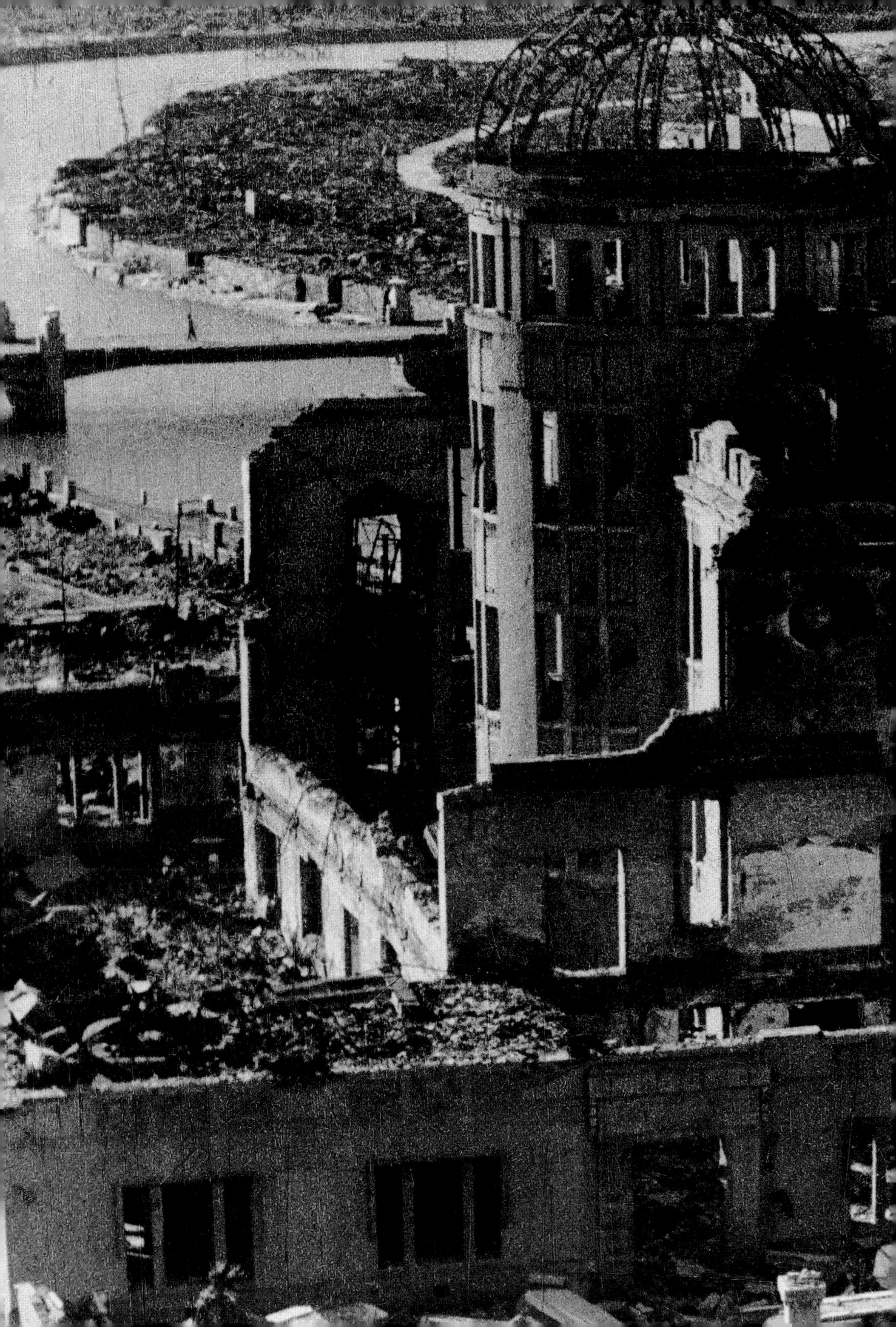

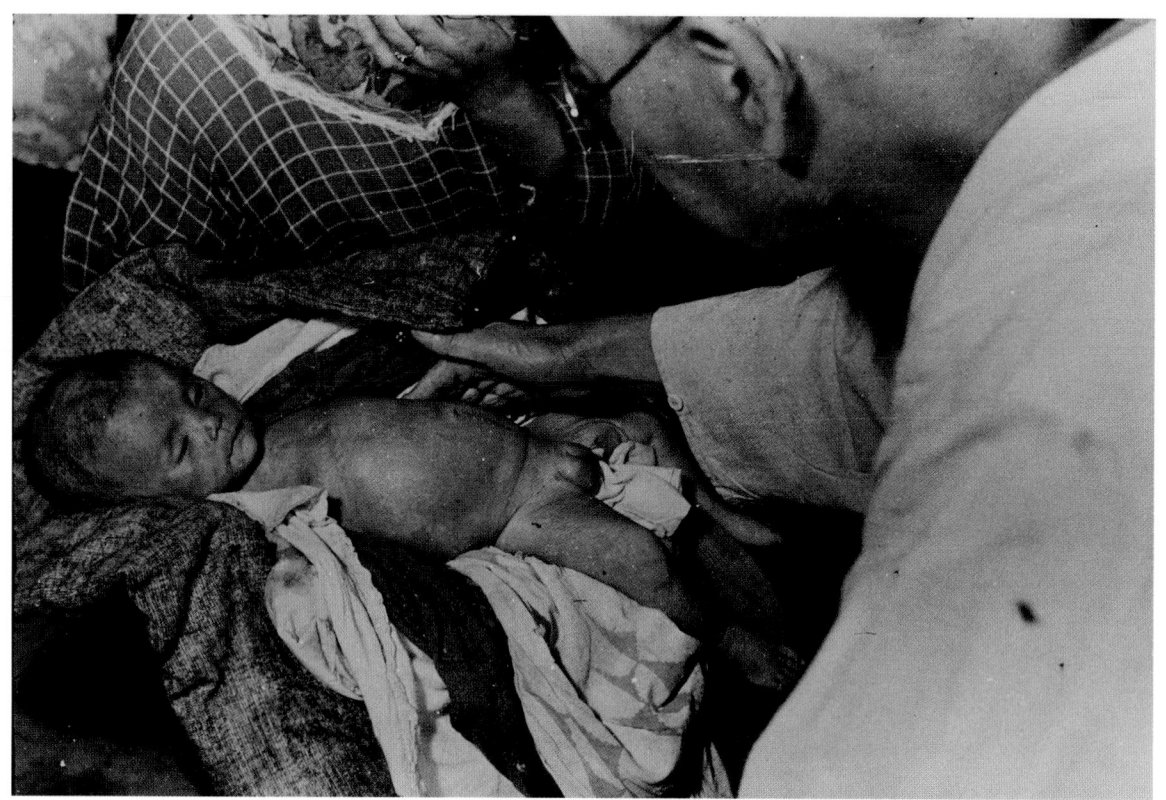

教室を改造した治療室に母親が駆け込んできた。医師が診察した時、この子はこと切れていた
= 1945 年 10 月 11 日、広島大芝国民学校臨時救護所（撮影：菊池俊吉）

Temporary first-aid station set up at the Hiroshima Oshiba Primary School. The mother rushed into the classroom, which was used as treatment room. The doctor checked on and found her child already dead. = Photographed on October 11th 1945 by Shunkichi Kikuchi

工作室をつかっての外来診療 = 1945 年 10 月 11 日、広島大芝国民学校臨時救護所（撮影：菊池俊吉）

Temporary first-aid station set up at the Hiroshima Oshiba Primary School. Using the craft room to treat outpatients.
= Photographed on October 11th 1945 by Shunkichi Kikuchi

外来患者の治療風景＝1945年10月11日、広島大芝国民学校臨時救護所（撮影：菊池俊吉）
Temporary first-aid station set up at the Hiroshima Oshiba Primary School. A scene of outpatients being treated.
= Photographed on October 11th 1945 by Shunkichi Kikuchi

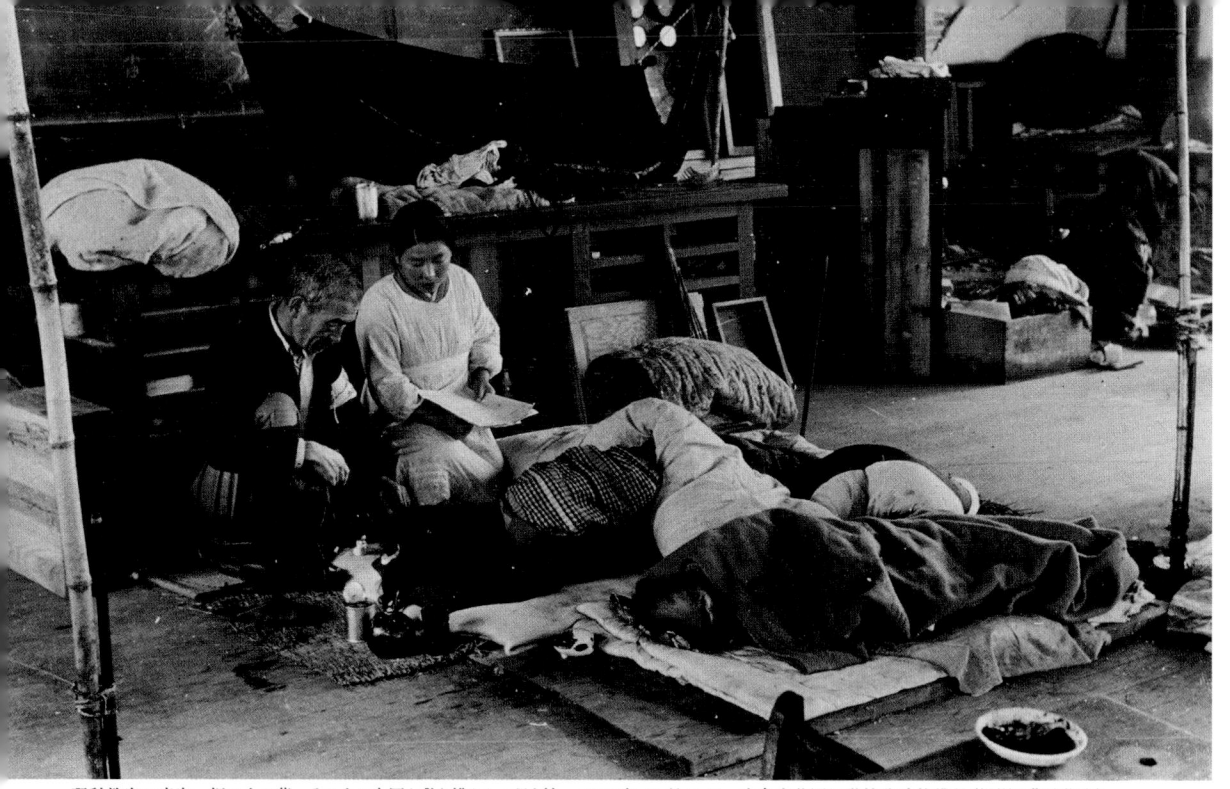

理科教室が病室。板の上に蓙、その上に布団を敷き横たわる母と娘＝ 1945 年 10 月 11 日、広島大芝国民学校臨時救護所（撮影：菊池俊吉）
Temporary first-aid station set up at the Hiroshima Oshiba Primary School. Science class room used as patient's room. On the wood floor, Mother and daughter lying down on futon beds on top of straw mat. = Photographed on October 11th 1945 by Shunkichi Kikuchi

原爆症の婦人（31 歳）。親子で被爆、外傷は全く無し。元気で娘の看病をしていたが、被爆後 1 ヶ月頃から体の不調を訴え
9 月中頃広島大芝臨時救護所に入院。10 月に入り皮下、歯茎出血、咳がひどく呼吸困難を訴え重体。撮影した日から 3 日後に死亡
＝ 1945 年 10 月 11 日、広島大芝国民学校臨時救護所（撮影：菊池俊吉）
Temporary first-aid station set up at the Hiroshima Oshiba Primary School. Woman aged 31 with radiation diseases. She and her daughter were exposed to radioactivity, but had no physical injury. She was fine just after the exposure and took care of her daughter. After 1 month, she complained physical disorder and was hospitalized here in September. She slipped into critical condition in October with subcutaneous and gums bleedings and dyspnea caused by bad cough. She passed away 3 days after this photo taken = Photographed on October 11th 1945 by Shunkichi Kikuchi

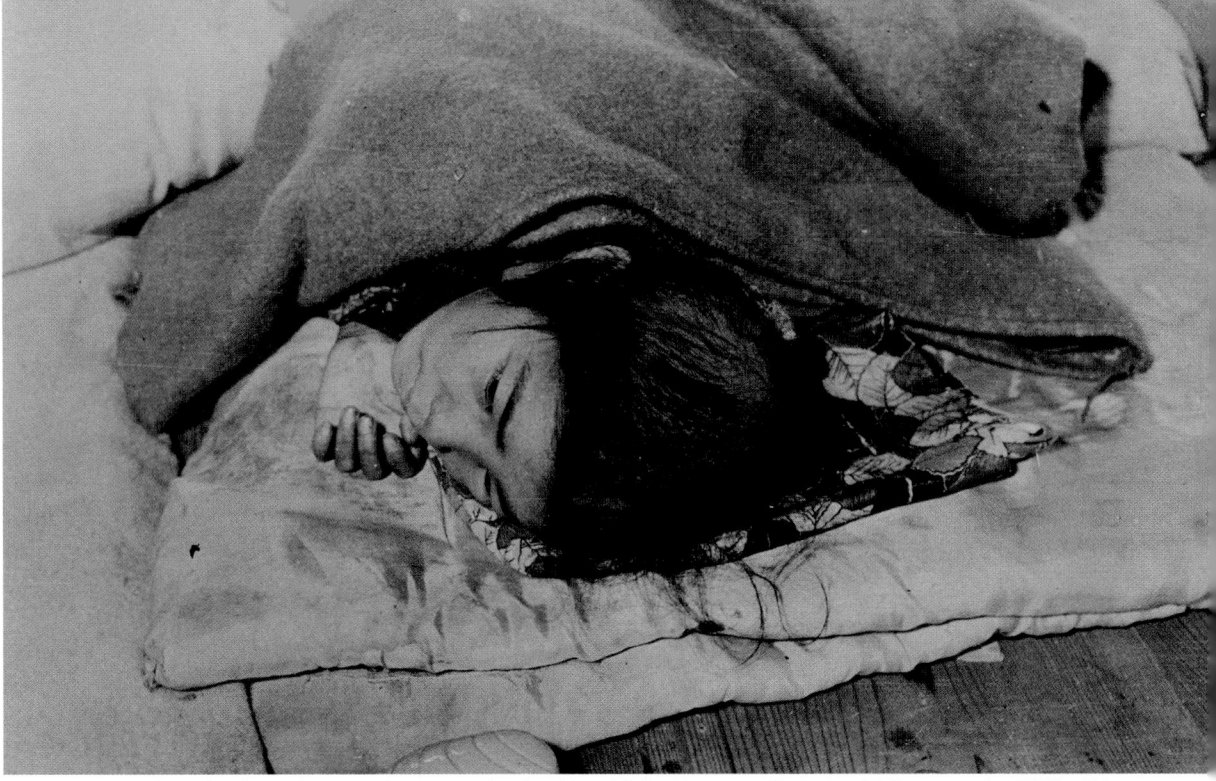

娘のヨウちゃんは 12 歳。広島市舟入町（爆心地より南西 2km 付近）の家で被爆。冷蔵庫が倒れてその下敷きとなり一時失神。そのため右の股関節を脱臼、右ひざと左足内側に外傷を受け、それが化膿してひどい状態だった。また後頭部にも、そいだような傷を受けていた。被爆後約 2ヶ月たったこのとき、原爆症状を示して脱毛、下痢、発熱が続いていた＝ 1945 年 10 月 11 日、広島大芝国民学校臨時救護所（撮影：菊池俊吉）

Temporary first-aid station set up at the Hiroshima Oshiba Primary School. This 12 years old girl, Yo, was exposed to radioactivity at her home located in Funairi-machi, Hiroshima City (approximately 2km southwest of the ground zero). She lost her consciousness for a while because of being pressed under a fridge. She had dislocation of her right hip joint and injuries on her right knee and inner side of her left leg. These injuries eventually festered. She also had injury like a cut by knife on back of her head. 2 months after the exposure, she had an onset of symptoms associated with the exposure including alopecia, diarrhea and fever = Photographed on October 11th 1945 by Shunkichi Kikuchi

12 歳の女の子。広島市舟入町で冷蔵庫の下敷きに。けがの他に脱毛、下痢の症状あり。母親と一緒に入院
＝ 1945 年 10 月 11 日、広島大芝国民学校臨時救護所（撮影：菊池俊吉）

Temporary first-aid station set up at the Hiroshima Oshiba Primary School. A 12-years old girl. She was pressed under a fridge in Funairi-machi, Hiroshima City. In addition to injuries, she also had symptoms such as alopecia and diarrhea. She was hospitalized with her mother
= Photographed on October 11th 1945 by Shunkichi Kikuchi

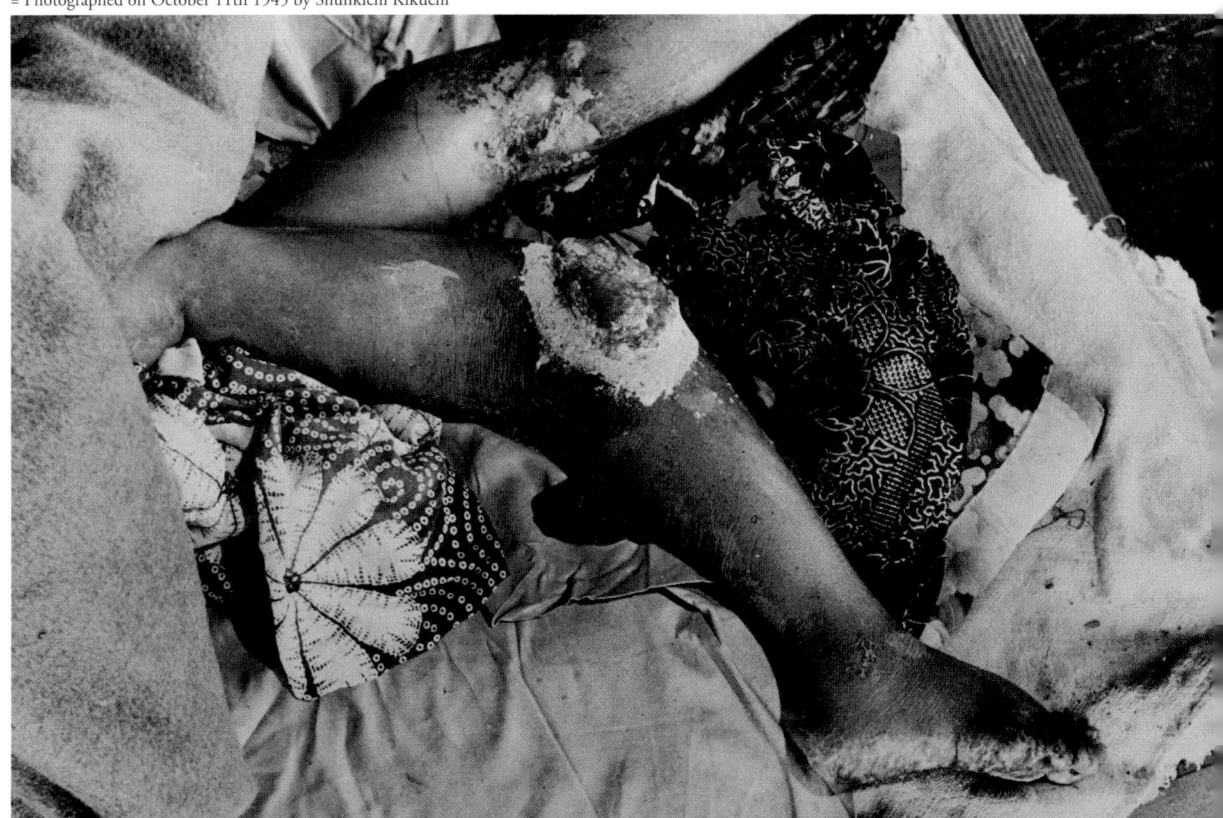

木造で大破したが、被害の少なかった部分で治療が行われた。10月、戦災保護法の期限切れで、各所の救急救護所が閉鎖された。
本校を含む5校は、以後日本医療団病院が解放され、被爆者の長期間治療に従事した＝1945年10月11日、
広島大芝国民学校臨時救護所（撮影：菊池俊吉）

Temporary first-aid station set up at the Hiroshima Oshiba Primary School. While the wooden building was heavily damaged,
medical treatments were provided in the less damaged areas. All of the emergency first-aid station throughout Japan were closed due to the expiration of the
Wardamage Protection Act in October 1945. After that, Japan Medical Foundation Hospital was used for the treatment of Atomic bomb survivors
for a long time = Photographed on October 11th 1945 by Shunkichi Kikuchi

爆心地より北に2.4km＝1945年10月11日、
広島大芝国民学校臨時救護所（撮影：菊池俊吉）

Temporary first-aid station set up at the Hiroshima
Oshiba Primary School. 2.4km north of the ground
zero = Photographed on October 11th 1945
by Shunkichi Kikuchi

運び込まれた少年を診察する長崎五郎医師＝1945年10月11日、広島大芝国民学校臨時救護所（撮影：菊池俊吉）

Temporary first-aid station set up at the Hiroshima Oshiba Primary School. Dr. Goro Nagasaki providing medical examination to a boy
who was just brought in = Photographed on October 11th 1945 by Shunkichi Kikuchi

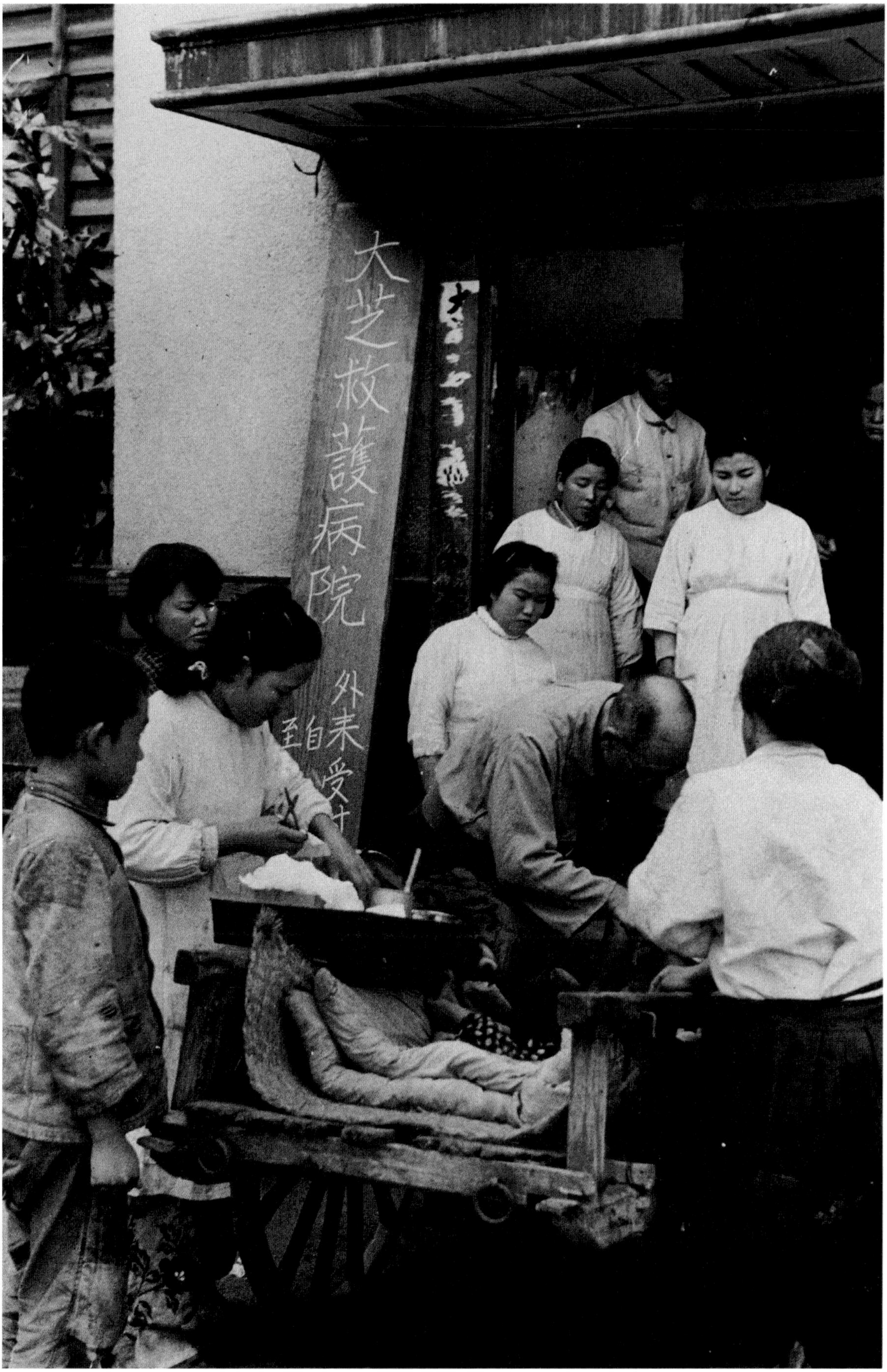
大芝救護病院

ガスタンクに残るはしごの影＝ 1945 年 10 月 15 日、広島市皆実町（撮影：菊池俊吉）

The shadow of a ladder left on the gasholder at Minami-machi, Hiroshima City = Photographed on October 15th 1945 by Shunkichi Kikuchi

ガスタンクに残ったハンドルの影＝ 1945 年 10 月 15 日、広島市皆実町（撮影：菊池俊吉）
The shadow of a handgrip on the gasholder at Minami-machi, Hiroshima City = Photographed on October 15th 1945 by Shunkichi Kikuchi

爆心地から南へ 800m。中国配電本社ビル。
爆風により北側の雨といが接続部でちぎれてつぶれていた
＝ 1945 年 10 月 15 日、広島市小町（撮影：菊池俊吉）
The building of Chugoku Haiden HQ, 800 meters south of the ground zero. Rain gutter at the north side was destroyed = Photographed on October 15th 1945 at komachi, Hiroshima City by Shunkichi Kikuchi

爆心地から東南東に 2km = 1945 年 10 月中旬、比治山からみた広島市段原東浦町（撮影：菊池俊吉）
View of Danhara-Higashiuracho, Hiroshima City from Mt. Hiji. 2km east-southeast of the ground zero
= Photographed in mid-October 1945 by Shunkichi Kikuchi

1945 年 10 月中旬、広島市（撮影：菊池俊吉）
Hiroshima City. Photographed in mid-October 1945 by Shunkichi Kikuchi

閃光の熱線で焼けた橙(ダイダイ) = 1945年10月中旬、広島市(撮影:菊池俊吉)
Bitter orange burnt by heat rays of blast flash = Photographed in mid-October 1945 in Hiroshima City by Shunkichi Kikuchi

爆心地から約 10km にある似島周辺の広島湾に放置された日本軍の潜水艦＝ 1945 年 10 月 17 日（撮影：菊池俊吉）
Submarines of Japanese Navy abandoned in Hiroshima Bay near Ninoshima island, located approximately 10 km north of the ground zero
= Photographed on October 17th 1945 by Shunkichi Kikuchi

元安川河口南約 4km、爆心地より 8 〜 11.5km の位置にある似島は、東側の浜に陸軍の検疫所があった。
東海岸の陸軍馬匹検疫所構内に、高さ約 4m の白木の柱をたて千人塚とし、次々に遺骨を埋めていった。
約 1300 人が埋葬されたと推定されるが、後年、遺骨は平和記念公園内供養塔に移された＝ 1945 年 10 月 17 日、広島湾似島検疫所（撮影：菊池俊吉）

Ninoshima Quarantine Station of Japanese Army in the east part of the shore of Ninoshima, located about 4 km south of the estuary of Motoyasu River,
8-11.5 km from the ground zero. At th site of the army horse quarantine station in the east coast, a gravepost called "Senninzuka (Grave of thousands)" made of
plain wood pole of 4 meters high was established and human remains were buried one after another. It is estimated that there were approximately
1,300 bodies buried there, and later these remains were moved to the memorial tower located in Hiroshima Peace Memorial Park
= Photographed on October 17th 1945 by Shunkichi Kikuchi

広島市中島町と大手町を結んで元安川にかかる。爆心地から100m。
ほとんど真上から爆風をうけたので橋上にぶつかった風圧は
両側に流れて欄干を川へ吹き飛ばし、同時に石の飾り灯篭が
ほぼ等間隔に橋の両側方向へ移動した＝1945年10月17日、
元安橋（撮影：菊池俊吉）

Motoyasu Bridge built over Motoyasu River, connecting Nakajima-cho and Otemachi, Hiroshima City. It was located 100 meters from the ground zero. Receiving the blast wave from above, the parapets of the bridge were blown away into the river and stone lanterns were moved to the left and right
= Photographed on October 17th 1945 by Shunkichi Kikuchi

爆心地より東に3.5km＝1945年10月20日、
広島市浄土真宗尾長説教場（撮影：菊池俊吉）

The Onaga Sermon Institute of The Jyodo-Shinshu (True Pure Land Sect of Buddism), 3.5 km east of the ground zero = Photographed on October 20th 1945 by Shunkichi Kikuchi

爆心地から400m。南東から北西に向って爆心地方向を望む。
広島県農業会広島支所の建物。玄関と奥の建物が壊滅して、
一つの建物とは見えない＝1945年11月頃、
広島市大手町四丁目（撮影：森本太一）

400 meters from the ground zero. Looking the ground zero direction from southeast toward northwest. The Hiroshima Branch building of Hiroshima Prefecture Agriculture Association completely collapsed.
= Photographed in November 1945 at 4 Chome, Otemachi, Hiroshima City by Taichi Morimoto

爆心地から400m。広島県農業会広島支所の建物＝1945年11月頃、
広島市大手町四丁目（撮影：森本太一）

400 meters from the ground zero. The Hiroshima Branch building of Hiroshima Prefecture Agriculture Association. = Photographed in November 1945 at 4 Chome, Otemachi, Hiroshima City by Taichi Morimoto

爆心地から400m。
広島県農業会広島支所の玄関
＝1945年11月頃、広島市大手町四丁目
（撮影：森本太一）

400 meters from the ground zero.
The entrance of the Hiroshima Branch building
of Hiroshima Prefecture Agriculture Association.
= Photographed in November 1945 at 4 Chome,
Otemachi, Hiroshima City by Taichi Morimoto

倒された楠の大木＝ 1945 年 11 月頃（撮影：松重美人）
Huge camphor tree knocked down. = Photographed by Yoshito Matsushige

爆心地から約 700m の広島本通り入口から東方を望む。左角の建物は安田生命。爆風で天井が抜け、陽がさしこんでいる。
右手前のビルは当時帝国銀行、現在のアンデルセン。その左の建物は安田銀行で、
中央の建物は大林組広島支店（現在、山口銀行）＝ 1945 年 11 月頃、広島本通り（撮影：松重美人）

Eastward view from the start point of Hondori Street, Hiroshima City, approximately 700 meters from the ground zero.
The building in left corner is Yasuda Life Insurance. Sun creeps in through the ceiling which was blown away by the blast wave.
The building in front right is Teikoku Bank which is now Hiroshima Andersen building. On left is Yasuda Bank.
The building in center is Ohbayashi-Gumi Hiroshima branch, (currently Yamaguchi Bank).
= Photographed in November 1945 by Yoshito Matsushige

爆心地から約 1.3km。
旧浅野侯のお庭で浅野泉邸といっていた。
モノクロ写真ではわからないが、
火炎の模様がはっきりわかり、
名園の面影が微塵もなくなっている
＝ 1945 年 11 月頃、
広島縮景園（撮影：松重美人）

Hiroshima Shukukei-en, Approximately 1.3 km from the ground zero. Garden of feudal lord Asano and was known as Asano Sentei (manison with fountain). You can see the fire destroyed all the beauty of this garden. = Photographed in November 1945 by Yoshito Matsushige

爆心地から北東 1.4km の
京橋の欄干上から撮影する。3 枚続き。
当時の中国新聞社・福屋・旧福屋・
旧日本勧業銀行広島支店が、
瓦礫の中に建物のムクロで残る
＝ 1945 年 11 月頃、
京橋から市の中心部を望む（撮影：松重美人）

View from the top of the rail of Kyobashi bridge, 1.4 km northeast of the ground zero, toward the Hiroshima City center. Chugoku Shimbun-sha, Fukuya New and Old Wings, and former Nihon Kangyo Bank Hiroshima branch. Those were all destroyed. = Photographed, 3 in a row, in November 1945 by Yoshito Matsushige

爆心地から北東 1.4km の京橋の欄干上から撮影する。3 枚続き。
当時の中国新聞社・福屋・旧福屋・旧日本勧業銀行広島支店が、
瓦礫の中に建物のムクロで残る＝ 1945 年 11 月頃、
京橋から市の中心部を望む（撮影：松重美人）

View from the top of the rail of Kyobashi bridge , 1.4 km northeast of the ground zero, toward the Hiroshima City center. Chugoku Shimbun-sha, Fukuya New and Old Wings, and former Nihon Kangyo Bank Hiroshima branch. Those were all destroyed. = Photographed, 3 in a row, in November 1945 by Yoshito Matsushige

爆心地から北東 1.4km の京橋の欄干上から撮影する。3 枚続き。
当時の中国新聞社・福屋・旧福屋・旧日本勧業銀行広島支店が、
瓦礫の中に建物のムクロで残る＝ 1945 年 11 月頃、
京橋から市の中心部を望む（撮影：松重美人）

View from the top of the rail of Kyobashi bridge , 1.4 km northeast of the ground zero, toward the Hiroshima City center. Chugoku Shimbun-sha, Fukuya New and Old Wings, and former Nihon Kangyo Bank Hiroshima branch. Those were all destroyed. = Photographed, 3 in a row, in November 1945 by Yoshito Matsushige

熱線による欄干の影＝ 1945 年 11 月頃（撮影：松重美人）

The shadow of the handrail by heat wave remains on the bridge floor. = Photographed by Yoshito Matsushige

住友銀行広島支店入口に残った人影のように黒く変色した階段＝1945年11月頃、広島市紙屋町（撮影：松重美人）
The stairs at the entrance of Sumitomo Bank Hiroshima branch. The black shadow looks like that of a person.
= Photographed at Kamiya-cho, Hiroshima City by Yoshito Matsushige

爆風で浮上がった瞬間に小石がはさまった石灯ろう。爆心地から約600m＝1945年末頃、国泰寺境内（撮影：川本俊雄）
Small pebble floated by the blast wave burying the gaps of the stone lantern at Kokutai Temple precinct, Hiroshima City. Approximately 600 meters from the ground zero. = Photographed at the end of 1945 by Toshio Kawamoto

爆風によって橋の欄干の笠石（登呂）がずれる。
右端の建物から、被災者のバラック住宅、
その後ろに広島富国館、
（屋根がのった）明治生命広島支店、
広島銀行集会所、日本生命広島支店。
笠石を挟んで、三和銀行広島支店、
安田生命広島支店、三井物産広島出張所、
住友銀行広島支店、その前には修復中の
農林中央金庫広島支所
＝1945年末〜1946年頃、元安橋、
橋の中央から東南の方向（撮影：川本俊雄）

View toward southeast direction from the center of the Motoyasu bridge, Hiroshima City. The Kasaishi (copestones) of the bridge railing shifted by the blast wave. You can see barrack housings for victims at right front. Behind that, Hiroshima Fukokukan, Meiji Seimei Hiroshima Branch, Hiroshima bank meeting-house and Nihon Seimei Hiroshima Branch. Across the Kasaishi are Sanwa Bank Hiroshima Branch, Yasuda Life Insurance Hiroshima Branch, Mitsui Bussan Hiroshima Branch Office, Sumitomo Bank Hiroshima Branch and probably in front is Norin-chukin Bank Hiroshima Branch under restoration.
＝ Photographed at the end of 1945 or the beginning of 1946 by Toshio Kawamoto

レンガ造りの瀟洒な建物は1909（明治42）年金融街として発展する大手町筋に誕生した。
原爆で、屋根や壁の一部が崩れ亀裂を生じ、爆風で全体が南に傾いた（爆心地の反対側）。
壁には無数の亀裂が入り、南壁（写真右側）の一部分は爆風の影響で「く」の字に折れ曲がり内部は全焼、2階の床は跡形もなくなりかろうじて金庫だけが残った。
この建物は再使用されることなく廃墟のまま1947年頃までその姿をさらしていた＝1945年末頃、日本生命広島支店内部（撮影：川本俊雄）

Inside view of the Nihon Seimei Hiroshima branch. This once elegant brick building was built in 1909 at Otemachi-suji. This street later developed into a financial district of Hiroshima city. Parts of roofs and walls were destroyed, cracked and tilted southward (opposite direction to the ground zero) by the blast wave. On right, the south wall dogleged. The insides were burnt down and the second floor was destroyed leaving nothing but the vault. This building was never reconstructed and was left untouched until 1947. ＝ Photographed at the end of 1945 by Toshio Kawamoto

婦人の背一面のケロイド。広島赤十字病院レントゲン技師として撮影した＝1947年4月30日、広島赤十字病院（撮影：黒石勝）

Keloid scars on the entire back of a woman. The photograph was taken by Masaru Kuroishi, an X-ray technician.
＝ Photographed at the Hiroshima Red Cross Hospital on April 30th 1947

KIKKAWA K
HIROSHIMA
APRIL 30 1947

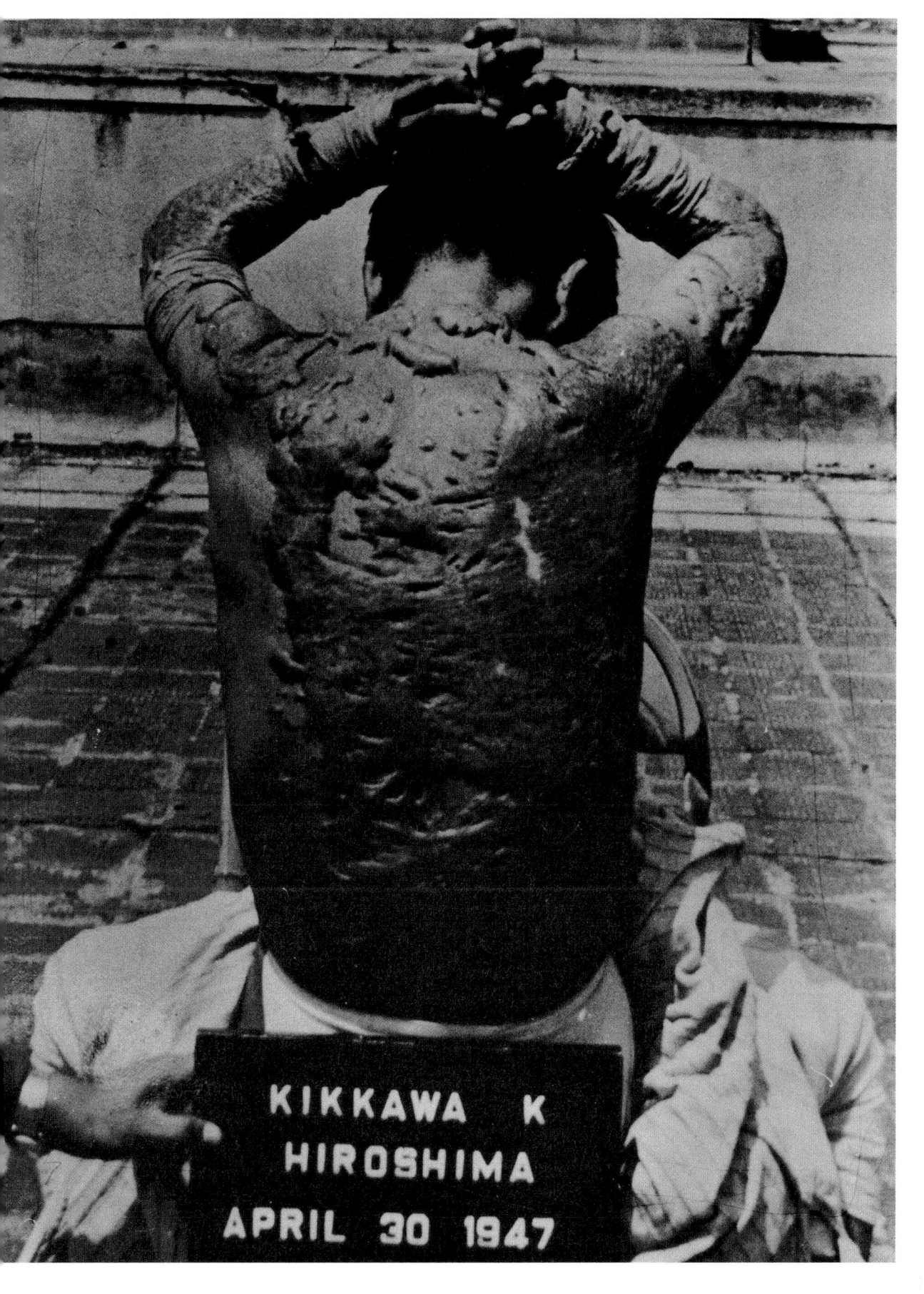

「原爆を撮った男たち」の証言

写真家・松本栄一　写真家・林 重男

（聞き手・小松健一）

——敗戦の1945（昭和20）年8月9日長崎に原爆が落とされたわけですが、松本さんは、その12日後の8月21日に東京を発って、まず長崎に向かった。25日に入り、14日間撮影をして、9月8日に広島へ。

林さんは、20年10月1日に広島の爆心地に立つわけですが、9月27日に東京を発って、28日に尾道、そして29日には宇品港に入って、30日から広島の撮影を始めている。10月11日にさらに長崎に向かって、12日間長崎にいた。

松本さんが約1カ月間、長崎、広島にいて、林さんも23日間取材をされていたわけですね。当時、松本さんは30歳、林さんが27歳というお歳だったのですが、最初に世界で初めて原爆というものが落とされた爆心地に立ったときの印象、驚きというようなことを、まずはじめに一言ずつお話しいただけたらと思います。

1発の爆弾で消えたまち

松本　皆さんで考えていただきたいのは、たった1発の爆弾が都市そのものを消してしまう現象を起こしていることです。これは私、当時新聞社におりまして、戦争中なものですから、何カ所かの空襲を受けた都市、市街を見て歩いております。それはいずれもB29が100機来たとか、200機来たとか、焼夷弾が何千発落とされたとか、爆弾が何百発落ちたとかいうことでの被害を見ていた目から、たった1発で本当にこれだけの広いところが、消えてしまったようにしてやられてしまったものか、この驚きが第一印象です。これは広島でも長崎でも同じような印象を受けました。

林　私は当時、文部省学術研究会議で編成されました原子爆弾災害調査研究特別委員会という、仁科博士を団長とする災害調査を目的とする調査団に組み入れられたわけです。

カメラマンの通弊として、人間を見ると、どうしても人間を主題にして写真を撮りたくなるから、あくまでも調査団にうまくマッチするような写真を撮ってこいと言われて、10月1日だと私、記憶しているんですが、広島の爆心地に立ったわけです。広島商工会議所という焼けたビルの上から1発でなくなった広島のまちを見たわけです。何といいますか、その無念さというか、戦争に負けたというか、その実感が一挙に私の胸に迫りまして、とりあえずこれを撮っちゃえと。まず第1発に撮ったのは、パノラマだったんですね。ぐるっと回り、360度をローライフレックスでつないで撮影しましたのが、広島の爆心地を望んだ第1発目のシャッターだったんですね。

11日間、広島の爆心地を撮影しまして、それから長崎に向かいました。長崎は広島のような地形ではありませんので、一望するということは無理です。ちょうど谷間に立ったようなところでして。そこでやはり、横長の写真をずうっとつないで撮っておりましたらば、偶然だったんですが、

救援物資のイモを満載した貨車が、轟然と音を立てて私の視界に飛び込んできました。一応全部つないだ写真を撮り終わったところで、幸いなことに足が１歩も動いていなかったために、入ってきた汽車をもう１回撮ったわけです。果たせるかな、後でつないで見ますと、その場所へ汽車がバチッと入ってくるものですから、一連の５枚つなぎの写真の中には、運よくばく進してくる列車が撮れました。両都市とも、もう１発でなくなったという感じは、共通してありました。

——敗戦直後の当時、爆心地での放射能の怖ろしさがまだよくわかっていないうちに、お二人とも被爆の地に立たれたわけですね。非常に危険だと言われていたところに。当時、林さんは結婚なさって、赤ちゃんが奥さんのお腹の中にできたばかりと聞いていますし、松本さんは朝日新聞の出版部の写真部員として、若い命をかけて、なぜカメラで原爆を記録しようと思ったのか。私も、写真家として、そのような立場に立たされたときに、果たしてお二人のような行動が取れるかどうかということも考えまして、ぜひお聞きしたいと思います。

カメラマンの使命感に燃えて

松本 これはニュースカメラマンとしての一つの宿命だと思います。一つは、自分自身で東京で聞いていた原爆というものの実際のあり様を見てみたいという、これは個人的な興味といいますか、そういったことが多分にありました。とにかく上からの命令に対しては素直に飛び出していく。これが新聞社勤めのカメラマンの一つの意気込みだったわけです。そういったことに惚れて、私もカメラマンになったわけですから、別に深く考えないで平常の出張取材の気持ちで出かけました。実際に放射能の威力というものを私らが知ったのは、終戦後の何年かたった後のことで、当時としては、ただ単におそろしい爆弾だったなという印象の方が強かったように思っております。

林 私は昭和18年に現役を除隊しまして、いよいよこれから本格的な戦闘になるというところで、軍の外郭団体で情報宣伝を担当する東方社に入ったのです。実はちょっと明かしておかないといけないんですが、仕事の内容というのは、当時の日本の占領地、つまり南方から華北全般にわたっての占領地をくまなく撮影に行かされまして、たくさんの資料を持ち帰って、日本の占領地はこれだけうまくいっているんだとか。あるいは内地で撮影しました軍用機の数々を、数百枚撮っておりますが、それをうまいことモンタージュしまして、たとえば北アルプスの上を飛んでいる爆撃機をインドの上空を飛んでいる爆撃機にしてしまったり、写真としての利用を最大限に、プロパガンダの一つとして使ったという経験を持っているんです。ですから、写真というものは絶対手

「原爆を撮った男たち」オリジナル写真展、
1991・7/24〜27 渋谷・山手教会で
（左から林重男、松本榮一、小松健一の各氏）

を加えてはいけない、1枚の写真の中にカメラマンの思った映像をたたき込むというのが、写真の本来の使命なんですけれども、そういう点からいくと、実に卑劣きわまることをやっておった。

　それで、戦い敗れて、私らの戦友はフィリピン上陸を前にして、ほとんど南海の藻屑と消えたり、悲惨な状態で終戦を迎えたわけです。幸い私は、そういう業務に携わっていたために死ぬことを免れた、そういう思いが、あの当時私の体の中にいっぱいたまっておった。彼らはどんな苦しい思いをして死んだんだろうと思えば、たかが1発の原爆で自分の体がどうなっても構わん。まして、先ほど司会の小松さんから言われた通り、私の家内が妊娠していることを初めて知らされたものですから、「3カ月だったらもう大丈夫だろう。おれは行くぜ」と友達に言ったわけです。友達は「よせよせ、そんなところに行って、禿になったらどうするんだ」と。いまでもその兆候はあるんですけれども（笑）、「子どもができなくなるぞ」、「いや、もうできたからいいんだ」といって、初めて友達に明かしたわけです。そういうような立場で、調査団の一員としてまいりました。

　松本さんの、ニュースカメラマンとしての宿命、私は調査団のカメラマンとしての宿命として仕事にとりくみましたが、何しろ、水はない、食料はない、にぎり飯1個の昼食では、残念ながら歩けないんです。それで、爆心地から、「あそこら辺があやしいぞ」と、行くんですけれども、途中で、"刀折れ、矢尽き"で足が動かない。どうにも前に進めない。何しろ食うものがない。水がない。行動範囲はおのずから絞られてきまして、情けないことに、後から写真を全部整理しますと、幾らたどっても、爆心地を中心にして10キロは行っていないんですね。

　長崎に行って顕著な違いがあったのは、ちょうど占領軍が長崎に上がってきて、実際に市のグラウンドで施設大隊が軽飛行機の発着所をつくっておりました。そして、城山小学校の校庭でたくさんの人が集団茶毘にされた光景を写真におさめた。もうそのときのショックというのは、本当にくやしくてくやしくて……。こんな光景になるまでして、何で日本は戦ったんだという思いで帰ってきたんです。

――お二人とも、それぞれの立場で約1カ月、広島、長崎に滞在して多くのカットを残したわけです。それが今日、世界で唯一の被爆直後の原爆写真として残されているわけなんですが、撮影のときのエピソード、広島や長崎での人びとの様子などお話しいただけたらと思います。

あなたの苦しみを写真に

松本　実は私と一緒に取材していた、もう一人の記者が道を歩いていて、「栄ちゃん、何だね、原爆というのはいやなにおいがするもんだね」と言うんです。ところがこれは、それから10数日間、長崎に滞在して、取材をして歩いている間にわかったことなのですが、まだ私が長崎に到着したころは、遺体がその辺に散らばっておりました。気をつけて歩かなければいけない。それほどたくさん遺体があったわけです。その遺体が8月の炎暑で、半ばびらんしております。それからウジがわいて、ハエが出ている。この腐乱死体からのにおいが、あの広い焼け跡に充満していたわけです。

　ところが、それから1カ月以上たった後「枕崎台風」というのが来ていますが、これで全部洗い流された。林さんが広島に入られたのはその後だから、もうにおい、遺体、そういったものがきれいになくなっている、そういった時間的な違いがあるんですね。

　実際に私が直面したことは、三菱兵器工場の中で後片づけをしている方を見つけて、被爆当時の話を伺って帰ったんです。そしてまた、2日、3日して、どうもあの人の話におかしいとこ

ろがあるから、もう1回確認しようじゃないかというので、2人で同じ方を三菱兵器に訪ねて行ったところが、つい2日ほど前に歯ぐきから猛烈な出血をして、夜中に高熱を出して、朝までに亡くなりましたと。これが、実は放射能による急性白血病の症状だったわけです。それで、これはやっぱり大変なことなんだなというのが、はじめてわかったわけです。

　毎日のように日が沈んで暗くなりかけると、あちらこちらでチョロチョロ火が燃え上がるんです。初めのころは、私は、防空壕で生活でもなさっている被災者の方が夕飯の支度をしているのだとばかり思っていたわけです。ところが、昼間歩いてみますと、方々に茶毘の跡があるんですね。骨が散らばっている。これで初めて、あの火はそれぞれの家族の方たちが、ご自分の肉親またはお友達、そういった方たちの腐乱してくる遺体にしようがなくて、皆さん、自分の手で茶毘をやっていた。

　一体こういうことが、普通の爆弾その他の攻撃を受けた都市で見られたろうか。実は私は写真を撮るときに、「あなたの苦しみをどうか写真に撮らせてください。その写真で、世界に、こんなにあなた方が苦しい思いをしたということを無言のうちに教えてあげたいから、1枚シャッターを切らせてください」ということをお願いして、シャッターを切ったわけです。ただ、残念ながら、お名前その他を伺ったメモを紛失してしまって、後々、いまだに私はあのお3人の方たちのその後を伺いたいと思って探しているんですが、どうしても消息がつかめません。そんなことが、やっぱり原爆の一つのあらわれだったのではないかと思っております。

——いままで発表されている原爆に関する写真を見て疑問に思ったことが一つあるんです。それは、広島の方では勤労奉仕などで出ていた、学徒動員の学生が、あるいはレントゲンの技師だとか、写真館の経営者、新聞社のカメラマン、気象台に勤務していて写真をやっていた方だとか、わりと広範囲な人たちが原爆に、原子雲に向かってシャッターを切っている。ですから、広島の原子雲の写真というものは比較的正確に確認できるのですが、長崎の原子雲の写真が非常に少ない。大村にあった海軍病院から軍医さんが撮ったのが1点残されているんですけれども、それも、広島みたいな正確な形での原子雲ではなくて、ちょっと見ると夏雲みたいにも見える。そして、一般の人たちも、当時の長崎県警の方と長崎造船所の方と市役所の方と、3人の方が記録しているとしかわかっていない。日本で一番最初に写真が伝わった長崎なんですが、長崎の方が非常に少なくて、広島がなぜあれ

撮影の合間に飯盒での自炊。
松本（右）、同行の半沢記者。広島で
写真提供・松本栄一

だけ多かったのか。率直な疑問なのです。

原子雲を撮ったのは17歳の少年

林　私もそう思いました。端的に言いますと、長崎の要塞司令部というのは、当時として、機密のかたまりみたいなところです。それから、広島は軍都と言われた、第五師団の司令部の所在地ですけれども、やはり物資の集散地ですから、その点、陸軍関係が全部取り仕切っていた、そういう違いがあるんですね。海軍と陸軍。ましてや終戦直前の「武蔵」、「大和」。あの軍艦が秘密裏に出航して、秘密裏に失ったという地ですから、それはすさまじいほど検閲がひどかったと思いますね。

　広島の原子雲をみごとにとらえたのは17歳だった山田精三さん。彼は中国新聞の新聞少年だったんですね。それで新聞社に毎日勤めていて、その日に限って休暇届を出して、友達と、爆心から約6、7キロ離れた水分（みくまり）峡というところに水泳に行こうと言って、二人で行ったんだそうです。

　それで、カメラが好きなものですから、雑嚢にカメラをしのばせて、弁当の材料を持って行ったところが、約6キロ離れた山中で、いきなりバーッと、目の前が灰色の世界になってしまって、直径30センチからの太さの松の木が、数分のうちにズズーッ、サササッと横になびいたというんですね。ところが彼は、その光景を、6キロ離れた原爆を見ながら、何が何だかさっぱりわからない。とにかく、「これはえらいこっちゃ」一体何だろうとひょっと見たら、キノコ雲がまさに上がってきたわけです。すかさず彼は、バッグからバルダックスか何かのセミ版のカメラを取り出して、1発撮ったんです。そして、「こりゃあ何だ？」と言っているうちに、もう1回巻いて撮ろうと思ったら、もうこの雲がファインダーいっぱいに広がっちゃって、2発目からは何も撮れない。運よく第1発目の、実にすさまじい、雲の下からドーンと突き上げて笠状になったところを1枚しか撮れなかった。山を下り始めたら、被爆者が上がってきたんですね。被爆者は指の先から全部、皮がた

90式携帯電話機の鞄、陸軍の航空服、焼け残りの登山靴、
全てを失った当時としてはまあまあの装備であった。
（長崎浦上の爆心地に立つ）昭和20年10月中旬　写真提供・林重男

れている、髪はぼうぼうで。「火薬庫が爆発したに違いないから、とりあえずおれは会社に帰る」と言って、中国新聞に帰って行くわけです。

ところが、広島駅の近所に来ると、もう火が渦巻いていて中に入れない。それでやっと川沿いに通っていって、上流川町の中国新聞の社屋に行って、彼は、3階の自分の仕事場までいくと中は全部ロールペーパーから何からめちゃくちゃになって焦げている。全部が火で焼かれている。

非常に仲のよかった加藤さんというおばさんが、あの原爆が落ちた8時15分は必ずベランダに出て掃除している時間なのだそうですよ。それで彼は、あのおばちゃんがきっとここで爆弾の被害に遭ったに違いないと思って、その部屋を探したんだそうです。狭い部屋だから、もうめっちゃくちゃになって、何が何だかわからないんだけれども、そのおばちゃんの挿していたサンゴのかんざしが1本落ちていた。「ああ、おれが水泳に行かなかったら、このおばちゃんと一緒におれもここで焼け焦げになっていたんだな」と、彼は懸命になって、もっとそのおばさんの遺物がないかと探す。そしてひょっと見たら、窓の壊れた鉄枠の一部に小指が引っかかっていたんだそうです。

残骸を見ますと爆心から真正面のところにある部屋なんですね。実際にこの被爆を免れて現場に立ち至った山田精三さんの話は、私はもうすごい思いで聞きましたね。

こういう話は枚挙に暇ないんですけれども、そのたびに私が思うのは、やはり核兵器の残酷さ、これはあの広島平和公園の碑にある通りに、「過ちは繰返しませぬから」という言葉を、われわれ胸に深く焼きつけて、こういう日本の歴史があったということを皆さんひとつ、お子さんたちに語り伝えて、世界中から核兵器がなくなるまでわれわれも運動を続けるつもりでおります。今日の私の拙い話で何か得るところがありましたら、お話くだされば幸いだと思います。

爆心地は浦上の上空560〜600メートル

松本 いまの林さんのお話の中で補足させていただきますが、なぜ広島、長崎であまり写真を撮っていないかというご質問がありましたけれども、いまの方はあまりご存じないことなんですが、この広島も長崎も両方ともが軍事要塞地帯に入るわけです。当時、要塞地帯でカメラなんか持っていたら、これはすぐ憲兵に引っ張られたものなんです。それほど厳しい世の中だったわけです。ですからいまのような、本当に10人いれば10人がカメラを持っているといった潤沢な時代ではございません。それに一般の人にはフィルムの入手難だということもあります。私が広島、長崎へ行った目的というのが、『科学朝日』という雑誌が、いまも朝日新聞から出ております。これのグラビアページで、原爆というのが一体どういうものかを紹介しようじゃないかということでいったわけです。私らが入ったときには、爆心ということは、言葉としては出ていましたが、ここがそうだというものは何もなかったんです。それで私たちが企画をしたのは、その爆心から1キロ離れたところでは建物がどういう壊れ方をしたか、2キロ離れたところではどういう壊れ方をしたかというようなねらいで撮影しようじゃないかということで出かけて行ったわけです。

ところが、一緒に行った半沢記者は、さすがに科学部で洗練された人でした。長崎に入って「栄ちゃん、これを見なさいよ、立木とか電信柱が真っすぐ立っているところが爆心の近くだよ。爆心から離れるに従って外側へ外側へと盃状に広がってものが壊れている」と。そういったことから、浦上のあの天主堂の下に行って、「この辺だ」と。そうしてさらに、私の、はしごの影が板塀に焼きついている写真がありますが、これが4.5キロぐらい離れたところにあった要塞司令部。そこに私が地図をもらいに行ったわけです。そうしたら、うちの構内でこういうものがあるという

で撮ったんですが、あの影と同じように、はしごを立てかけて、そうしてその影の角度を見た。その角度を計りながらずうっと浦上へ持っていって、地図の上で計算してみると、大体560メートルというのが出てきた。ですから、浦上のこの辺で、確かに上空560メートルから600メートルぐらいの間で爆発しているというのを、この科学部の記者が、まず示してくれたわけです。

それから私たちの取材が始まったんですが、いま申し上げましたように、地図の上で1キロ、2キロメートルという線を引くのに地図がないんです。これもやはり要塞地帯なものですから、地図なんていうのは市販されていません。そこで、要塞司令部に言ったり、警察の当時ありました特高という特別高等警察です。大変こわいところなんですが、そこへ行って手に入れたのが、真っ白けの、白地で何も書いていない、ただ輪郭だけがかいてある地図をもらった。こういったことは、いままた新たに思い出してきました。

——そのような大変なご苦労をして撮影したフィルムを日本を占領したアメリカ軍に没収されそうになったと聞いていますが。

写真家の撮影したフィルムは軍人の銃と同じ

林　はい、ありました。松本さんの場合と私は立場が違いますので、私ども原子爆弾災害調査研究特別委員会として行った記録を、戦後、昭和20年の11月と記憶していますが、アメリカ軍が直接私らの東方社にまいりまして、撮影したフィルムを全部出せと言って来ました。その場に私、立ち会っておりますからはっきり申しますが、そのときの写真部長が木村伊兵衛さんだった。それで向こうにアメリカ軍の通訳と将校、木村さんがこっちで、机一つで対峙していた。私は衝立一つへだてて聞いていました。木村さんに、盛んにアメリカ軍の将校が通訳を通して、フィルムを全部ここに並べろと強要するわけです。木村さんがそこで何をおっしゃったかというと、「われわれにとって撮影したフィルムは、あなたが腰の右につけている拳銃と同じだ」と、将校に指差して言っているんです。「その拳銃をここに置きなさい。そうしたら、われわれの部員が撮ってきたフィルムを全部ここに出しますよ。交換しましょう」と。さすがにその将校は、それだけはできなかった。それで、「拳銃を渡すわけにはいかん」と。「そうしたらわれわれもフィルムを渡すわけにはいきません」と、非常に勇気のある答えで彼らの要求を突っぱねた。そのためにわれわれのフィルムは、いま現在でも残っております。片や、一緒に被爆地へ行った日本映画社の映画班のフィルムは、全部没収されました。それでアメリカに持って行かれたのです。「しかし、この写真をわれわれはほしいんだけど、どうしたらいいか」とアメリカの将校が木村さんに言うわけです。「そんなことは簡単だ。この写真を全部プリントすればいいんだから。プリントして持っていらっしゃい」と、こう言ったんです。「それなら、ことしのクリスマスまでにプリントできるか」、「ああできます」。「じゃ、プリントしろ」と命令を出したんです。そうしたら、「ちょっと待ってくれ、われわれには戦争に負けたために写真を焼く印画紙がない。薬がない。乾かす器材がない。これがあれば、すぐにでもできます」と。そんなことはアメリカ軍にはわけはない。「じゃ、全部計算しろ」と将校。それで木村さんが「おおい、林くん、ちょっと計算してくれ」と衝立越しに言ったわけですよ。私は計算しているふりをして、大ざっぱに大体このぐらいと、全部値を出したんです。大目に。印画紙を何百箱、ガロン計算で、薬品は、現像液が何ガロン、定着液が何ガロンと、アメリカの将校にわかりやすいようにガロン計算で出した。それに印画紙を乾かす乾燥機が3台、こう出しましたら、彼はこれを見てOKと言って帰り、その全材料が届いたのは3日後でした。3台の

クォータートントラックという小さなトラックに積んできまして、材料をドーンとわれわれのいる玄関の前に突きつけたんですね。この時、こんな豊かな国と戦争したのがまちがいだったとつくづく思いました。

——当時、映画プロデューサーの相原秀次さんが記述している中では、54人ぐらいの人が、広島、長崎で原爆の記録を撮っているだろうと。そのうちすでに半数の方がお亡くなりになって、林さんたちと一緒に入った、私たち日本写真家協会（JPS）の先輩でもある菊池俊吉さんも、昨年の11月に急性白血病で突然お亡くなりになられたわけです。約1カ月間も、それも被爆直後に入っていらした松本さん、林さんをはじめ、いまご健在でいられる原爆を記録した人たちの健康が心配なのですが……

写真に写らない放射能の恐さ

林　いわゆる放射能について両面からお話しすると、写真に写らないのは放射能ですね。また、感光するのも放射能なんですね。私どもは最初行きますときに、せっかく撮った写真が全部放射能でかぶってしまうんじゃないかと。これに対する処置をどうしたらいいかというので、一番関心事がそこにあったんですが、撮影しましたフィルムを、日本映画社関係の人が急遽東京に行くというので持って帰ってもらって、テスト現像したら、大丈夫だという電報が入って、私どもは撮影を続けたわけです。

そして、これは時効ですから、お話ししますが、私が入りましたのは、さっきお話のあった「枕崎台風」が上陸し、通過した後のわけですね。私が行ったとき、まず不思議だったのは、家が1軒もないということですね。当然バラックが建ってしかるべきだという話も聞いていたのに、これは何というきれいなことだと。それで一望、見渡して写真を撮る前に、一瞬、おかしいなという疑問が起きた。あまりにもきれい過ぎる。それは、いわゆる軍司令部のあるところですから、爆弾が落ちた後、兵隊を使って、作戦路と称する主要道路の二号線は全部掃除したんですね。それで軍車両が通れるようにきれいにしたとは言いながら、あまりにもきれいだったので、これはどういうことだろうと思って宿舎に毎日帰るわけです。

帰ると、東京大学の先生方の助手をしておられる方が、毎日の測定値を宿舎で全部記録していくわけです。毎日「おかしい、おかしい」と言っているんですね。いったい何がおかしいんだろうと思っても、なかなかそのおかしい原因を聞き取ることができないんです。

東京へ帰って、明くる年になって、突然箝口令が敷かれたんですね。「これはしゃべってはならん」と。われわれが行った広島では、放射能の測定値が非常に低かったんですね。それで、もしこれを軽々しく言ってしまうと、アメリカ軍の核爆弾に対する認識を、「それみたことか、大したことないじゃないかという宣伝に利用されるから、これは絶対口外してはならない」と。何と、その原因は、台風だったんですね。台風がすべてを流していった。

これは先年、私も松本さんもモスクワに行きまして、ノーボスチ通信社にいったときにチェルノブイリ原発事故を撮影したカメラマンと一緒に会談したんですが、そのときにも、やはりいろいろ向こうの写真を見せてもらったら、ものすごく建物を洗うんですね。プリピャチの町をほとんど噴水で洗ってしまう。洗った水は流せないから、またプールに戻して、それを缶に入れて土の中に埋めて捨てる。こういう大変につけの重い仕事をやっておるんですね。ですから、やっぱりあのときにも台風が大分放射能を流し去ってくれたんだろうなということが、後年はっきりしました。放射能は写真に写らないので、われわれは大変くやしがったんですが、何とかして放射能を写す

方法はないかと思ったら、やはりチェルノブイリで若干それを証明してくれた。あるテレビの画像で、放射能だということを証明してくれたけれども、あれも若干、眉唾じゃないかという説もあるんですが、確かに画像の走査線が乱れておりますね。そういう未知の放射能に対して、ずいぶん怖れたものでした。

松本 僕の場合は、林くんよりもまだ1カ月も前ですから、十分に残存の放射能はあったと思うんです。最近、広島や長崎の原爆病院をお訪ねしますと、いま入院されている方たちは、大体親戚の手伝いに入ったとか、遺族を探したとかいうような、いわゆる直接の被爆をされた方でなしに、後から入られていわゆる二次放射能によって汚染された方が多いんですね。それを見てまいりますと、私などというのは、本当にこんな幸運な男があるのかと、自分でそう思っております。

いまノーボスチ通信社の話が林さんから出ましたけれども、この通信社を訪ねたときも、第1の質問が、「おまえたち、広島、長崎に入るときに、防護服は一体どういうものを着て入ったのか」ということだったんです。「冗談じゃない。まだ僕らが広島、長崎の被災地を撮影した時点では、放射能からの防護ということは考えていなかった。それほどの怖ろしさがあるものとは知らなかったから、普通の服装のままで入っていた」と。とにかく3週間、両方合わせて1カ月近い間を歩き回って、これという異常がいまだに出てこないというのは、こんなに幸せなことはないと思っております。

この間も、一緒に行った科学部の記者と、社の古い連中が集まる旧友会の会場で二人で「お互いに、死ぬときはきっと癌で死ぬだろうけれども、死んだら献体をして、放射能がどういう影響を残していたか調べてもらう方がいいんじゃないか」と話しました。

――最後に、お二人の方をはじめ、50人以上の方が命の危険を冒して、世界で最初の核兵器の使用によって生じた惨状を写したわけですけれども、そうした核の絶対の事実というか、そういうものがわずか50年あまりの歳月の中で、私たち日本人だけではないんでしょうけれども、人々の意識の中で薄まりつつあると思うんです。いまから17年前に、日本の写真家、写真評論家など552人の人たちの呼びかけでできた「反核・写真運動」は、この間、細々ですけれども、そうした先輩たちが命をかけて撮ってきた遺産を後世に残そうということで、フィルムの複製、あるいはオリジナルプリントの収集、原爆を撮影した人たちの調査活動をこの間ずっと続けてきました。それぞれ非常に忙しい人たちが、ボランティア活動でやってきました。この運動をこれからさらに進めていかなければならないということをいまのお話を聞きながら改めて思いました。原爆を記録した人間として今後の運動に対する期待や、政府や国に対しての要望などがありましたら、最後に一言お願いしたいと思います。

一刻も早く被爆者の救済を

林 私が願うのは、いまも病の床に伏せておられる35万数千人の方々のことです。私は前から申し上げているんですけれども、日本はまだ被爆者に対する援護法は制定されてない国家なんです。何とも情ない。いまバブル経済のつけが盛んに新聞紙上をにぎわしていますけれども、一体日本人はどうなってしまったんだろう。あれだけの金が特定の人の間で左右されるならば、あの何分の一でもまわせば被爆者に対してちゃんと制定された法令ができる。いまになって1日も早くというのはおかしな話ですけれども制定しなければ、あの方たちは、死んでも死にきれないと思いますね。

現に、先ほどもお話がありました私と一緒に広島に入った友人の菊池くん。彼は私よりも2つ

年上でありましたが、ちょっと虚弱体質だということも災いしたのかもしれませんが、昨年の10月に発病して、亡くなったのが11月5日でした。奥さんの話によれば、急に具合が悪くなって、お医者さんに調べてもらったら、これは大病院で精密検査をする必要があるというので、早速大きな病院に行きましたら、急性白血病で、白血球が通常の人の数十倍になっていた。急遽入院したところが、そのときすでに肺炎を併発して、あっという間に亡くなってしまいました。

これなども因果関係は立証できないとのお医者さんの言葉だったそうです。われわれの先輩の長崎を記録した山端庸介さんは、被爆後20数年にして肝臓がんで亡くなられました。山端さんが長崎の刑務所跡に撮影に行って昼食にしたときに、急性放射能障害によって食べたものを全部吐いたそうです。そういう被爆1日後の写真を百数十枚のフィルムにおさめて、しかも想像もできないような放射能を浴びて、食べたものを全部吐いた。果せるかな、やはり彼の手記によれば、「原爆のためとは言えないかもしれないけれども、おれはそう思っている」と言って亡くなったそうです。

こういう話を思い出すと、何十年たっても、その障害の影はひたひたと、いま申し上げた30数万の被爆者の上にものしかかっているのではないかと思って、それを考えると、1日も早く法令を制定するように、皆さんにもお力を貸していただきたい。

松本 この間、広島の市長ともいろいろお話ししているときに出たことなんですが、実は私、はじめに申し上げているように、長崎に入ったのが8月25日でございます。爆弾が落ちたのが8月9日です。そうしますと、いわゆる被爆者に対する被爆者手帳というのは、罹災してから2週間以内の人には、証明があれば被爆者手帳というのがもらえるんだそうです。ところが私の場合は25日で1日違いなんです。それで、あなたには差し上げられませんということを市役所の担当の方から言われております。その話を私、市長としたんですけれども、私みたいに達者でいるものは、あなた1日違いだからあげられないよと言われても、さほどに感じはしないけれども、実際にいま病院で苦しんでいられる方に、「あなた1日違いだから被爆者手帳には該当しないんだというようなことを断れますか。そういうむごいことをあなた、言えるんですか。何かここで、国がだめならば、自治体が何か救済の方法を考えてあげることができないのか」ということを市長と盛んにお話ししたんですけれども、「そこが松本さん、法律というのはどこかで線を引かなきゃならない」ということを言っておられる。そういうことを聞きますと、本当にまだまだ、被爆された方々への援護、救済、こういったものが決して十分なことではないと思いました。

私たちが撮った原爆の写真を見て、平和というものがどんなに大切なものか、そういうことをひとつお互いに考える材料にしていただきたいと思います。願うことは、こういった運動を1日も早くやらないで済むような世の中にしたい。それが私どもの念願でございます。どうか、皆様方のお力添えよろしくお願いいたします。

——松本さん、林さん、今日は貴重な体験談やご提言、本当にありがとうございました。

(1991年7月26日 於東京山手教会)
司会・構成／小松健一
写真／川原 勇
協力／「反核・写真運動」
◎日本写真家協会会報 第88号(1991年11月25日発行)に掲載されたものに一部、加筆・補正をした

解説

「広島の原爆を撮った男」

新藤健一

広島と長崎の原爆を撮ったカメラマン、写真関係者は「反核・写真運動」の調べによると
氏名が分かっている方々だけで47人になります。撮影者名を列挙します（順不同）。
黒石勝、北 勲、松重三男、岸本吉太、山本儀江、松重美人、尾木正巳、岸田貢宜、尾糠政美、谷川辰次、山田精三、深田敏夫、
富重安雄、相原秀次、松本栄一、菊池俊吉、林重男、田子恒男、中田左都男、山端庸介、川本俊雄、小川虎彦、
川原四儀、木村権一、斎藤誠二、鴉田藤太郎、森本太一、林寿麿、空博行、森末太郎、松田弘道、塩月正雄、宮武甫、保野公男、
加賀美幾三、三木茂、菅義夫、山崎文男、筒井俊正、山中真男、二瓶禎二、眞島正市、堺屋修一、弥永泰正、津場真雄、
桝屋富一、佐々木雄一郎の各氏です。

不安と恐怖が渦巻き、耐え難い悲惨な人類未曾有の修羅場で歴史を記録してきた「原爆を撮った男たち」の体験と証言を
『広島原爆写真集』と『長崎原爆写真集』でそれぞれに、紹介します。

地獄だった広島　中国新聞の松重美人

　1945年8月6日午前11時過ぎ、中国新聞社のカメラマン、松重美人は広島市の京橋川にかかる御幸橋西詰で作業中に被爆した広島女子商業学校、県立第一中学校生徒たちにカメラを向けた。
　「8月6日、火の中をあれだけ歩いたんですが、熱さは感じなかったんです」。
　ネオン華やかな広島の小料理屋で松重は原爆投下直後の様子を正座して語り出した。

撮影こそが使命

　「午前11時、御幸橋で2カットを撮影した。写してから裏側にまわり被災者の正面からも撮影したかった。でも、あまりにもむごたらしく報道班員の腕章を付けていたにもかかわらず行けなかったんですよ」。

陶板に焼き付けられた被災時の写真前に立つ松重美人氏＝広島市の御幸橋
＝1995年1月（撮影：新藤健一）

　広島に原爆が投下されたとき、松重は前日から報道班員として師団司令部で夜を明かし食事のため自宅に戻っていた。松重の家は爆心から2.7キロにあった。妻は自宅で理容店を営んでいた。「私は上半身裸で血だらけになりながら家内の手を引っ張って素足で外に出た。その内、空が真っ赤になり、闇夜のようになった。心臓が張り裂ける感じになりました。気がついたら前のイモ畑に横たわっていた」。
　「30〜40分たってから家に戻り壁土に埋まったカメラを掘り出した。家内は赤い太陽を鏡越しに見たといっているが、私は音も聞いていない。爆風がきたが、はっきり覚えていないんですよ」。爆風で地上の砂が舞い上がり降ってくる灰で広島の上空には黒い霧状の雲が垂れ込めた。
　1995年1月、松重の案内で御幸橋に出かけた。橋のたもとに松重撮影の大きな写真記念碑がある。「家から徒歩で10分、御幸橋付近で30分ぐらいウロウロした。被爆直後、薄日が差していたが空は暗かった」。「食用油を塗っ

た被災者が数百人おられました。その側には1～2年生の女子中学生がいました。彼女たちは建物の強制疎開を手伝っていた学徒でした」。

松重の脳裏には「阿鼻叫喚の修羅場」があった。髪は焼け縮れ、顔、腕、背、足の火ぶくれが破れ、やけどの皮膚がボロ布のように垂れ下がる。まさに地獄画だった。西詰めの中央から1枚、ようやくシャッターを切った。「1枚撮ればカメラを持っていると勇気がでるもの」。近づいて2枚目を撮った。「水をください」というかすかな声が聞こえた。写真に写った右側の女性たちに「写真を撮るのが私の使命です」と断るのがやっとだった。答えはなかった。「この一言はいわなければならないとじっと考えていた」。「何か罪の意識があったからでしょう」と松重がポツリと語る。

「写真上の黒いのは煙です。真ん中には赤ちゃんがいる女性です」。顔が焼け焦げた姿をファインダー越しに見た目はうるんでしまった。「助けてくださいよ、という声は、いまも耳に残っています」と目を閉じる。

松重は午後2時すぎ、再び外に出た。「広島大学のプールは水がなくなり死体でいっぱいでした。水を求めた被災者が沸騰しているプールに飛び込んだのでしょうね。防火水槽に身を突っ込んだ遺体もありましたよ」。

「紙屋町では爆風で胸が押しつぶされた人、目を明けたままの遺体を目撃しましたが、一度はカメラを向けましたが、可哀そうでやめました」。その後、死者を葬った広島湾の似島では何日も何日も煙がのぼっていた。

星空の下で現像

中国新聞社に保管されているネガを松重から見せてもらった。立ち会ってくれた写真関係者の話だとネガは一時、行方不明になったという。あまりにも貴重なネガなので総務部の金庫にしまい、編集関係者はその存在を忘れてしまったからだ。歴史の記録は6×6判の大きなフィルム。

いま、ネガは編集局の金庫に桐の小箱に納められて保管されている。り災証明を書く警官が写ったネガは左端部分が切り取られていた。ネガを永久保存しようと毎年、繰り返してきた水洗作業の結果、乳剤がはく離したための緊急措置だ。膜面には銀塩がメッキのようにふいている。傷の部分は茶褐色に変色、全体は黄色みを帯びていた。現像にまつわるエピソードを教えてくれた。「当時、新聞社が疎開していた広島市郊外の牧場で夜、星を見ながら現像した。水洗は近くにある小川だった」。後世、このネガが貴重な記録になるとはこの時、思わなかった。

中田左都男撮影の広島　埋もれていた同盟通信社の27枚

広島に原爆が投下された直後、同盟通信社大阪支社の中田左都男カメラマンは大阪海軍警備府の要請で大阪大学理学部浅田常三郎教授に同行、海軍調査団員として広島市に入った。国策だった同盟通信社は終戦と同時に戦犯に問われないよう自主的に解体、共同通信社と時事通信社、電通に分かれた。この3兄弟は共同が生ニュース、時事が経済ニュース、電通が広告会社になり今日に至る。私はこの共同通信社に長く勤め大阪支社写真部のデスクもしていたから中田カメラマンは大先輩になる。しかし中田先輩の広島取材について全く知らなかった。

大阪大学理学部の礎を作った浅田常三郎教授は東京帝国大学理学部の出身。1923（大正12）年4月、3年生になった浅田は物理学の長岡半太郎教授の研究室に入り物理を学んだ。翌24年3月、大学卒業後は長岡教授の助手として理研に入った。因みに長岡半太郎の長男、治男は理化学研究所理事長、次男の正男は日本光学工業（ニコン）社長を勤めた。

27枚の写真は広島平和記念資料館の「相原資料」（旧文部省学術研究会議　原子爆弾災害

調査研究特別委員会）の中にあり撮影者不明のままだった。遺品になった浅田常三郎教授の手帳に中田の名前があり、中田写真の確定ができた。中国新聞の西本雅美編集委員による追跡取材の成果だった。西本記者は当時、私にも問い合わせしてきた記憶がある。中田左都男が広島市の西練兵場で撮った「眼球が飛び出した被災者」の写真は当時、共同通信社にいた私が米ニューヨークのデーリー・ニューズから入手、日本新聞博物館で公開した戦争写真に含まれ、ACME（米通信社UPIの前身）が1945年9月2日に配信していた。

同僚だった小路春美の証言

同盟通信時代、中田左都男と一緒だった小路春美（元共同通信大阪支社写真部）は「中田さんは報道班員として同行し、8月10日、市街を撮影した。一行が放射能測定などしている間に撮影したものと思う。当時の同盟通信社大阪支社は戦災で焼失し、中之島難波橋にあった。広島の被災地を撮影したフィルムは大阪の砂田写真部長と中田さんが相談の上、未現像で本社に送り、本社で処理し、東京から配信した」と証言する。

中田左都男は1994年、74歳で死去しているが以下、小路が共同通信社友会報（2007年3月31日付）に記した一文を引用させていただく。

昨年（2006年）9月上旬、中国新聞社から電話がかかった。この年寄りに何の用か、とおどろいた。
「中国新聞の西本と云いますが、実は終戦の頃（昭和20年）同盟通信大阪支社におられた中田左都男さんのことについてお尋ねしたいのですが」それを聞いて思い出した。
やはり昨年の春か夏だったか、さだかではないが、岡本広島支局長から、中田さんについ問い合わせがあった件だな、と。
内容は「昭和20年頃、大阪支社に中田左都男というカメラマンがいたか」「広島原爆資料館の被爆写真の中から同盟中田左都男撮影の写真が出てきたので、中田さんのことを詳しく知りたい」というものだった。
当時の頃のことを思い出しながら①私が昭和19年、南方従軍から帰り、大阪支社へ転勤になったとき知り合った人②当時、海軍警備府があり、同盟から中田記者、小路カメラマンの2人が阪警付き報道班員として登録していた③本土空襲があると、甲子園球場の西側にあった海軍戦闘機基地へ同行した④中田記者は私より若く関西学院出身、学生時代はラガーだった。終戦と同時に退社して、OB会にも出席していないのでその後のことは不明⑤原爆写真は、投下後、大阪海軍警備府から調査団が出ており、報道班員だった中田記者がその一員として同行したのではないか。詳しくは聞いていないが、そのときに撮影したものと思う。中国新聞の西本さんに聞かれるままに電話口で話をした。

中田記者が8月10日から11日に撮影した広島の写真には①石油配給統制倉庫のトタン屋根被害状況②八丁堀付近の電車通りで被爆し、全焼した路面電車③爆心地から北東の西練兵場で被爆した遺体④中区堀川町にあった久保田醤油の煙突⑤被災した7階建ての中国新聞社新館と

撮影者不明のまま共同通信社にファイルされていた
同盟通信社・中田左都男カメラマン撮影の広島原爆写真

右隣に旧館ビル⑥旧中国新聞社屋上から見た東方面の廃虚⑦山陽線神田川鉄橋で脱線転覆した貨物列車の積んでいたドラム缶が爆発、49両のうち26両が全焼⑧列車転覆現場の神田川鉄橋では復旧に当たる工兵隊員らが復旧工事⑨爆心地から北東に1.9キロ、鉄筋コンクリートの広島駅の天井が爆風で崩落した——など、広島が壊滅的被害をこうむった実情が克明に写されていた。

8月19日付で朝日、毎日（東京・大阪）、読売、中日、23日付で中国（被災で代行印刷）、西日本、北海道新聞が掲載した。

小路の証言が続く。

2、3日後、西本さんから「共同通信、新聞通信調査会にも問い合わせたが当時のことははっきりわからない。新聞通信調査会で、共同OBの小路さんを紹介された。明後日にお宅に伺いたい。中田さん撮影の写真をぜひ見てもらいたい」との電話。取材熱心な西本さんに感心しながら快諾した。

当日の朝、中国新聞編集委員西本雅美氏が来宅。取材調査を詳しく聞いた。

一、原爆資料館にある被爆写真数千枚の中から同盟中田左都男撮影の写真が32枚見つかった（8月10日撮影）。中に未発表のものもあるので私の電話をもとに取材にかかった。
一、大阪海軍警備府の求めで、大阪大学理学部教授浅田常三郎氏（1984年死去）一行が海軍調査団として広島市に入った。中田さんは報道班員として同行し（浅田教授の手帳に中田氏の名前）、8月10日、市街を撮影した。一行が放射能測定などしている間に撮影したものと思う。
一、西本さんの持ってこられた被爆写真を見ると粒子かなり荒れているので、小型カメラ、支社写真部備品でライカ（ドイツ製の有名カメラ）と思われる。
中国新聞の取材でわかったことだが、中田さんは、1994年、74歳で死去、奥さんも5年後に死去されていた。
一、東京本社から配信された中田さん撮影の被爆写真は終戦が報じられた8月19日付で朝日、毎日（東京・大阪）、読売、中日、23日付、中国（被災で代行印刷）、西日本、北海道新聞など確認できた。
「惨禍の広島市、原子爆弾投下で瞬時にして焦土と化した市街の一部」の説明で、各紙同様の説明。表、裏2頁の紙面で、3〜4段と破格の扱いだった。
米軍進駐に伴い、9月14日付で「プレスコード」が出る前に報じた被爆写真だった。
一、中田記者が撮影した写真32枚が見つかったが、未発表のものもあるので取材経緯などを調べて紙面に出したい。中田記者は20年10月、同盟解散と同時に退社しており、名簿、共同、時事と取材したが名前も取材の足跡もわからなかった……

中国新聞西本さんの話を聞いて、中田左都男さんを知っているのはどうやら私一人らしい。中田情報は退社とともに消えていたらしい。

広島・長崎を撮った東方社の林重男（「反核・写真運動」代表委員）

「こういう表現はいけないけれど実にきれいだった。9時ごろ広島の秋空に朝日がドームに輝いていた」。廃墟になった広島の街を背景に、広島県産業奨励館（原爆ドーム）を撮影したときの感

林重男氏が撮影した広島県産業奨励館(原爆ドーム)の連続写真＝1945年10月上旬

想だ。

林重男は現役兵として3年間、ソ満国境にいた。除隊して軍の対外宣伝組織だった東方社に入った。1943(昭和18)年6月には写真部長だった木村伊兵衛とともに、幻のグラフ誌といわれた「FRONT」の取材で中国にも行ったこともあった。

木村の勧めで林は1945(昭和20)年9月27日、文部省学術研究会議 原子爆弾災害調査研究特別委員会の記録映画班(日本映画社)の写真担当として同僚の菊池俊吉とともに約2週間、広島に入った。林は物理班を担当。現場に行くと、調査団の人たちは測定器を設置するための穴掘りで忙しく、撮影指示を出す余裕がない。「カメラマンの裁量でそれらしいものを撮ってくれ」と言われた。

「なぜかバラックも道路も何もない灰色の世界だった」。疑問は林が東京に帰ってから解けた。9月中旬、中国地方を通過した枕崎台風による豪雨がバラックや放射能のチリを海に流してしまっていたからだ。カメラはライカと二眼レフのローライを使用した。高い撮影場所を探し広島県産業奨励館(原爆ドーム)北に残った4階建ての広島商工会議所屋上の望楼に上った。後年、写真は世界的に有名になった。

「一発の爆弾でこんなになったとは…」。林にとって信じられない破壊力だった。「火葬した跡に残った遺骨の量にも驚いた。紙ペラのような骨を見たが、こんな爆弾は使ってはいけないと思った」。

1945年10月中旬、東方社に連合国軍総司令部から原爆ネガの提出命令がきた。木村が「ネガを出せ」という米将校と交渉した。

「木村さんはそんなにネガを出せというのなら、あなたのピストルと交換しようとがんばった」。結局、プリントを相手の希望通り一種に付き10枚焼くことで話がついたが印画紙がなかった。

「米軍の担当官に、ネガは我々カメラマンの生命線だ。持って行くなら、あなたのピストルを置いていってほしいといったんですよ。木村さんは、うちには資材がないといって、印画紙や薬品、乾燥機の提供まで頼んだんです」。

3日後に印画紙や現像資材を大型トラック2台と小型トラックに乗せ持ってきた。「これには負けたよ。戦争に勝ってないことを物量でも感じた。木村さんはもし米兵がピストルを渡したら射つつもりだった」。話が木村のことになると、林は顔をくしゃくしゃにして涙を流していた。

医学的写真を撮影した菊池俊吉(「反核・写真運動」よびかけ人)

林重男とともに「原子爆弾災害調査研究特別委員会」記録映画班に同行した菊池俊吉は医学班を受け持った。何回か「反核・写真運動」の会合でお会いしたが、菊池は常に寡黙で当時のことについて多くを語ってくれなかった。その理由をいま考えると医療班に同行していたカメラマンとして、被ばく者の悲惨な状況下、解剖を含め「厳しい情景をつぶさに目撃してしまったからではないか」と推察する。その一方、菊池が残した写真はシャープで医学的にも貴重な記録となっている。

菊池は「反核・写真運動」が出版した『原爆を撮った男たち』(1987年、草の根出版刊)の中

で「最終的に、これらの写真は映画には使用しなかったが、記録写真として残ったわけである。はじめの段階で、映画にも使うかもしれないし、歴史の1ページとしての普通写真も残したいという思いであったときいている。この映画のプロデューサー加納竜一氏が相原秀次氏にも打診、そして木村伊兵衛さんに会いスチール3名の同行を決めたそうである。原爆写真を残すきっかけをつくった功労者であると思う」と語っている。写真は広島での21日間で、ライカ判705枚、6×6判82枚を写した。これらの写真は広島平和記念資料館に保存されている。

以下、菊池俊吉が「反核・写真運動」に残してくれた詳細な写真説明と『原爆を撮った男たち』を参考に菊池俊吉の医療班取材を整理してみた。

「仕事としては原爆記録映画のスチール班である。さて何をどう撮るのか、撮らねばならないのか、原爆そのものもほとんどわからず、映画のスチールというのもはじめての経験。林重男君が物理班に、私と田子恒男君が医学班を受けもつことになる」。医学班は、医学映画に経験豊富な山中真男、演出補助、撮影助手、ライトマン、スチールと8名で、スタッフは全員で33名、一番人数の多い班であった。

最初の撮影は陸軍病院宇品分院だった。9月中旬、広島地方を襲った台風の影響で停電が続き、ライトが使えないので撮影は中庭で行われた。「撮影は、どんな姿勢で被爆したか、熱線をどの方向から受けたか、そして脱毛・原爆症の有無。爆心からの距離はどのくらいかを、主なねらいとし8名の人たちの病状を写す」。「この病気は、それまでにはなかった症状だったことぐらい、私にもわかった。ただ、それまでは、聞いたこともない放射能とか原爆症という言葉が出たり、とまどいの多い撮影のはじまりである」と菊池は後年、話している。

解剖の撮影ではライトが使えないのでスチールだけとなった。残された写真説明には「男性、八月入院一〇月死亡、被爆地は横川（爆心より二キロ）製油作業中火傷を受ける。病歴・顔面蒼白活気ナシ、心音清純、梢幽微、腎部一部化膿、食欲不振、全身倦怠感アリ」とある。

使用したカメラは、ライカⅢB2台、レンズはズミタール50ミリF2、ヘクトール73ミリ、エルマー135ミリ。それとローライフレックス1台、接写用プロクサーである。フィルムは「さくらパンF」DIN18（ASA50相当）。低感度のため暗い病室での撮影はライトに負うことが多々あったという。

広島赤十字病院での撮影は外来治療室からはじめ皮膚科・耳鼻科・小児科・外科・内科の各診療状況を写した。

爆心地近くで負傷した若い兵士の後ろ姿を撮影した写真説明には「佐々木氏（二六歳）、爆心地近くの中国軍管区兵器部言受傷、火傷程度、二度広範囲にわたる、脱毛、下痢、発熱四〇度。見るからに痛々しく、写すのが申しわけない気になる」と書いていた。被写体となったのは、呉市住む佐々木忠孝氏。当時、広島市中区にあった中国軍管区兵器部に所属し、爆心地から北東約1キロの広島城堀端で被ばくした。菊池は「（佐々木氏は）後年テレビ（だったと思う）に出演、あのときはライトの熱でピリピリと痛かったと話しておられた。回復されたわけである」と『原爆を撮った男たち』で述べている。

10月6日は袋町国民学校救護病院を撮影。階段下が診療室で教室が病室。2階が県の衛生課と薬務課となっていた。学校は爆心から約500メートルと近く、コンクリートの外形は残ったが内部は焼け、児童、先生とも全滅に近かった。

10月11日は大芝国民学校救護病院に移った。ここまでかなりの被害者を写し神経もマヒしはじめているが、「入院中の母と子に出合い、原爆の非情と実体を見せつけられた思いになった」と菊池は述べている。「親と子を写すカメラも非情である。仕事とはいえ、申しわけない気持で写させてもらう。そこは理科室であるらしく、床は板張りの病室。普通の病院より悲惨さを見せつけられる。病歴をきくまでもなく重態の様相である」。

写真説明によると「母ヨネ三一歳　九月一八日入院、紫斑、歯齦出血ありたり、現症状・咳、呼吸困難、娘ヨオ12歳　受傷地・船入町、屋内冷蔵庫倒れその下敷きとなる。一時失神す、右股関節脱臼、右膝外側左下肢外傷潰瘍状、右後頭部サッカ創、脱毛、下痢ヨウの看護中、母一ヵ月後に原爆症となり重態」とある。菊池は「なんらの外傷もなかったのに突然の原爆症に慄然とする思いであった」記している。

次いで13日は草津国民学校救護所で解剖を撮影した。菊池にとっても初めての体験だった。「構内の物置が臨時の解剖室となる。京都府立医大荒木教授の執刀。廿日市工業救護所より回送の78歳の女性。なれないこととはいえ、その臭気にはまいってしまう。カメラを持っていなかったら逃げ出したいところ」と写真説明に付記して書いている。

広島での最後の取材は京大医学部の調査団に同行、「山津波の犠牲になった大野陸軍病院、そして初期の救護活動にかかった似島を写し医学班の撮影が終わる」とある。1990年11月5日、74歳で逝った菊池俊吉の死因は急性白血病だった。

個人のネガ管理には限界　朝日の松本栄一（「反核・写真運動」運営委員長）

「広島が爆撃された翌日には、もう原子爆弾という言葉を朝日社内で聞きました」。元朝日新聞社カメラマン、松本栄一は毎年、原爆記念日が近づくと各地で開かれる平和勉強会の講師として忙しかった。20年ほど前だが東京・池袋で開かれた講演会をのぞいてみたことがある。

「科学朝日の記者と2人で4日がかりで長崎に入り、浦上の見えるところに出たら、焼け野原なんですよ。なるほど、1発でこれか……。しばらく、そこに立ちすくみました」。

「放射能が危険という意識はありませんでした。でも、三菱の兵器工場で後片付けをしていた人に取材して、翌々日にもう一回会おうとしたら、『昨日亡くなりました』と。急に発熱して、歯茎から猛烈に出血。急性白血病と診断されたそうです」。（『AERA』戦後50年記念増刊「原爆と日本人」1995年8月10日号）

「核兵器破壊力は今の写真の比ではない。写真家の務めとして何とか核の廃止運動に私の写真を使ってもらいたい。何回でも写真を見ていただき感慨を新たににしてほしい」。「体験継承も仕事だ」と語る松本は新聞社を退いた後も労を惜しまず平和の尊さを語り歩いている。

「毎晩、焼け跡の中で火が見えました。被災した人たちの晩飯の支度だろうと思ってたんですが、昼間みると、遺骨が散らばっている。ある晩、火が燃え始めたので訪ねたところ、やはり荼毘でした」。「死体は新聞には載せられないから、撮るんじゃないと言われていた。だけれど、長崎の人たちの苦しみを見たら『これは知らせなきゃいけないんじゃないか』と思った。苦しみを訴えるためにも写真を撮らせてくださいと、お許しをいただきました」。

スライドを終えて、松本栄一は「わたしにとって原爆写真はひとつの証ともいえる」と語り、こう続けた。「写真を撮ることだけでなく、できるだけ被爆者の方に会うことも自分の仕事と思っている」。

ライカとフィルム（映画用の100フィート巻き）2巻をデスクから手渡されて松本は8月下旬に長崎

原爆写真の考証作業を行う、
左から林重男、菊池俊吉、松本栄一、丹野章、松本徳彦の各氏
＝1985年、東京・四谷（撮影：新藤健一）

と広島に向かった。「長崎から福岡に列車で何本かフィルムを送ったのですが、帰京して確かめたら、原爆の写真を使っちゃいけないということで捨てられていたのにはびっくりしました」。

東京では連合国軍の検閲に出すため1コマにつきキャビネ各3枚を焼いて持っていったが、即、没収された。さらに松本は当局にネガの提出を求められた。当時、朝日新聞は屋上で、共同通信社は日比谷公園にネガを集めて焼いていた。そこで松本は「ネガは焼いた」と報告した。実際には会社のロッカーにしまって保管していたが定年退職の時「あなたが隠してもっていたのだから、持っていってくれ」といわれ、結果的には自分で持つことになった。

「昭和26（1951）年、アサヒグラフの編集長が原爆写真のことを知っていて発表することになった。当時は通常、8万部印刷するのだが、刷り増しして80万部も売れた」。初めての原爆写真の公表だった。

だが松本にとって悩ましいのは、ネガの保存だ。朝日新聞は松本栄一が退職したとき、松本に「一度焼却したはずのネガだから」と言って"退職金代わり"の意味合いで本人に返した。この話は私も松本栄一から直接聞いた。なんとも粋な計らいだが、このネガは人類共有の負の遺産である。朝日新聞は新聞社の社会的役割を考えていないのだろうか。

その後、松本はこうも語っていた。「僕のネガも銀が浮いていて焼きづらくなっている。昔、広島の市長と食事した時、ネガの保存の話をしたら、後で職員3人がネガを頂きたい、とやって来たのには驚いた。役所は人が変わったら終わり。まだ自分で保管したほうがよい。将来、国会図書館のような国の施設で保存できればいいのだが……」。個人のネガ管理には限界がある。公的保存施設の設置は時代の要請でもある。

核被災の惨状を、次世代に引き継ぐ

ロシアのプーチン大統領は2015年3月、国営テレビに出演して、ロシアが約1年前にウクライナからクリミアを併合した際、核兵器の使用を準備していたことを明らかにし、世界を驚かせた。プーチン氏は番組の中で、クリミア情勢がロシアにとって思わしくない方向に向かっていた時、「ロシア軍の核戦力を臨戦態勢に置く可能性があったか」と聞かれて「我々はそうする用意ができていた」と答えたのだ。

米国もイラクやアフガンで限定的な核兵器を使ったという情報がある。真相が明らかになるにはしばらく時間がかかるだろう。しかし、米国は1958年9月の金門馬祖事件の際、中国本土5カ所に核攻撃を準備し、一触即発の危機にあった。この時、沖縄の嘉手納米空軍基地にあったF101ジェット戦闘機には核爆弾MK7が積み込まれていたのだ。

沖縄返還を目前にした佐藤元首相は「核抜き本土並み」をキャッチ・フレーズに「非核三原則」を制定したわけだが、日米間では万が一の有事に際しての「事前協議」の話を詰めていたのが真相だ。それは有事に際して核を搭載した米艦船が日本領海に入る時に「事前に協議する」という項目で、これが実は「密約」だったわけだ。

米国は核装備をした艦船の通過・寄港は日本への「核持ち

文部省学術研究会議 原子爆弾災害調査研究特別委員会の「広島長崎における輻射温度および爆風圧」の調査・研究班の一員として参加した東京帝国大学工学部助教授だった菅義夫氏のご子息が、「反核・写真運動」に管理・運用を委託された写真（フイルム）の考証作業をする、右から松本栄一運営委員長、川原勇事務局長、佐々木俊成運営委員、小松健一運営委員＝1995年8月、東京（撮影：新藤健一）

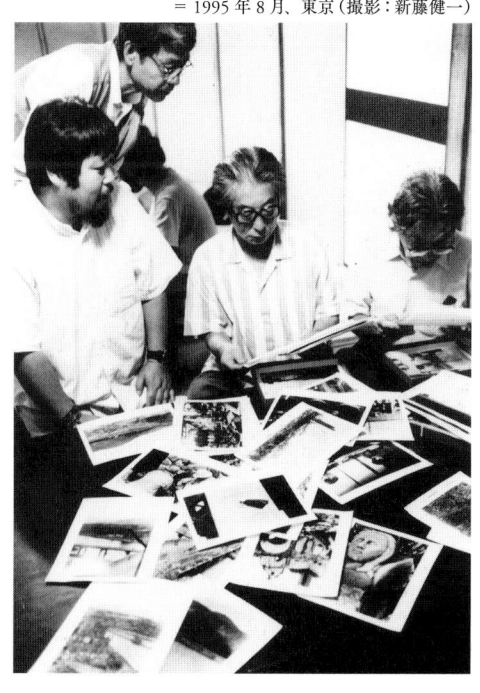

込み」に当たらないという解釈である。いま沖縄県名護市辺野古では普天間飛行場の移設先という名目でキャンプ・シュワブ基地を再編、新基地を建設する工事が進んでいる。キャンプ・シュワブを観察すると平屋の事務棟中庭には核シェルター入口の階段があった。さらに最近までは県道と接するゲート前には核兵器取り扱い部隊の存在を示すマークもあったのだ。

　では、なぜ、日米両政府は辺野古の海を強引に埋め立てるのか。その本当の理由は原子力空母や原子力潜水艦が寄港できる港湾施設とオスプレイを含む航空機用滑走路、さらには核兵器を含む辺野古弾薬庫の再整備計画があるからだ。

　いま世界には核弾頭が約1万5700発あり、その9割をロシアと米国が占めている。戦後70年が経ち、戦争の記憶が薄れてきた。国会では憲法を無視した「戦争法案」と呼ばれる安保法制の審議で与野党がぶつかった。そして若者たちが再び、戦場に狩り出されるキナ臭い時代の到来が目前に迫っている。

　だからこそ、核被災の惨状を、次世代の若者に引き継ぐ原爆写真の調査と保存は私たちの責務だと考える。核のない、戦争のない平和な時代を守るため、再び、過ちを繰り返してはならないのだ。

（文中敬称略）

あとがき

　今年もまた、あの忌まわしい、そして忘れてはならない広島、長崎に原爆が投下されてから70回目の夏が巡ってきました。
　「反核・写真運動」は、1982年当時の国内外の「核兵器を廃絶して平和な世界を」の大きな運動の高まりの中で発足しました。
　川島浩、杉村恒、丹野章、東松照明、細江英公の5人の写真家が発起人となり、発足時には、日本のジャンルを超えた写真家、写真評論家、写真団体の代表など552人が呼びかけ人となりました。
　代表委員には、秋山庄太郎、入江泰吉、立木香都子、田中雅夫、春木栄、福田勝治、藤本四八、吉川富三、渡辺義雄の9氏が選ばれました。

　　「反核・写真運動」の趣旨は次の通りです。

1. 核兵器の廃絶と軍縮を実現するために国連、世界各国の政府ならびに日本政府に働きかける。
1. 日本政府と国会に核兵器を作らず、持たず、持ち込ませず、という「非核三原則」を厳密に守り、今後いかなる政府内閣のもとでも継続される保障を求める。
1. 世界各国の写真・写真関係者に、核兵器廃絶のために行動するように働きかける。
1. 被爆直後の惨状とその後の被爆者の苦しみの記録を包括的に集め、写真集の出版、写真展の開催など映像を通じて反核運動に役立てる。
1. 原水爆禁止世界大会に代表を派遣するなど、目標達成のために必要な行動をおこなう。

　振り返ってみるとこの33年間、節目、節目に写真家として何が出来るか、模索しながら活動してきました。そして先に書いた代表委員の9氏ならびに、発起人で卒寿を迎えた丹野章氏と、細江英公氏を除いた先達たちはすべて鬼籍に入られました。
　現在、運動を担っている私たちは3世代目となりますが、それぞれ還暦を過ぎ、ほとんどは70歳代となっています。次の世代へバトンを渡すことは急務となっているのです。
　人類へ初めて原子爆弾が投下されてから今年で70年。この歴史的な年に、多くの方々のご協力で、私たちがこの間運動してきた集大成とも言うべき『決定版　広島原爆写真集』、『決定版　長崎原爆写真集』の2冊の本を世に送り出すことができました。同時に東京で「原爆投下70年──広島・長崎写真展」も開催しました。

本写真集に作品を使用させていただいたのは、広島を撮影した23人、長崎を撮影した11人、合せて27人の方々です。その大多数はすでに亡くなられ、今回はご遺族の方々にもご協力を仰ぐことになりました。
　この先達たちは、広島では原爆炸裂2分後、長崎では15分後から撮影を開始しています。
　当時、放射能障害が定かではない危険な時期、それも戦時中の極限状況下で撮影し、敗戦後は、米軍の占領下で記録したフィルムの保存に全力で努力しています。
　私たちは、自らの生命の危険を顧みず、被爆直後の惨状と、その後の被爆者たちの苦しみ、悲しみの記録を撮り続けた先達たちの意思をしっかりと継承し、歴史の証として貴重な記録を後世へ伝えていく使命を果していくことを改めて誓います。

　本書を刊行するにあたり、推薦文を寄せていただいた写真家の細江英公氏、ヒロシマ・ピース・オフィス代表で前広島市長の秋葉忠利氏、日本原水爆被害者団体協議会事務局長の田中熙巳氏をはじめ多くの方々にお力添えをいただいてきました。ここに感謝申し上げます。
　英文キャプションの監修では、共同通信元外信部長の横山司氏に多大なお世話になりました。感謝申し上げます。装幀を担当していただいたデザイナーの宗利淳一氏に深謝いたします。
　また長崎の写真を特別に提供いただいた山端庸介氏の長男、山端祥吾氏と、資料を提供していただいた孫の青山雅英氏のお二人にも感謝申し上げます。
　そして、出版にあたり、この実現が不可能とも思える企画を快くお引き受けいただき、様々な便宜をはかってくださった勉誠出版株式会社の岡田林太郎社長をはじめ社員の皆さまにも心から感謝致します。

合掌

2015年 風待月
小松健一
新藤健一

撮　影　者　一　覧

（50音順）

尾木正己（おき・まさみ）
1914～2007年。当時、呉海軍工廠火工部所属。同所で被爆。炸裂約40分後の原子雲を火工部があった吉浦町から数点撮影。その後、市内の惨状を数十点撮影した

尾糠政美（おぬか・まさみ）
1921～2011年。当時、陸軍船舶司令部写真班。広島市南区宇品海岸にあった司令部で被爆。重傷者らが収容された似島の検疫所で翌7日に撮影を始め、各臨時救護所でも市民の惨状を撮った

加賀美幾三（かがみ・いくぞう）
文部省学術研究会議 原子爆弾災害調査研究特別委員会の「広島長崎における輻射温度および爆風圧」の調査・研究班に助手として同行して広島、長崎を9月上旬～中旬まで撮影。眞島正市東京帝国大学教授、筒井俊正同大助教授、菅義夫同大助教授、助手・二瓶禎二の5名がメンバーであった

川原四儀（かわはら・よつぎ）
1923～1972年。当時、陸軍船舶司令部写真班。同所で被爆。翌々日の8日から市街や臨時救護所を撮影。終戦になるまで数百枚撮影するが、米軍の進駐を知った軍の指示で焼却された。しかし25点の原爆写真を保管していた

川本俊雄（かわもと・としお）
1902～1968年。当時、広島県警察本部写真班。5日に西条町に出張し、6日正午過ぎに広島市に入り、8日から撮影を行った。1945年12月までに建造物、交通機関の被害など約100点を撮影した

菊池俊吉（きくち・しゅんきち）
1916～1990年。当時、東方社カメラマン。1941年に東方社入社。文部省学術研究会議 原子爆弾災害調査研究特別委員会の記録映画班の医学班に属し、スチール写真担当として参加。広島（9月30日～10月22日）を787点撮影した

岸田貢宜（きしだ・みつぎ）
1916～1987年。当時、広島師団司令部報道班。広島市で「キシダ写真館」を営んでいたが、広島師団司令部報道班員として、市中心街を原子爆弾炸裂の4時間後から撮影。翌7日になって、この未曾有の惨状を後世に残さねばと決意し、フィルムのある限り撮影した

岸本吉太（きしもと・よした）
1902～1989年。当時、広島市田中町で写真館経営。その自宅で被爆。9月上旬から市内各地の撮影を開始。中国配電（中国電力）の求めで45年11月から市内各地の電気施設被害も撮影。3ヶ月間で100点近く撮った。その後、広島市を1年おきに10年間撮り続けた

北勲（きた・いさお）
1902～1991年。当時、広島中央気象台勤務。官舎で被爆。8月9日から2ヶ月間、焦土と化した瓦礫の街を約40点撮影した

木村権一（きむら・ごんいち）
1904〜1973年。中国新聞写真部を経て当時、陸軍船舶練習部。ここで被爆。練習部のあった南区から、炸裂15分後の原子雲とその後、炎上する市外を撮影

黒石勝（くろいし・まさる）
1913〜1990年。当時、広島赤十字病院レントゲン技手。8月7日に、家族が疎開していた福山市から市内に戻り、主に患者を医学的資料として50点ほど撮影した

菅義夫（すげ・よしお）
1902〜1985年。当時、東京帝国大学工学部助教授。文部省学術研究会議 原子爆弾災害調査研究特別委員会の「広島長崎における輻射温度および爆風圧」の調査・研究班に物理学者として参加。筒井俊正助教授、加賀美幾三助手らが撮影した当時のフィルムを保管していた

筒井俊正（つつい・としまさ）
1900〜1977年。当時、東京帝国大学工学部助教授。文部省学術研究会議 原子爆弾災害調査研究特別委員会の「広島長崎における輻射温度および爆風圧」の調査・研究班の班員として広島、長崎を9月上旬〜中旬まで撮影。眞島正市東京帝国大学教授、菅義夫同大助教授、助手・二瓶禎二、加賀美幾三の5名がメンバーであった

中田左都男（なかた・さつお）
1920〜1994年。当時、同盟大阪支社写真部。大阪海軍調査団に同行して、原爆投下4日後の8月10日に広島に入って撮影した

二瓶禎二（にへい・ていじ）
文部省学術研究会議 原子爆弾災害調査研究特別委員会の「広島長崎における輻射温度および爆風圧」の調査・研究班に助手として同行して広島、長崎を9月上旬〜中旬まで撮影。眞島正市東京帝国大学教授、筒井俊正同大助教授、菅義夫同大助教授、助手・加賀美幾三の5名がメンバーであった

林重男（はやし・しげお）
1918〜2002年。当時、東方社カメラマン。1943年に東方社に入社し、文部省学術研究会議 原子爆弾災害調査研究特別委員会の記録映画班の物理班に属し、スチール写真担当として参加。広島（9月30日〜10月11日）、長崎（10月12日〜22日）を撮影した

深田敏夫（ふかだ・としお）
1928〜2009年。当時、崇徳中学在学中。学徒動員で陸軍兵器補給廠で被爆した。ポケットにしのばせていたカメラ、ベビーパールで兵器廠があった霞町から炸裂後5〜10分後の原子雲を続けて4点撮影した

眞島正市（まじま・まさいち）
1886〜1974年。当時、東京帝国大学工学部教授。応用物理学者。文部省学術研究会議 原子爆弾災害調査研究特別委員会の「広島長崎における輻射温度および爆風圧」の調査・研究班の班長として広島、長崎を9月上旬〜中旬まで撮影。筒井俊正同大助教授、菅義夫同大助教授、助手・二瓶禎二、加賀美幾三の5名がメンバーであった

松重三男（まつしげ・みつお）
1911〜1989年。当時、広島県職員・レントゲン技師。病気療養していた安古市町の自宅で被爆。8月6日炸裂後、2分後と30〜40分後の原子雲を撮影。その後、自宅の2階から数十台通り過ぎる被爆者を乗せたトラックなどを撮影

松重美人（まつしげ・よしと）
1913〜2005年。当時、中国新聞社編集局写真部員ならびに中国軍管区司令部報道班員を兼務。爆心地から2kmの翠町の自宅で被爆。8月6日午前11時頃から御幸橋の被爆した市民など当日に6点を撮影した

松本栄一（まつもと・えいいち）
1915〜2004年。当時、朝日新聞出版写真部。終戦直後の『科学朝日』で原爆特集が企画され、長崎（8月25日〜9月15日）、広島（9月18日〜25日）の撮影に特派された。撮影したネガがすべて焼却されることを知り、密かに自分のロッカーの中に保管していた

森本太一（もりもと・たいち）
1917〜1978年。当時、オリエンタル写真学校卒業後、写真家。軍隊に召集されて被爆。8月下旬から数十点、広島市内を撮影した

山田精三（やまだ・せいぞう）
1927〜。当時、広島一中（夜間部）生徒。中国新聞社で働く。爆心地から6.7kmの府中町の水分峡を散策中に、もっとも早い時期である炸裂2分後の原子雲を2点撮影。2枚目は雲の塊が大きすぎてファインダーに入らなかった

陸軍船舶司令部写真班（りくぐんせんぱくしれいぶしゃしんはん）
尾糠政美、川原四儀、木村権一が所属していて、手分けして撮影した。多くは焼却されたが、数十点のネガを保管していた

本書に収録した写真は、「反核・写真運動」が撮影者ならびにご遺族（著作権継承者）の許諾を得て収集してきたものである。
ただし、以下の写真は本書のために新たに提供いただいたものである。

中田左都男撮影写真：広島平和記念資料館提供

編者プロフィール

「反核・写真運動」
核兵器の廃絶と非核三原則の厳守を求め、ジャンルを超えた写真家、写真評論家、写真業界の代表など552名の呼びかけにより、1982年に発足。広島・長崎を撮影した原爆写真の収集、ネガの複製保存、デジタル化、出版物の刊行、展示などの活動を行っている

小松健一（こまつ・けんいち）
1953年岡山県生まれ、群馬県に育つ。世界の厳しい風土の中で自然と共生する民族をライフワークに地球巡礼をしている。また、日本人の近現代の文学、作家の原風景を切り口にして日本人の暮らしと風土、沖縄、環境問題など社会的テーマを追い続けている。公益社団法人日本写真家協会会員、協同組合日本写真家ユニオン会員。主な著書に、『ヒマラヤ古寺巡礼』（インデックスコミュニケーションズ、2005年、日本写真協会賞年度賞）、『雲上の神々―ムスタン・ドルパ』（冬青社、1999年、第2回藤本四八写真文化賞）など多数。「反核・写真運動」運営委員 事務局長

新藤健一（しんどう・けんいち）
1943年、東京生まれ。元共同通信社カメラマン。帝銀事件・平沢被告の獄中撮影やダッカ事件、朴大統領暗殺事件、湾岸戦争、アフガン戦争、イラク戦争、スーダン、ソマリア紛争を取材。共同通信社写真部デスク、編集委員。定年後は明星大学、東京工芸大学、立教大学非常勤講師を歴任、東日本大震災を取材。『見えない戦争』（情報センター出版局、1993年）、『疑惑のアングル』（平凡社、2006年）の著書がある。潜水士。「反核・写真運動」運営委員

決定版
広島原爆写真集

2015年8月6日　初版発行

監修
「反核・写真運動」

編者
小松健一・新藤健一

発行者
池嶋洋次

発行所
勉誠出版株式会社
〒101-0051　東京都千代田区神田神保町3-10-2
TEL：(03) 5215-9021　（代）FAX：(03) 5215-9025
〈出版詳細情報〉http://bensei.jp/

印刷
太平印刷社

製本
大口製本印刷

ブックデザイン
宗利淳一・齋藤久美子

© "Anti-Nuclear Photographers' Movement of Japan" 2015, Printed in Japan　ISBN978-4-585-27023-2 C0072

本書の無断複写・複製・転載を禁じます。乱丁・落丁本はお取り替えいたしますので、ご面倒ですが小社までお送り下さい。送料は小社が負担いたします。定価はカバーに表示してあります。